Why You Should
The Pragmatics of
Deontic Speech

Why You Should
The Pragmatics of
Deontic Speech

James W. Forrester

Published for Brown University Press by
University Press of New England
Hanover and London

This project has been supported by the National Endowment for the
Humanities, a federal agency that supports the study of such fields as
history, philosophy, literature, and the languages.

Printed in the United States of America

∞

Library of Congress Cataloging-in-Publication Data

Forrester, James W.
  Why you should.

  Includes index.
  1. Deontic logic. 2. Pragmatics. I. Title.
BD145.F67 1988   160   88–40111
ISBN 0–87451–453–3
5 4 3 2 1

In memory of a good man,
my father,
William Forrester

Contents

Acknowledgments

This book began as a seminar paper for the 1982 National Endowment for the Humanities Summer Seminar on Human Action, given at Bloomington, Indiana, by Professor Hector-Neri Castañeda. The paper was discussed during the seminar, and Professor Castañeda prepared detailed comments on it. In addition, Arthur Walker, Anatole Anton, and Joaquin Zuñiga all wrote comments on the paper, and I am grateful to all of them for their helpful remarks. I owe a special debt to Professor Castañeda for his comments and other assistance, for his example, and for his remarkable abilities as a slave driver!

I wrote the first draft of this book during the summer of 1983. I was materially assisted by a National Endowment for the Humanities summer stipend during that period. I am deeply grateful to this organization both for the 1982 seminar and for the 1983 stipend. They made this book possible. I completed additional drafts of the book during a sabbatical in the fall of 1984, and I am indebted to the University of Wyoming for granting me this leave.

Michael Bender provided both the stimulus and valuable information for my discussion of the lawyer's dilemma in chapter 2. Anne Slater deserves thanks for suggesting that I read Durkheim and Radcliffe-Brown, as does Francis Heck for his consultation on the translation of a French word. The staff at the University of Wyoming, College of Law Library, and especially Karolyn Durer, were of great help to me in finding and checking legal references. I owe a very large debt to an anonymous reader for Brown University Press, whose trenchant criticism of earlier versions have led to some much-needed improvements. I am also grateful to a second reader for many valuable suggestions.

One member of the 1982 summer seminar was my wife, Mary Gore Forrester. She, of course, has published a book, *Moral Language* (University of Wisconsin Press, 1982), so that my book is to some extent an infringement on territory she knows far better than I do. Her knowledge, help, and criticism have been of enormous value to me from the start of this book, and as some footnotes will reveal, she has saved me from some bad blunders.

After having thanked all these people, I would like to proclaim that they are responsible for any remaining errors. But they aren't. They probably tried to talk me out of those errors. Anyway, I'm responsible.

Aristotle suggests there is no point in trying to learn ethics unless one is already possessed of good habits. The same, I suppose, might be said of trying to write books on deontic matters. If I am at all in a position to write this book, by the criterion of having good habits, a large amount of the credit belongs to the book's dedicatee.

August 1988   J.W.F.

Introduction

This is, as far as I know, the first book devoted to the pragmatics of deontic speech. Moreover, again as far as I know, it is the first systematic study of deontic pragmatics.

Deontic speech is the language of obligation and permission. If I say that one has a moral obligation to visit the sick, or that one has a legal obligation to pay one's taxes, or that one may under the rules of etiquette drink red wine with fish, I am using deontic speech. The literature on that topic is quite ample.

There are somewhat fewer accounts of pragmatics, however. Pragmatics is the study of how the conditions under which a speech act is made contribute to the effect of that speech act. For example, H. P. Grice has argued that there are standard rules by which conversations are conducted; a listener has reason to expect the speaker to abide by those rules. Since the rules do not form part of the meaning of the sentences uttered, Grice's rules are usually taken as belonging to the province of pragmatics rather than to that of semantics.

I know of no previous attempt to work out systematically the rules of pragmatics that govern deontic speech. This is therefore a pioneer effort. Now pioneering has its joys, but it also carries some special responsibilities.

For instance, the prospective audience for a book on deontic pragmatics is not already sold on the merits of this project. There are at present no graduate seminars devoted to the pragmatics of deontic speech, nor has anyone yet suggested that my topic be made the center of a college's general education curriculum. Neither learned journals nor popular magazines yet ring with the noise of combat amoung rival students of the subject.

I must, then, do more than simply present what I take to be the maxims of deontic pragmatics; I must also try to create an audience for my subject. To do so, I need first to show why the subject deserves attention. After I have set forth my account of deontic pragmatics, I then need to explore at length how the maxims can be fruitfully applied.

That is why this book, like Gaul, is divided into three parts. In the first part, I try to explain why one should take an interest in the pragmatics of deontic speech. Chapter 1 indicates the sorts of basic questions about morality from which this study began. Chapter 2 argues that a principle often regarded as a cornerstone of deontic logic should be regarded as pragmatic. In chapter 3 I examine the purpose of deontic speech. I have labeled part 1 "Why."

I have read books that loudly trumpet the wonders of a particular method of doing philosophy but that somehow never manage to display that method in action! I have tried to avoid that pitfall by presenting in part 2 the heart of the book, my system of deontic pragmatics. Part 2, entitled "What," contains seven chapters. Chapter 4 gives an overview of the maxims of deontic pragmatics, while chapters 5 through 9 are devoted to an investigation of individual maxims. In chapter 10, I consider whether the list of maxims is complete.

In part 3, entitled "How," I apply the system presented in part 2. Chapter 11 is an examination of the way pragmatic principles functioned in a well-known court decision. Chapter 12 takes up the question of whether there is any general procedure for settling cases where rules conflict. Chapter 13 asks whether there is any point to calling the maxims I have identified pragmatic rather than semantic. And in chapter 14 I return to the question raised in chapter 1 of the use of deontic pragmatics in fighting ethical relativism, skepticism, and nihilism.

If you are already convinced of the value of deontic pragmatics and of the best ways to apply its principles, feel free to skip parts 1 and 3. If the field becomes a well-established one, future books (and perhaps future editions of this book) may well be shorter and more concentrated. This book is, I confess, a long one. But I think it is no longer than necessary. And everyone knows that pioneers like to talk a lot.

Creating an audience requires more than trying to show the importance of my subject; it has had its effect on the style of this book as well. I have tried throughout to make the book as readable, as free from jargon, and even, at times, as humorous as I could. I could afford to be dry only if I knew people must read my work.

I am a philosopher, and this is a philosopher's book; but I have not written it solely for philosophers. As I noted above, such an audience does not yet exist. More importantly, I believe that the subject of deontic pragmatics will be of interest to people outside philosophy: to people in linguistics, to those in jurisprudence, and, I hope, to the general educated public. I have tried to write this book to appeal to this wider audience.

Since my aim is to consider systematically the rules governing the effective utterance of statements of permission and obligation, I devote most of my consideration to those utterances themselves, as they occur in common speech, in the law, and in other contexts. I spend comparatively little time on what other philosophers have had to say, for my object is different from theirs: I am trying to construct a systematic pragmatics of deontic speech, and, as far as I know, other philosophers were not. Hence, although I believe I am doing philosophy, I rarely discuss either philosophy or philosophers.

Now it would be absurd for me to pretend that I am the first to consider the principle that 'ought' implies 'can', or the principle of universalizability, or the nature of legal reasoning. Many of my topics, and much of what I say about them, have parallels or antecedents in the work of others. Where I am aware of parallelism or debt, I have tried to acknowledge it. Once again, though, my purpose is different from that of any other author of whom I am aware, so that often an apparent parallel disappears upon closer examination. There are therefore fewer acknowledgments than the scholarly reader might expect.

I need to make one final disclaimer, although this one arises from the field of deontic pragmatics itself and not from my efforts at pioneering. This point has to do with the rather untidy character of many of my arguments.

The principles of pragmatics, whether deontic or otherwise, do not hold in all cases. Violations of the principles occur, often giving rise to what Grice called 'implicatures'. When I present and apply the maxims of deontic pragmatics, therefore, I make constant use of such terms as 'generally', 'normally', 'for the most part', and so on. The looseness of my arguments is often a function of looseness in the subject matter.

But enough of disclaimers. Let us turn to the first major question: Why should we study the pragmatics of deontic speech?

I | WHY

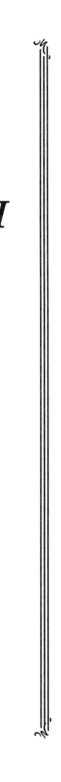

1 | Why This Book?

Anyone who teaches an introductory philosophy course has heard the same dialogue time and time again. Students bring up the same question, which they take to be merely rhetorical, class after class.

The polite form of the question is, "Why should I be moral?" A less polite, but more common, form is, "Who cares?" The students conscientiously take notes on moral theory or theories, on a thousand careful distinctions, and perhaps on a few absurdities desperately thrown in for laughs. (I use William Wollaston for that purpose.) But the notes they have taken in zoology or in English composition might actually prove of some use when they begin to open up a cat or a sentence. They want to know what use, if any, their notes on moral theory will ever be. And the burden of proof is on the teacher.

If Professor Doe is lucky, her students challenge her out loud, giving her a chance to respond. Maybe this time the students won't notice if their professor has no good answers. If they do notice, and at least the bright ones will, they tune the professor out completely.

If the teacher is unlucky, the students never do say what they're thinking. Instead, they just sit there, smugly wondering how the professor can say such foolish things. Surely not even Dr. Doe can believe that! But such speculation does not occupy the students long enough to prevent them from tuning out. When there seem to be only three options open, of which one involves fooling the students and two involve boring them, the value of philosophy is at an all-time low.

For whether they got it in school or imbibed it with their mothers' milk, most students come to their first philosophy class absolutely convinced that morality and moral theory are useless. They may be absolutists on Sunday morning, but the rest of the week they know it's all relative. They may be a bit vague on what it's all relative to— the individual, his country, his culture, or whatever—but that detail is petty. So why take notes on the travails of utilitarianism? If a person or their culture is utilitarian, then that's right for them, and if not, then ditto.

What does Professor Doe say to that? Obviously, she must meet the challenge. Even teachers that are themselves ethical relativists have a professional duty to get students thinking about the matter.

Professor Doe might try to push the idea that morality is a form of self-interest. The students know better than that: "If I can get away with something, then why not?" The teacher tries Plato's rejoinder: to be moral is to be mentally healthy. That response gives at least some students pause, for they realize that mental health is a Good Thing. Meanwhile, the teacher is squirming inside her skin, thinking about the confusion of different types of norms and laws, the occasional disutility of health, and other problems. Does she conceal these difficulties, thus fooling the students, or reveal them, thus confirming the students' original belief that there's no reason to be moral? Neither alternative is very attractive.

Perhaps the teacher takes up a theological version of the self-interest account. Whether God is thought of as using eternal negative reinforcement or only the eternal positive kind, we had all better be good. Of course, being good may not be enough to get you a place on the winning side, but, as Pascal advises, you can always pretend you're among the Elect and act morally. After all, that's your best shot at the reward.

Even if the teacher can square it with her conscience to say all this, the odds are the students won't be ready to accept all the theological baggage her position involves. And the bright ones should recognize that, from a religious point of view, the motivation recommended here is at best suspect and at worst anathema.

What then? Claim that morality is a form of life? I have yet to meet a student uncorrupted by prior philosophy courses who sees anything at all in this position. When the teacher starts talking about playing the morality game, students are confirmed in their belief that to be moral is only to play a game—and a pretty dull game at that. No color graphics at all, and it costs a lot more than a quarter!

Should Professor Doe suggest that to be moral is to be rational (or reasonable)? If she regards rationality as self-interested conduct, she's back in a familiar soup. And if she puts forward some notion of reasonableness that goes beyond self-interest, it will not only be the bright students that will say to themselves: "Then why should I bother being reasonable?" The transcendent beauty of being reasonable seems visible only after many years of philosophical training.

Well, I teach introductory philosophy courses. How do I deal with this predicament?

I have no unique and strangely satisfying doctrines to impart to students. Like a great many other teachers, I claim that there are certain threshold conditions that any acceptable moral theory has to meet, and that these threshold conditions provide a good reason for being moral. I appeal to the relativist audience by pointing out that more than one moral theory passes the threshold, and that there is no rational basis for choosing one above another of these successful theories. I try to appease any latent hunger for Sunday morning absolutism by pointing out that these threshold conditions are sufficient to condemn certain sets of values. The Nazis offend against universalizability, the utilitarians against a need for an adequate theory of justice, the Dobu against the requirement that false beliefs not play a crucial role in one's moral code, and so on.

Is all for the best, then, in my classroom? The students take careful notes on my list of threshold conditions. They write down my claim that these conditions provide good reasons for acting. I am content, for no hands are raised. But all the time, most of the students are thinking, "I say it's spinach, and I say the hell with it!"

I need to give a clear and persuasive justification for my claims about threshold conditions if I hope to wake students from their dogmatic slumbers.[1] Where can I find such a justification? Do I point to the universal condemnation of the Nazis? Alas, students today think the Nazis came somewhere between the Medes and the Persians— part of that boring old dead stuff they had to take in high school two years ago (except, of course, that they didn't have to take it). The Nazis committed mass murder? Well, it was long ago and far away, and anyway they were just doing their own thing, weren't they?

So I scuttle the Nazis for more up-to-date examples. Idi Amin was good for a while, but he's long gone. The Ayatollah? That's old news, and besides, doesn't a guy have a right to his own religion? If I can think of any more recent examples, either the students haven't heard of them or their awareness is so dim that the relativist reflex remains undisturbed.

Should I call attention to moral arguments and moral education? Well, to do so I must show the students, without begging the question, how these phenomena differ from mere barroom shouting matches or exercises in indoctrination. And the audience won't be receptive.

In desperation, I remind the students of their Sunday-morning beliefs and urge a bit of consistency on them. This is when some student who actually remembers a bit of his nineteenth-century American literature course declaims: "A foolish consistency is the hobgoblin of little minds, adored by little statesmen, philosophers, and divines." He emphasizes the word 'philosophers' unnecessarily, of course. As the teacher is reeling, the student adds: "Do I contradict myself? Very well, then, I contradict myself. I am large. I contain multitudes." *Exeunt omnes*, mentally at least, to generous self-applause.

I would not have rehearsed this dreary catalogue if I did not think a philosophy teacher has a way of getting through to students. The strategy I suggest is based on beliefs that are neither new nor startling, although they inevitably surprise some of my students.

I try to demonstrate that the presence of a shared morality is invaluable for a group—not essential, but invaluable—and that the purposes of having a shared morality can be achieved only when the morality in question meets certain conditions. Those conditions are, of course, our old friends, the threshold conditions.

I think this position is defensible and, what is more, true. By the last chapter of this book, I will have the materials to clarify and justify that statement.

---

1. One could, of course, look down one's philosophical nose at the very idea of being persuasive, but nobody actually faced with a class can afford to do so.

Certainly, both clarification and justification are needed. Just what are these mysterious "purposes of a shared morality," and just how do specific threshold conditions further them? Or again, how can one explain the moral force these threshold conditions seem to have if our justification of them is, at bottom, pragmatic? Those of us who condemn the Nazis do not do so because we think they were impractical or their moral beliefs inefficient!

One major motivation for reading this book is to look at the fresh answers I try to provide to these and other difficult problems.[2] A teacher of philosophy can follow the strategy I outline with a clear conscience.

But I am not so foolish as to bite off an utterly impossible morsel to chew. Although I will have much to say about morals, my primary focus will be on the language of morals.

My chief topic is even more restricted: I am interested in the *uses* we make of moral language, and particularly in how we use statements of obligation, permission, and the like. In a phrase, my concern is with the pragmatics of deontic language. However, in the third part of this book, I shall be applying what I take to be the leading principles of deontic pragmatics, and at that point, I try to answer the broad questions with which this book begins.

Even the presentation of the rules of deontic pragmatics is not quite as narrow as the preceding paragraph might suggest. For the term 'deontic' is not restricted to moral matters. People ought both to keep their promises and to pass the salt when asked—although both the sources and the strengths of these obligations are no doubt quite different. While working on deontic pragmatics, then, I will be including more than the problems of moral theory that generated this book.[3]

During this study, I take up the question of the uses of moral codes. For the employment to which we put any specialized area of

2. Although finding answers to the basic question of ethics is a major reason for reading the book, and although providing those answers was my original motive in writing it, it would be wrong to regard these considerations as defining the central concern of this book. My chief purpose is rather to lay out the structure of deontic pragmatics. The application to ethics is, strictly speaking, a sideshow. But I am not so fond of my subject as to suppose that a burning desire to know the principles of deontic pragmatics motivates most readers! Also, when I return to the question "Why be moral?" in chapter 14 my main argument will by no means be new. What is new is the way in which knowledge of the pragmatics of deontic speech shapes the details of that argument.

3. I cannot take for granted, of course, that the different types of deontic systems have anything like a common pragmatics.

language depends on the purposes of various institutions in a society—
and particularly on the purposes of those institutions vitally connected
with the area of language under study. For example, Robin Lakoff's
work on the pragmatics of politeness obviously required her to know
how manners function in society. Just as obviously, her study helps
her readers understand how manners do function.[4]

This book is therefore not a study of language for language's sake.
What I have to say about the pragmatics of deontic language should
tell us something about the aims of morality and other deontic institutions, as well as the means by which those aims are best fulfilled.
Ultimately, I hope my work will help any teacher faced with a roomful
of students asking, "Who cares?" to give an answer that will satisfy
both teacher and students.

4. Robin Lakoff, "What You Can Do with Words: Politeness, Pragmatics, and Performatives," in A. Rogers, B. Wall, and J. P. Murphy, eds., *Proceedings of the Texas
Conference on Perfomatives, Presuppositions, and Implicatures* (Arlington, Va., 1977),
79–105.

2 Why Naught Implies Kant

I intend to show in this chapter that a certain well-known deontic principle, usually considered a key part of the very logic of 'ought', is instead best regarded as falling under the pragmatics of deontic speech. If I am right, the chapter should serve as an advertisement for the importance of the study of deontic pragmatics. The principle in question is usually ascribed to Kant, and I shall call it Kant's Principle. This principle holds that persons are obligated to perform only those acts they are able to perform. In three words, 'ought' implies 'can'.

I read an altered version of part of this chapter as a paper, "Responsibility and Incapacity," for the 1987 Mountain-Plains Philosophy Conference.

To many philosophers, Kant's Principle appears to be plain common sense. There is clearly something wrong in supposing that a person ought to act in a way that he or she is unable to act. It also seems reasonable to think that the wrongness in such a supposition consists in misuse of the word 'ought'. The person who uses an 'ought' without a 'can' is therefore mistaking the logic of 'ought'.

An example will help show how Kant's Principle can be applied. Suppose Jane believes she ought to do whatever her guru tells her to do. But one day, the guru, under the false impression that Jane has an estate worth five million dollars, tells her to give him a certified check for that amount before another day has passed. Jane is quite literally unable to raise anything close to that amount of money. What is she to do?[5]

According to standard accounts of deontic logic, Jane's problem does not exist. Kant's Principle tells her that she ought to do something only if she is able to do it; therefore it is false that she ought to give the guru the certified check. She might continue to regard the guru as an issuer of 'oughts' for her, but on this matter his requirement is a dead letter. I suggest instead that Jane's inability to give the guru the money does not imply that it is false that she ought to do so. There can be, I shall argue, 'oughts' without 'cans'.

I am far from the first person to reject " 'ought' implies 'can' " as a part of deontic logic. As far as I know, E. J. Lemmon was the first to deny that 'ought' logically implies 'can', while R. M. Hare, in *Freedom and Reason*, argued that the relation between 'ought' and 'can' is that of presupposition.[6] Since then, several people have made similar points—including a founding father of deontic logic, G. H. von Wright.[7] Any originality in this chapter thus lies in its argument, not in its conclusions.

E. J. Lemmon, in a pair of influential articles, argued that a person can have contradictory obligations: he or she can be obligated both to

---

5. It is useless to attack the example by claiming that Jane wrongly accepts the guru as a source of genuine obligation for her. The same dilemma arises for anyone who asks, "What is my duty when some genuine source of obligation binds me to perform an impossible task?"

6. As a reader of this book pointed out, Hare explicitly denies that 'ought' *implicates* 'can', however. See R. M. Hare, *Freedom and Reason* (Oxford, 1963), 59.

7. E. J. Lemmon, "Moral Dilemmas," *Philosophical Review* 71 (1962): 139–58, esp. 150 n. 8; R. M. Hare, *Freedom and Reason* (Oxford, 1963), 51–59; G. H. von Wright, "On the Logic of Norms and Actions," in Risto Hilpinen, ed., *New Studies in Deontic Logic* (Dordrecht, 1981), 28.

perform a certain action and to fail to perform that action. And of course, it is impossible for the person both to perform and to fail to perform a given action (action-token, that is). Hence Lemmon believed a person could be obligated to do the impossible.[8]

Lemmon used a number of examples to make his point. Perhaps the most compelling of these is Sartre's famous case of his student, a young man torn between joining the Free French Forces and remaining at home to help his mother.[9] This young man, Lemmon concluded, had a genuine conflict of obligations. He could not both leave and remain, and he was obligated to do both. He was therefore obligated to do the impossible.

The usual response to such attacks upon Kant's Principle—attacks based on the phenomenon of contradictory obligations—is to distinguish between obligations that are genuine and those that are only *prima facie*. In a conflict situation, there are a number of contenders for the role of one's duty, and these contenders may well be incompatible with one another. But when the contest is settled, no matter which group of contenders wins out, a person then has a consistent set of obligations.[10]

If we apply this standard way of analyzing conflict situations to the case of Sartre's student, one fact stands out. The standard analysis does not presuppose that a person is always or, for that matter, ever able to discover which of his duties are genuine and which are not. The standard method requires only that Sartre's student, if he has a duty at all in this matter, has a duty to do something possible.

Now according to this analysis, Sartre's student had a genuine duty. I do not know what it was, nor, apparently, did either Sartre or the young man himself. He might have been obligated to join the Free French, he might have been obligated to stay with his mother, he might have had no obligation to do either of these actions—but he

8. E. J. Lemmon, *op. cit.* Also E. J. Lemmon, "Deontic Logic and the Logic of Imperatives," *Logique et Analyse* 8 (1965): 39–71. As a reader of this book noted, the sorts of dilemmas Lemmon raises (and that I shall raise later in this chapter) present difficulties for Kant's Principle only if one further assumes that if A ought to do P and A ought to do Q, then A ought to do both P and Q. Such a principle seems eminently consistent with common sense, however.

9. Jean-Paul Sartre, *Existentialism and Humanism*, trans. P. Mairet (London, 1948), 35–46; quoted by E. J. Lemmon in "Moral Dilemmas," 153–54.

10. For example, see Azizah al-Hibri, *Deontic Logic: A Comprehensive Appraisal and a New Proposal* (Washington, D.C., 1978), 50–53. The reader will note that I am making no distinctions here between duty and obligation.

cannot have been obligated to do both. By this method, then, conflicts are restricted to the realm of the *prima facie*. Genuine duties cannot conflict.

Another method of dealing with conflict situations, bearing some resemblance to the standard one, is that of Hector-Neri Castañeda.[11] In Castañeda's version of deontic logic, all deontic operators receive subscripts, tags that indicate the source of obligation or permission. Operators with different subscripts are, in effect, different operators. Castañeda can then easily allow that there are obligations to perform contradictory acts, as long as those obligations derive from different sources. He does believe, though, that it is impossible for obligations with the same subscript to conflict.

Both Castañeda's and the standard response to supposed conflicts of obligation presuppose that genuine obligations, or obligations deriving from the same source, never conflict. There seems no *a priori* reason why this should be so, and we shall shortly be looking at three cases in which it definitely appears not to be so. It also seems more than a bit facile to say that Sartre's student had a genuine obligation to do something possible, without providing any way of discovering what that genuine duty was.

I am positivist enough to have grave doubts about the worth of saying that there is an answer to the young man's terrible dilemma when neither he nor anyone else has any way of discovering that answer or of determining whether a proposed answer is correct. I can't imagine even the most fanatical Kantian giving this advice: "Young man, there is no need to worry. You have no real problem at all. If you have a duty in this case, rest assured that you will be able to fulfill that duty, whatever it may be. Unfortunately, you may never know what that duty, if there is one, consists of." The value of such advice is minimal.

One might, if one wishes, accept as vacuously true the claim that genuine obligations do not conflict. According to this strategy, whenever we come across an apparent conflict, we can rest assured that at least one of the conflicting obligations is not genuine, for lack of conflict is built into the very meaning of 'genuine obligation'. To ensure that counterexamples will never arise, all we need do is choose a suitable redefinition of 'genuine obligation'.

But taking the "high priori" road avoids accidents only at the cost of getting nowhere. Any redefinition is worthless without a reason

---

11. Hector-Neri Castañeda, *Thinking and Doing* (Boston, 1975), 195–201.

for accepting it. And that reason, in this case, must consist of some independent criterion for suppposing that what we normally take as genuine obligations never do conflict. If there is such a criterion, it will do all the work, and the new definition is so much fruit salad. The Humpty-Dumpty solution of making lack of conflict part of the new meaning of 'genuine obligation' is therefore either unjustified or superfluous.

The preceding discussion of Sartre's student shows at least that Kant's Principle, when applied to some concrete situations, fails to resolve dilemmas. A Kantian, however, could always retort that a principle can be both useless and true. I therefore need to show that there are in fact some genuine 'oughts' without any corresponding 'cans'. To do so, I will consider at length three separate cases that, I shall argue, present genuine obligations that cannot be fulfilled. In each of the three sorts of cases, people have good reason to think themselves obligated to do the impossible. In many instances, this is exactly what they do think; and, I shall argue, they are right.

The three cases I present differ from each other in the source of obligation. In the first case, drawn from an interpretation of Christianity, the rules of an ethic prescribe a duty that the ethic claims cannot be met. In the second case, a fictional account from the Vietnam War, there is no conflict in the rules, but the rules do permit the issuance of contradictory commands. In the third case, which derives from American legal ethics, the rules of a professional code of conduct do, given the facts of a particular situation, conflict with one another.

CASE 1: THE DEMAND FOR PERFECTION

In this first example, the apparent impossibility of performance does not arise from a conflict in rules. The case comes from a reading of certain passages of the New Testament. The reading I outline here does not come with a certificate of orthodoxy, but it is certainly a possible interpretation. And persons who think along these same lines could have no other conclusion than that Christianity obligates a person to do the impossible. As I shall try to show, there have, in fact, been people who have come to just such a conclusion.

I begin with the Gospel According to St. Matthew 5:48: "Be perfect, just as your Heavenly Father is perfect." A reader—call him Gus— takes this passage literally. He thinks it imposes an obligation on humans to be perfect. Gus does not pussyfoot by supposing himself obligated only to be as good as he can be or as good as is humanly possible. Gus thinks himself obligated to be perfect—no ifs, ands, or buts!

So far, Gus has no problem in his theory, whatever practical difficulties he might face. The idea of perfection does not contain any obvious internal inconsistencies, and hence there may well be possible worlds in which Gus is perfect. But Gus continues his reading of the New Testament and comes upon the Pauline Epistles. There he finds that, in fact, he will fail to keep the obligation to be perfect. After reading St. Paul, he now believes that all persons are in a fallen condition. Without special Grace, they will without exception fall short of perfection. Gus is saddened by this fact, but he still might believe that perfection is possible for him. Many possibilities are never realized.

Then Gus's eye hits upon Romans 8:8: "So then they that are in the flesh *cannot* please God" (italics mine). Gus knows Greek and checks the passage—sure enough, that is exactly what St. Paul said. Once again, Gus decides to take the passage literally. Not only will he fail to fulfill his obligation to be perfect, he can't fulfill it. He is thus obligated to do the impossible.

Rather than try to explain away the passage from Romans, Gus makes it an integral part of his theology. He posits that all men are sufferers from original sin. It is therefore logically necessary, on this hypothesis, for all people after Adam, unless they receive special Grace, to act sinfully at some time or another, if they act at all. Those unlucky enough to miss receiving such Grace cannot fulfill their duty to be perfect and thus to please God.[12]

A believer in Kant's Principle would find Gus's position inconsistent. But Gus, at least, clearly does not believe that the violation of Kant's Principle somehow annuls his obligation to be perfect; rather, he believes that St. Paul's statement that everyone has sinned means precisely that we all had an obligation that we failed to carry out. For Gus, that he cannot help but fall into sin is no excuse, much less a cancellation of his duty of perfection.

Is Gus simply a philosopher's strawman, or has anyone actually thought as he does? I suggest that Gus is essentially no different in his arguments and conclusions from a most genuine and eminent historical figure: St. Augustine of Hippo. In his *Confessions*, St. Augustine spends a good bit of time reconstructing his actions during infancy. He

---

12. On the point of whether the necessity is logical or not, see pp. 30–31.

was, he concludes, an abject slave to lust (*libido*). When he nursed, he tells us, his selfishness was truly appalling. Why does St. Augustine make these bizarre claims?

The reason, I think, is that St. Augustine believes lust to lie at the root of all sin.[13] The infant Augustine, being sinful, must therefore have been lustful. But why suppose the infant was sinful? The most likely answer is that St. Augustine thought sinfulness inseparable from action for us fallen humans.

This interpretation of St. Augustine receives confirmation from Book 3 of the *De Libero Arbitrio*. There, in sections 170–179, Augustine takes up the thorny question of whether sin can be avoided through the exercise of free will. His answer is that it can be—as long as you are Adam or Eve before the fatal lunch (or, presumably, if you happen to be Jesus). If sin were natural for man, St. Augustine says, then no one (no One?) should blame a person for sinning. But sin is not natural—yet it is inseparable from us in our fallen condition. "Since man is as he is, he is not good, and does not have it in his power to be good" (section 174).[14] The infant Augustine must, therefore, have been bad, in other words, lustful.

This interpretation explains what strikes a modern reader as the oddest feature in Augustine's account of his infancy: it is all reconstruction on the basis of theory. Augustine does not draw at all on reminiscences of his mother or of old family friends; he tells how it must have been, not how it was. Augustine invented behavior to fit his belief that a human unaided by Grace cannot help but fall into sin.

St. Augustine knew well that babies sometimes die before they have a chance to commit obviously damnable acts, such as stealing pears. Given that babies are worthy of damnation, then, they must be doing something nasty. Hence, his theory leads St. Augustine to expect lustful acts from the newborn. Infant damnation has been a thorny subject among traditional theologians. St. Augustine's beliefs certainly indicate that he would not balk at the notion. To be sure, infants were not usually baptized in Augustine's day, but, as the saint well knew, even baptism does not remove lust. A baptized infant, cleansed from original sin, will still commit atrocious sins out of lust. Baptized infants are like the infant Augustine, as reconstructed by the grown Augustine's theology, and are good candidates for damnation.

13. See the translation of *De Libero Arbitrio Voluntatis*, entitled *On Free Choice of the Will*, Part 1, trans. Anna S. Benjamin and L. H. Hackstaff (Indianapolis, 1964), 21.
14. Ibid., p. 127.

Let us then ask not about my mythical Gus but about the real St. Augustine: where would Kant's Principle fit into his view of human obligation? Nowhere that I can see. Augustine instead seems to accept what I might call the Augustinian Principle: If I ought, then Adam could have. I ought to be perfect, and therefore Adam could have been perfect—but there is no way that I can be perfect. For that inability is, he says in the *De Libero Arbitrio*, part of my punishment, apparently for Adam's sin.

Augustinians have been accused through the ages of believing that humans without Grace are obligated to do what they cannot do. In 1653, Pope Innocent X, in the bull *Cum Occasione*, condemned five propositions supposedly extracted from the *Augustinus* of Cornelius Jansen, father of the Jansenist movement. The first proposition read: "Some of God's commandments are impossible for just men [to observe], even when they wish and strive [to keep them], if the grace which makes them possible is lacking."[15] Marc Escholier, in his book on Port-Royal, notes that, of the five condemned propositions, only this first one appears almost word for word in the *Augustinus*.[16] Jansen, then, followed St. Augustine in rejecting Kant's Principle.

We need not pick out St. Augustine alone among Church Fathers for rejecting Kant's Principle. Many theologians took the same line. For example, I believe it was Tertullian who was known as the *tortor infantum* for his eager acceptance of infant damnation. For him, and not for him alone, inability to behave properly is no excuse from damnation. Tertullian, I am sure, would have found Kant's Principle anathema.

So would the founders of Protestantism. To take a single sentence from many on the subject by Martin Luther: "For example, the commandment, 'You shall not covet' [Exod. 20:17], is a command which proves us all to be sinners, for no one can avoid coveting no matter how much he may struggle against it."[17] And the first petal of the Calvinist "tulip" is, of course, Total Depravity.

---

15. Reproduced in *Port-Royal: The Drama of the Jansenists*, by Marc Escholier (New York, 1968), 315. As one reader of this book pointed out, the sense of 'impossible' is left unclear.

16. Escholier, ibid., p. 71.

17. Martin Luther, "The Freedom of a Christian," trans. W. A. Lambert and H. J. Grimm, in John Dillenberger, ed., *Martin Luther: Selections from his Writings* (Garden City, 1961), 57.

I am not urging that we subscribe to the views of these Church Fathers. I find them morally repugnant. That they sound so strange to us today might be a sign that there really is such a thing as moral progress. But like it or not, these people had a developed view of human obligation in which 'ought' does not imply 'can'. They believed that people are obligated to do what they are utterly unable to perform because of their fallen nature.

Augustinian views are far from dead. As a matter of fact, when I was an undergraduate I heard a bishop take a position even more extreme than the one I have attributed to St. Augustine. The topic of the bishop's lecture was announced as "Christian Ethics"; a Kantian listening to the talk would conclude that the title, at least according to the bishop's construal of his topic, was a contradiction in terms!

The bishop's argument went something like this: Any natural action of a human in the current fallen state of mankind must lack all moral worth whatsoever. For either that action is, in God's eyes, a proper one, or it is not. If it is not, then clearly it lacks moral worth. But if the action is proper, then either the agent knows of its goodness or the agent does not. If the agent is ignorant of the act's goodness, then neither the individual nor the act merits any credit. But if the agent is aware of the goodness of what he or she is doing, then the agent necessarily takes pride in the deed. And pride, being terribly evil, automatically cancels all the moral worth of the action. Therefore, nothing we do can be of any moral worth. Since only actions that have moral worth are free of sin and can serve to fulfill our obligations to God, nothing that we do can serve to fulfill our obligations. Nothing.

In other words, the bishop concluded that 'ought', at least for us sinners in our duties to God, implies 'cannot'. I attributed to St. Augustine the relavitely mild positon that *some* acts of any human agent must be sinful. But the bishop claimed that *all* acts, or at least all acts with any moral significance, must be sinful.[18]

If I remember correctly, the bishop realized full well the implications of his argument. Indeed, I think he regarded the utter anti-Kantianism of his position as a *virtue*, not an embarrassment. This attitude is evidence, if any is needed, that even though Kant's Principle may be second nature to most moral philosophers, the world is not composed solely of moral philosophers!

How could the bishop think of his anti-Kantianism as a virtue? Perhaps he, like so many others, saw little point in being fair to evil-

18. I am sure the bishop would contend that all moral duties are ultimately duties to God.

doers. Compare the low opinion some people have of the Fifth Amendment's provisions against self-incrimination. Many years ago, a law was enacted that required all illegal bookmakers to report their revenue and its source to the local authorities on pain of penalty for tax evasion. This law was a blatant attempt to get people to incriminate themselves. I well remember one person's reaction at the time: "That will get them!" Yes, indeed. If bookies can't avoid punishment no matter what they do, so much the better, for evil people deserve anything that is done to them. This attitude was, I suspect, the bishop's as well—except that for "bookies" he read "people in general." Such a way of looking at things is distressingly common.

Most deontic logicians are far more fair-minded than this, and by including Kant's Principle among their moral beliefs, they show those beliefs to be far better than the bishop's. But to say that a person's moral beliefs are vicious is one thing, to say that they are nonexistent (as by the remark, "He must be using the word 'obligation' in some odd way that has nothing to do with morality") or self-contradictory is quite another.[19] The bishop should not have held the beliefs he held, but that 'should' is moral, not logical. Moral theories of the Augustinian stripe and worse deserve condemnation, to be sure, but to treat them as if they didn't exist, to suppose that Kant's Principle is built into every genuine moral theory and code, is absurd.

The point is important enough to bear repetition. Moral systems that deny Kant's Principle are vicious. In the same way, rulers who deliberately issue orders that cannot be carried out, to give some color of excuse to their future vindictive actions, are morally contemptible. "Vicious," "morally contemptible"—these are not the terms by which we call attention to logical mistakes. St. Augustine's reasoning is pretty good. His faults are not in his logic.

CASE 2: THE DUTIFUL SOLDIER

The second example I shall take up is quite different from the niceties of Augustinian theology, but it too raises difficulties for the upholder of Kant's Principle. In this case, a single source of authority, acting under

19. I do not want to suggest that Kant himself thought that his opponents held a nonexistent morality. But he did think they held a self-contradictory morality. And since a self-contradiction allows us to infer whatever we please, it is hard to see how a self-contradictory theory could require some performances of us and forbid others. Hence, it is hard to see how a logically self-contradictory theory, or least one known to be such, could serve as a system of morality.

rules that are themselves consistent, prescribes contradictory actions as obligatory. The example I shall discuss is a fictional one, although the circumstances in which it arises bear a recognizable resemblance to reality.

Lieutenant Broderick is serving in the United States Army at the time of American involvement in the Vietnam War. Broderick has been told that the army is in Vietnam to help the Vietnamese people. By no means should he treat villagers as if they are enemy combatants. He has been told all about the rules of civilized warfare, and he has learned that the United States armed forces subscribe to those rules. He understands and accepts all he has been told; and then he is sent to Vietnam.

Broderick receives orders to lead his troops into a certain village, which is known for having given a certain measure of support to the Viet Cong. He is told that certain insurgent personnel are presently living in the village. His task is to destroy the insurgent infrastructure in the village—both enemy troops and those who have aided them. At the same time, his orders remind Broderick not to harm the peaceful inhabitants of the village.

What courses are open to Lieutenant Broderick as he conscientiously attempts to carry out his orders? He has no trustworthy informants in the village, and no good outside source of information. Villagers might denounce one another as Viet Cong sympathizers, but Broderick has no clear way of telling when these denunciations are to be trusted and when the villagers are merely furthering private feuds. Bribery is effective in securing denunciations—so many that Broderick realizes that, if he acts on all information gained from bribery, he will inevitably harm some innocent people.

Persuasion is another course open to Broderick, but only in very abstract theory. The lieutenant is not eloquent enough—perhaps nobody could be eloquent enough—to bring the Viet Cong and all their sympathizers to the side of the Saigon government. If Broderick backs up persuasion with bribery, he only causes the enemy to be somewhat more affluent.

Forcing some of the villagers to leave will harm innocent civilians, and after Broderick leaves, they will return anyway. Destroying their livelihoods is likely to create even more animosity toward the Saigon government.

Lieutenant Broderick concludes that, prison space being unavailable, the only way to destroy the enemy infrastructure is to kill a number of the villagers. There is simply no other way of fulfilling that part of his orders. He must use his best judgment as to which villagers are to be killed and which are not. The lieutenant is well aware, however, that, in following this course, he cannot avoid killing some, perhaps many, innocent people, and that would contradict his orders not to harm the innocent. What should he do?

Broderick's dilemma raises the familiar problem of false positives, a problem that bedevils attempts to base one's actions on predictions of an infrequent type of behavior. Most of the villagers are likely to be innocent; hence, lacking reliable information,the lieutenant cannot kill villagers without killing the innocent. Yet, Broderick cannot carry out his orders to destroy the enemy infrastructure in any other way.

Quite possibly, the army is at fault for putting Broderick into such a position. The question is debatable: a certain consequentialism, even with respect to life or death matters, seems unavoidable in time of war. But Broderick has no leisure to debate the question. He has his orders.

Broderick's orders are not self-contradictory. They generate what looks like a contradiction only when combined with background information about the available ways of destroying infrastructure. Even then, although the acts prescribed are contradictory, the orders combined with background information are not. There would be no self-contradiction even had the orders blatantly read: "You ought to destroy the enemy infrastructure and you ought not to destroy the enemy infrastructure." Only the statement that Broderick obeyed his orders would be a self-contradiction, not the orders themselves.[20]

We might suppose that Broderick answers his dilemma by deliberately setting out to do the impossible.[21] Many people have tried to

---

20. We would have a self-contradiction only if it is the case that Broderick ought to destroy and it is not the case that Broderick ought to destroy. 'Ought not' is different from 'not ought'; we can infer the latter from the former only by assuming that a person cannot have duties to do contradictory actions, and that would be assuming the very point at issue. A similar situation occurs with the logic of belief. It is contradictory to say that a person both believes a proposition p and doesn't believe p (at the same time, in the same manner, and so on). But it is not a contradiction to suppose that a person both believes p and believes not-p. Indeed, this often happens. Suppose that p is a complex set of propositions, and the subject fails to see that not-p contradicts that set. Thus in epistemic logic, one need not and probably should not adopt the principle that 'believes not-p' implies 'not believes p'. Similarly, in deontic logic one need not—and I am arguing that one should not—adopt the principle that 'ought not to do A' implies 'not ought to do A'. (The *moral* principle, yes; but not the *logical* principle.) In this respect, these two logics differ from most modal systems, where 'necessarily not-p' implies 'not necessarily p'. But even in standard modal systems, that implication is a matter of the special detachment principles governing the modal operators, not a matter of nonmodal logical rules.

do the impossible: the history of attempts to build a perpetual-motion machine or to square the circle is proof. Even if you know a task to be impossible, you might try your hand at it anyway, for any number of reasons. You might want to find out how close you can come to doing what can't be done, or you might be interested in just where the insuperable stumbling block lies, or you might see no better course to take. Let us suppose Broderick to be of this last type.

Broderick resolves not to take innocent lives. To destroy the enemy infrastructure, he therefore attempts to persuade and bribe all villagers to be loyal to the Saigon government, even though he knows these methods will fail. He knows he can't carry out both provisions of his orders. Still, he makes a stab at doing so. He fails.

At the court-martial, Broderick is charged with dereliction of duty: he failed to destroy the enemy infrastructure of the village, as he was ordered to do. Of course, had he succeeded in doing so, he would be facing a different court-martial, for he would have disobeyed orders by deliberately harming innocent civilians. Either way, he stands a good chance of conviction.

Whatever the lieutenant's decison might have been, the army is determined to hold him responsible for his actions, and those actions will inevitably violate his orders. Broderick thus has obligations as an officer of the United States Army that he cannot possibly fulfill.

As I already stated, this case is fictional, but the circumstances have been known to arise. The issuance of orders impossible to fulfill, coupled with the insistence that those orders are to be disregarded at one's peril, is not unheard-of in armies.

Can we say that Broderick's orders were a dead letter because of the impossiblity of carrying them out? The army wouldn't regard them as such. Nor does Broderick reason in accordance with Kant's Principle, for he conscientiously tries to do the impossible. He thinks himself bound by his orders.

Perhaps the army and Broderick should not treat those orders as in force? I agree completely with this suggestion. Whatever Broderick does in his predicament, it is immoral to make him bear the blame. As with the Augustinian theologians, however, wickedness is not illogicality. The problem isn't that the army does not play the deontic game; it's that the army plays the game in a reprehensible way. Nothing is wrong with the army's reasoning, but plenty is wrong

21. His counterparts in the British Army would do just that, according to the bartender in the comic strip "Andy Capp." Speaking of the title character, the bartender says: "He's ex-Army. When given two contradictory orders, obey 'em both" (Daily Mirror Newspapers, Ltd., 21 October 1984).

with its ethics. As with the Augustinians, then, we can conclude that the army's behavior in the case of Lieutenant Broderick reveals a bad code of ethics, not an illogical or nonexistent one. Moral theories do not forfeit their status as moral theories when they deny Kant's Principle—what they forfeit is their merit.

CASE 3: THE CONSCIENTIOUS ATTORNEY

Moral viciousness is not so apparent in the third case I shall discuss. In imposing an obligation impossible to perform, the canons of the American Bar Association (A.B.A.) are certainly in some sense at fault, and again, the fault does not seem a logical one. But as we shall see, the sin of the canons resembles impracticality more than immorality.[22]

Smith is indicted on charges of using the mail to defraud. To represent him at the trial, he retains Jones as his attorney. The case against Smith is strong, but, fortunately for him, Smith has a very persuasive manner. If he testifies that he knew nothing of the actual fraud and throws all the blame on his former assistant, who is to testify against him, there is a good chance the jury will have at least a reasonable doubt of his guilt. During a pretrial conference with his attorney, Smith announces his intention to testify to this effect. He also remarks to his attorney that the testimony will be false, for he did in fact know of the fraud. Smith has thus revealed an intention to commit perjury. What should Jones, as an ethical attorney, do?

This dilemma is, at the least, a difficult one. As an officer of the court, Jones must not countenance what he knows to be perjury. As Smith's attorney, however, Jones is obligated at a minimum to do nothing to injure his client's case. Revealing the client's perjury would certainly be such an injury, while keeping silent might lead to Jones's disbarment.[23]

There are a number of ways out of the dilemma, including provi-

22. In my discussion, I am depending on a speech given by Michael L. Bender to the Colorado Trial Lawyers Association. I learned of this speech from a news report by Zeke Scher in the 25 August 1984 issue of the Denver *Post*. I am grateful to Mr. Bender for sending me an outline of his speech, entitled, "The Insoluble Dilemma: The Perjurious Client in a Criminal Case."

23. As it did in *Board of Overseers of the Bar* v *Dinen*, #Bar–83–46, Maine Superior Judicial Court, 29 December 1983. This citation comes from the Bender speech mentioned in note 22.

dential ones. Smith might have a fatal heart attack before the trial, or he might get religion, renounce his intention to perjure himself, and enter a plea of guilty. Jones might find a flaw in the prosecution's case sufficient to win acquittal without his client's testimony. But let us suppose Jones has no such miraculous deliverance. What can he do?

He can and should attempt as strongly as he can to dissuade Smith from committing perjury. According to the *American Bar Association Standards for Criminal Justice*, the attorney must take this action, again on pain of disbarment.[24] But Smith is no fool. He will not forfeit his only chance for acquittal just to get his attorney off the hook.

Jones could refuse to call his client as a witness. But then he may be infringing on his client's constitutional rights to due process and to representation by counsel. For according to the *New A.B.A. Model Rules of Professional Conduct*, "In some jurisdictions these provisions [*read* the constitutional rights just mentioned] have been construed that counsel present an accused as a witness if the accused wishes to testify, even if counsel knows the testimony will be false."[25] If the case is being tried in such a jurisdiction, Smith's constitutional right to testify cannot be denied him.

Faced with his dilemma, Jones has no alternative but to attempt to withdraw from the case.[26] But to do so, Jones needs the permission of the court. And when he asks for permission, Jones will undoubtedly be asked his reasons for wishing to withdraw. After all, withdrawing is very likely to harm his client's case and should not be done except for very strong reasons.

Jones, of course, has excellent reasons for withdrawing. But should he tell the court that his client intends to commit perjury? No, according to the A.B.A. *Defense Function Standards*: "If, in advance of trial, the defendant insists that he or she will take the stand to testify perjuriously, the lawyer must withdraw from the case, if that is feasible, seeking leave of the court if necessary, but the court should not be

---

24. "If the defendant has admitted to defense counsel facts which establish guilt and counsel's independent investigation established that the admissions are true but the defendant insists on the right to trial, counsel must strongly discourage the defendant against taking the witness stand to testify perjuriously" (*A.B.A. Standards for Criminal Justice: Standards Relating to the Prosecution Function and the Defense Function*, [New York, 1982] vol. 1, chap. 4, sec. 7.7). This citation I also owe to Michael Bender, *op. cit.*

25. Ibid., sec. 3.3(a)(4), quoted in Bender, *op. cit.*

26. In the Maine case cited previously, the fact that the attorney did not try to withdraw contributed to his disbarment.

advised of the lawyer's reason for seeking to do so." [27] Surely such an advisement would prejudice the client's case.

Perhaps Jones decides he cannot in this case let himself be bound by A.B.A. rules, even though he faces disbarment for disobedience. After all, he might reason, the code of a professional association is less important than obeying the law. Unfortunately for him, he might be in a jurisdiction where that code is in effect the law. Michael Bender notes that in both state and federal cases, courts have adopted the A.B.A. *Defense Function Standards* as proper procedure in instances such as the present one. [28]

Jones, then, attempts to withdraw but gives no reason. His request is denied. It is time for him to present his defense. What should he, as an ethical attorney, do?

Under the *Defense Function Standards*, he must protect himself as best he can. First, Jones must make a record of the fact that Smith is testifying against advice of counsel (but Jones must not reveal this fact to the court). Jones may question Smith in a normal manner in those areas in which he does not expect Smith to commit perjury. But when he expects Smith to begin lying under oath, Jones must avoid normal questioning. Instead, he should ask Smith if he "wishes to make any additional statement concerning the case." After the testimony is over, Jones must act as if it had not been given: he may not "later argue the defendant's known false version of facts to the jury as worthy of belief, and may not recite or rely upon the false testimony in his or her closing argument." [29]

I think these suggestions reveal how insoluble Jones's difficulties are. Certainly an attorney who followed the A.B.A. recommendations to the letter would be, in effect, shouting to the judge that his client was perjuring himself. Would not the judge, then, in instructing the jury, call attention to the defense counsel's curious behavior and its

27. *A.B.A. Standards*, vol. 1, sec. 7.7, provision (b). This citation is also from Bender, *op. cit.*

28. Bender, *op. cit.* The cases include *Goodwin* v *State of South Carolina*, 305 So.E.2d 578 (So. Ca. 1983), and *Thornton* v *United States*, 357 A.2d 429 (D. Col. Ct. App. 1976). The decision in *Thornton* was upheld on appeal, and it has been the basis of a number of cases since. However, in *Johnson* v *United States*, 404 A2d 162, p. 163, the court notes that by its understanding of *Thornton*, restricting one's questioning in such an instance and making no use of the testimony is not a denial of the client's right to counsel. Hence, the dilemma cannot arise in the District of Columbia.

29. *A.B.A. Standards*, vol. 1, sec. 7.7, provision (c); cited in Bender, *op. cit.*

probable cause?[30] Under any circumstances, I think it hard to deny that the result would most likely be injury to the client's case. The fact is, the *Defense Function Standards* simply give up trying to resolve the dilemma. If the attorney cannot withdraw, and if he cannot persuade his client to testify either truthfully or not at all, then he has two duties that actually conflict. He both should and should not countenance what he knows to be perjury. The A.B.A. can do no better here than to let the attorney start building his own case for the disciplinary hearing to follow.

Michael Bender is, then, perfectly correct in calling poor Jones's predicament "the insoluble dilemma." Jones cannot both countenance and fail to countenance Smith's perjury, and yet he is obligated to do both. Jones, then, is obligated to do the impossible.

Should we then conclude that the A.B.A. rules are, as Kant's Principle would indicate, logical absurdities? Unfortunately, it is not just those rules that are at stake here. I have tried to indicate in describing the various alternatives open to Jones that, given Smith's unshakable intent to commit perjury, there is ample justification for ascribing each of these contradictory duties to Jones. In this case, the duty of upholding the law conflicts with the duty of serving as a faithful representative. These are actual duties that most people would uphold, although they actually do, in a case such as this, conflict. Lacking a clear-cut procedure for determining which duty takes precedence, the attorney has no way of resolving his dilemma.[31]

The case of the perjurious client, then, does not square at all well with Kant's Principle. To say that the rules giving rise to the lawyer's dilemma are therefore no rules disregards the fact that those rules embody what most people believe to be actual duties. To say that one or the other of the duties is, in the given case, not genuine is certainly

30. Not according to Warren Burger. Writing in 1966, before he became chief justice, Burger made suggesions very similar to those in Ibid., sec. 7.7, c. He then added: "Since this informal procedure is not uncommon with witnesses, there is no basis for saying that this tells the jury the witness is lying. A judge may infer that such is the case but lay jurors will not." But then, should the judge keep from the jury this piece of legal knowledge that might be relevant to their decision? (The quote is from Warren Burger, "Standards of Conduct: A Judge's Viewpoint," *Am. Crim. Law* 5 (1966): 11–16, especially 13; cited in *Butler v United States*, 414 A. 2d 844 [D.C.App.], p. 871.)

31. Michael Bender notes that, under the *New A.B.A. Model Rules of Professional Conduct*, there is a clear rule of precedence. The attorney must report perjury to the court, whatever the effect on the client's case.

not helpful, and only dogma would lead anyone to that conclusion. And to say that such cases just won't arise ignores the fact that they have arisen. At least one disbarred lawyer can testify to that effect!

CONCLUSIONS FROM THE THREE CASES

With these three cases, I am questioning the principle that what one ought to do is always *logically* possible. Obviously anything logically impossible is also physically impossible. In this universe, no amount of sustained effort will allow a person to make *pi* a repeating decimal. "Ummon said, 'All you monks roam about all over the earth on Zen pilgrimages, but you don't know the meaning of Daruma's coming from the West. The outside post knows it all right. Why don't you somehow find out the post's knowledge of that meaning?' "[32] A monk who took Ummon's order literally would be betraying his own lack of enlightenment, but not all monks are enlightened. Imagine the poor, literal-minded monk respectfully addressing the post and, necessarily, getting nowhere.

If in these three cases a person was genuinely obligated to do the logically impossible, then clearly that person was also obligated to do the physically impossible. It is not always easy to differentiate physical from logical possibility, however; and in at least two of the three case, one might well argue that logical possibility is not at issue. In case three, a trial lawyer is unable to do all he ought. One might contend either that the inhibition is logical or that it is physical. Likewise in case one, the Augustinian who claims that a person without Grace cannot be free from sin might be speaking of physical or of logical impossiblity.[33] Only the Augustinian theory of Divine Grace can settle that question, and I am not theologian enough to venture an interpretation of that theory.[34]

32. R. H. Blyth (selected by Frederick Franck), *Zen and Zen Classics* (New York, 1978), 247.

33. I am grateful to a reader for Brown University Press for pointing this out.

34. To settle the question in this case, we would have to determine just how Grace operates for the Augustinian. Does it provide a boost in the person's ability to avoid sin, something like enough extra fuel to allow a vehicle to get to a preset destination? If so, then the impossibility overcome by Grace would seem a physical one. But if Grace literally produces a new person, one with an ability to avoid sin altogether, an ability lacking in the old person, then there is a good case for the claim that the old person logically could not be perfect.

However, even if cases one and three are taken as instances of physical (and not logical) impossiblity, the physical impossibility would be of a most important kind. Neither the trial lawyer nor the unregenerate human are able to exercise the human agency necessary for them to do as they ought. Now if 'ought' does not imply 'logically can', it certainly doesn't imply 'agency can'. Hence, whether or not my cases show that one can be obligated to do the logically impossible, at the very least they show that one can be obligated to do what one lacks the ability to exercise the agency to do. Therefore, the cases succeed in calling into question an important version of Kant's Principle.

One way of defending Kant's Principle is to deny the reality of the three cases. Now the case of the Augustinian theologians is clearly a matter of impossibility engendered by theory. One can avoid the difficulty simply by avoiding the theory in question (although some have embraced that theory eagerly). The case of Lieutenant Broderick was fictional, although the opportunity for such a case to arise was ample and evident. But the case of the perjurious client is no fiction, even though my Smith and Jones are inventions. Clients have announced to their attorneys their unshakable intention to commit perjury, and the lawyer's dilemma has resulted.

One cannot defend Kant's Principle, then, by saying that exceptions exist only in theory or in the sort of far-fetched desert island example only an ethical theorist could love. One might try to defend it by disallowing the principle that if a person has a duty to do A and a duty to do B, that person has a duty to do both A and B. But this principle seems too commonsensical to give up completely. And it will not help much to tell the lawyer whose client intends perjury that, although he as a duty to countenance the perjury and a duty not to countenance the perjury, he might not have a duty to do both. The lawyer, whatever he does, will still be acting against a duty.

There are, I conclude, cases in which Kant's Principle simply does not hold. Therefore, Kant's Principle cannot be part of the logic of deontic speech.

But if Kant's Principle is not part of deontic logic, what is it? My three cases suggest strongly that it is a substantive moral principle, present in the better moral theories and lacking in the worse ones. In other words, one morally ought not to impose, accept, or infer any obligation that cannot be performed by the individual upon whom the obligation is placed.[35]

---

35. A position similar to this one has been defended by Morton White. See, for instance, his *What Is and What Ought to be Done* (New York and Oxford, 1981), 70.

That Kant's Principle is a substantive moral principle is, I think, true, but it is not the whole truth. For to take Kant's Principle as a substantive moral claim needs justification. St. Augustine, the United States Army, and at least a part of the American legal system implicitly reject that principle. We cannot therefore simply assume its correctness without offering some evidence or argument. Any argument *ex consensu gentium* must fall foul of the simple fact that too many of the peoples just do not go along with Kant's Principle. And to declare roundly that it is a moral principle, and that's all there is to say, is no better propaganda than it is philosophy.

Instead, we shall attack the question of the status of Kant's Principle by looking one more time at what the Augustinian God expects of us. Let us suppose that the infant Augustine is indeed caught in the toils of lust and is therefore exceedingly sinful. Allow further that the infant, not having developed reason, has no real choice in the matter of his lustful behavior. (When he is an adult and is reasonable, he will have a choice—as long as he is either Adam, Eve, or Jesus!) From God's point of view, then, the infant does what he ought not to do and hence merits damnation, although he could not but do exactly what he is doing.

A God like that is certainly worthy of moral condemnation. But, putting that aside for the moment, I suggest that, in an awful way, the behavior of St. Augustine's God is somewhat silly. I mean that God's behavior, as St. Augustine paints it, is peculiarly pointless. Why should He require an infant to behave in a way that the infant cannot begin to live up to? Why should anyone, much less God, do such a thing?

Presumably, setting obligations is a purposive activity. One makes requirements, at least in many instances, in order to get people to do certain things and to refrain from doing others.[36] If so, then to set an unfulfillable obligation is to act contrary to at least one major purpose of setting obligations. And in the three cases I have discussed, the purpose of the deontic speech did seem to be to guide actions.

I am suggesting that the Augustinian God, although not illogical, is using the language of obligation contrary to at least a major purpose for having and using such language. His offense is against pragmatics, not against semantics.

---

36. If, as St. Paul seems to suggest in places, the purpose of the Law is to ensure that all humans are guilty of sin, then St. Paul's God strikes me as guilty of a peculiarly nasty form of bad faith. See, for instance, Romans 3:19. My next chapter will include an extended discussion of the purposes of making deontic speeches.

We can say the same of the army in the Broderick case. What is the point of knowingly issuing an order that cannot be fulfilled? Certainly not the straightforward point of trying to get the lieutenant to take a particular action, that which the orders say that he should do. Contradictory orders, then, offend against the whole institutional purpose of order giving.

And the lawyer faced with a perjurious client simply has no good course of action available. Faced with conflicting obligations, he can only hope to avoid sanctions whatever he chooses to do. There is really no point in reciting his duties to court and client in this case: he cannot meet at least some of them.

I am claiming that Kant's Principle is a matter of pragmatics, not a matter of logic. But an obvious difficulty would present itself if I should claim that Kant's Principle is *merely* a matter of pragmatics. The activities of the Augustinian God are offensive. To call them merely impractical or inefficient is to damn with all too faint damns. The same can be said of the actions of Broderick's superior officers.

This very point will come up more than once in this book. I shall, for example, accuse Nazis of offenses against a pragmatic principle of universalizability. Few people would think it adequate to accuse Hitler of merely failing to pursue his ends in the most effective manner. Clearly, what I take to be pragmatic principles may also serve as important substantive moral rules. But that is not always the case. After all, I have stressed that the American Bar Association does not deserve to be charged with wickedness. The relation between pragmatic deontic principles and substantive moral rules is complex, and I do not address that matter until chapter 14, after I have explained the rules of deontic pragmatics. For now, I think it enough to have shown that Kant's Principle is in fact a pragmatic rather than a logical one. In H. P. Grice's terms, 'ought' does not imply 'can'; rather, 'ought' implicates 'can'.

But if so, what is the source of this implicature? What principle lies behind our usual willingness to suppose that what a person ought to do, he can do?

H. P. Grice finds the basis for all implicatures in his Cooperative Principle: "Make your conversational contribution such as is required, at the stage at which it occurs, by the accepted purpose or direction of the talk exchange in which you are engaged."[37] This statement, of course, is only a schema for a principle, a skeleton in need of flesh

---

37. H. P. Grice, "Logic and Conversation," in G. Harman and D. Davidson, eds., *The Logic of Grammar* (Encino and Belmont, Cal., 1975), 67.

for its bare bones. Where a "talk exchange" is deontic, the applicable version of the Cooperative Principle obviously depends on the purpose or purposes of deontic speech.

The purpose of deontic speech is a subject important and complex enough to warrant a chapter to itself. We will then be fairly clear about the "Why" of deontic pragmatics, and it will be time to turn to the "What."

3

Why We Use Deontic Speech

We employ deontic speech for many purposes. In this chapter, I will show that we may regard one use as central: to cause people to act or to refrain from acting in certain ways. I call this the *directive use* of deontic statements.

It takes little insight to see that the same deontic sentence may be used directively on one occasion, nondirectively on another. Suppose the department secretary reminds me I should attend a meeting at two o'clock. If she makes this speech in time for me to get to the meeting, it's likely that she is trying to direct my activities. But if she makes the same speech only when she knows that it's too late for me to get to the meeting, her purpose must be nondirective.

Richmond Thomason suggests that when we use deontic operators in contexts where we cannot hope to direct action, our usual intent is to make a judgment.[38] There may be a number of different reasons for making such a judgment—some directive, some not. My secretary may wish to induce guilt in me, or she may be trying to get me to do better in the future.

The judgmental use of deontic language is perhaps as common as the directive use.[39] I may say that the president ought to veto a certain bill, even though I have no influence on the president's actions; or a present-day historian might claim that Henry VIII should have made a different case for the illegality of his first marriage, although the historian has no chance of altering the past. In both cases, the use of 'ought' represents a judgment, not a directive.

But if directive oughts are distinct from and perhaps no more common than judgmental oughts, how can the former be primary and the latter merely derivative? I would not assert that the centrality of the directive use is a matter of historical precedence. Even proof that in the early days of deontic language all such talk was purely directive would have no clear bearing on why people today use that language. By the same token, I am not claiming that users of deontic language today have the directive use uppermost in their minds. Even if one could show that the judgmental use is more prevalent than the directive, my point would not be invalidated.[40] Nor am I making some sort of reductionist claim. The two uses are different: judgment is not direction in disguise. Rather, I shall argue for accepting a *theory* that organizes the data (that is, the uses of deontic speech) in a certain way. The theory in question seeks to explain, on the basis of directive use, all the nondirective ways in which deontic language is used.

I do not doubt that other ways of organizing the data could be found. Perhaps one might explain all the uses of deontic speech on the basis of the judgmental use, or one might take more than one use as primitive. My assertion is only that we can organize the data as I have done, and that such organization will prove fruitful.

38. Richmond Thomason, "Deontic Logic as Founded on Tense Logic" in Risto Hilpinen, ed., *New Studies in Deontic Logic* (Dordrecht, 1981), p. 170.

39. I do not mean to imply that the directive and judgmental are the only uses of deontic language, although I believe they are the most common. Later in this chapter, I shall look briefly at some other kinds of uses.

40. As I shall argue on p. 39, there is reason to think that at times people do base judgmental uses on directive ones, but my case does not rest on this point.

Aristotle's concept of 'focal meaning' is useful in clarifying what I mean by a central use. According to Aristotle, an operation is called surgical because 'surgical' literally describes the nature of the operation, while a scalpel or a textbook are called surgical because of their relationship to a surgical operation. To call the operation, the scalpel, and the textbook all surgical is to use the term ambiguously. But the meaning of 'surgical' in the latter two cases focuses in upon the meaning of the term in the first case.[41]

Likewise, I suggest, we can come up with a notion of 'focal use'. If there is one use for a type of speech that, by reference to it, will explain other uses, then the others can be said to focus in on that central use. Specifically, my contention is that we can explain judgmental uses of deontic language by reference to directive uses. For, I believe, a judgmental use can be regarded as the directive use in a counterfactual situation.[42]

For example, consider the case of J. J. Scarisbrick, a historian who argued that Henry VIII should have followed a different strategy.[43] I suggest that we regard Scarisbrick's purpose in making this claim to be the following: to give the counsel the historian would have given Henry had he been in a position to direct the king's thinking about the Divorce. The judgmental 'should', then, is the directive 'should' that one would offer if he were in a position to speak directively.

This is only a first approximation to an adequate account of judgmental uses. For would Scarisbrick, in fact, have advised Henry VIII to change his tactics? Henry, from all the historians I have read, was a man powerfully in love with his own ideas and none too fond of being contradicted. A prudent historian might well decide that silence was the best course.

Clearly, I need to specify the contrary-to-fact condition more carefully. Perhaps we can imagine Scarisbrick saying: "If I had been able to direct Henry's thinking about the Divorce, and if I had nothing

41. Aristotle *Metaphysics* 4. 2. The term 'focal meaning' is G. E. L. Owen's happy substitute for the half-English of '*pros hen* equivocation'. The standard English version of Aristotle's works is J. Barnes, ed., *The Complete Works of Aristotle: The Revised Oxford Translation* (Oxford, 1984).

42. If I were claiming that in some way the directive use of 'ought' is *really* primary, I would need to show that we cannot understand the directive use on the basis of the judgmental use (as a reader of the book suggested). Since I am not claiming that, I need not show any such thing—which is good since I have no idea how I could show it!

43. J. J. Scarisbrick, *Henry VIII* (Berkeley and Los Angeles, 1968), 183–97. Scarisbrick does not explicitly use deontic language, but he is clearly saying what he thinks Henry should have done.

to fear or hope for from Henry, and if I intended to give Henry the best advice I knew of, I would have told him to change his tactics."[44] But this account is also too crude, for one might reasonably ask what the historian means by the phrase "the best advice." In this instance, he probably means "the most practical advice for Henry in pursuing the king's aim of getting his marriage declared a nullity." Sometimes, however, the best advice is intended to advance something other than the advisee's short-term goals. The advisor might be trying to advance the advisee's long-term goals, or the goals the advisor thinks the advisee should have, or the advisor's own goals. Again, the best advice might be not prudential but moral or legal. Hence, we need to clarify the vague notion of "best advice" in any satisfactory counterfactual analysis of a judgmental ought.

After all, a counterfactual analysis presents what purports to be a causal situation. To determine the merit of any such analysis, we decide whether, under causal laws, the situation spelled out in the 'if' clauses would indeed produce the situation spelled out in the 'then' clauses. One cannot predict with any accuracy the outcome of a situation without some detailed awareness of the situation. Therefore, should the historian say, "... if I intended to give Henry the best advice I knew of," without spelling out what "best advice" means here, we can not tell whether his counterfactual is a good one or not. After all, there have been Anglican historians and Catholic historians, nationalists and non-nationalists, Anglophobes and Anglophiles. The 'best advice' of each of these is likely to differ from that of the others.

The 'if' part of my counterfactual seems to be mushrooming. One might reasonably begin to wonder whether a person could ever specify all the relevant conditions that must be met to have a good counterfactual. Certainly one could never specify all the conditions that must *not* obtain if the given result is to occur. Is there any hope for the counterfactual analysis?

There is hope, I think. In the first place, one should be able to list all the positive conditions that would have to obtain for one's prediction in the counterfactual situation to have a rational expectation of success. That the prediction is not certain does not seem a crip-

---

44. As a reader of the book pointed out, this counterfactual cannot give the *meaning* of "Henry VIII ought to have changed his tactics." For if it did, then two historians with different notions about what Henry should have done would not, in fact, be disagreeing. Each would only be stating what he himself would have said to Henry. This consideration makes it clear that I am giving a theory about use, not an analysis of meaning.

pling disability—as long as one is not claiming meaning equivalence between the original sentence and the proposed analysis. And I am not.

Further, it is often clear from context what the nature of this best advice would be. A religious leader says, "Hitler should not have brought about the deaths of millions of innocent people." A person who subjects this statement to the analysis I propose will have no doubt that this best advice is given from the moral point of view and does not attempt to satisfy Hitler's own practical interests or aims.

Counterfactual analysis therefore seems possible. And there is a large advantage in construing judgmental oughts as directive oughts in a counterfactual situation. If we understand directive oughts, and if we have a grasp of the counterfactual situation and the relevant causal laws, we should be able to understand judgmental oughts. And if our grasp of directive oughts enables us to give at least partial truth-conditions, we could do the same for judgmental oughts. In other words, we can understand judgmental uses by reference to directive uses.

At times, this is how people actually do understand judgmental uses. Readers might or might not accept an historian's claim that Henry should have changed his tactics. One way readers make that decision is to reflect on what the historian has revealed of his own beliefs and motives and to conjecture how these would have affected his advice to Henry. If, for example, the historian is someone with a contemporary axe to grind, someone on the order of Hilaire Belloc, we take that fact into account in determining what he would have said to Henry. With that point determined, we are in a position to judge the historian's claim that Henry should have done otherwise. In general, readers will often use something like my counterfactual analysis in assessing a judgmental ought, and in doing so, they will look for the historian's aims. The advice to "put yourself in his shoes" is so common as to be banal.

To be sure, we rarely have so clear an understanding of directive oughts that we can give truth-conditions for them. When the directive ought issues from a coherent body of rules, which clearly apply without conflict to the situation at hand, then we can perhaps determine the truth or falsity of the directive. This state of affairs seldom occurs in all its purity. Once again, though, I am not urging an analysis of what the historian means. We can and do often understand what conditions must hold if we are to have a reasonable expectation that a directive ought is true. For all practical purposes, that is enough.

After all, the weight of my argument does not rest on the claim that people actually go through the counterfactual analysis I propose. That they do so is only icing on the cake.[45]

What holds for judgmental oughts holds for other sorts of oughts as well. Informative, ironic, and other uses of deontic language do not reduce to either the directive or the judgmental use; but the same sort of theory I deployed for judgmental oughts applies equally well to these other uses.

Next to the directive and the judgmental, informative uses seem most common and most important. Certainly, we often use deontic language to inform someone of something: of the state of the law, perhaps, or of the nature or intensity of our feelings. The belief that one should bear witness or, in the Quaker phrase, "speak truth to power" suggests that some people find great value in telling a person what she should or should not do, even when they are fully aware there is no chance of getting her to agree. When one promulgates a law, at least one point in so doing is to let others know what the law is. And as a parent of teenagers, I have more than once resorted to the *pro forma* protest. To be sure, there is some element of judgment in all these uses, but the chief aim seems to be that of informing.

Above all, the purpose of making a first-person deontic statement is normally to inform.[46] If I say, "I ought to go to the store," I might be trying to get myself to take action, and I might be judging myself and perhaps blaming myself for not doing so. But it is far more likely that I am simply informing another person of what I take to be my duty.

We can analyze most of these cases of the informative ought along exactly the same lines as we analyzed the judgmental ought. Certainly, the person who speaks truth to power would not normally be angry if the power listened and agreed. In telling a wicked ruler what he should do, the witness-bearer can be understood as giving directions in a counterfactual situation: if you could be directed by

---

45. One should not mistake the icing for the cake. As I noted above, I am not trying to reduce one role to another, to say that judgmental oughts really are nothing but directive oughts in a counterfactual situation. I am attempting to build a theory, not to uncover a well-masked reality. (See pp. 36–37.)

46. This point, along with the example of the recalcitrant teenagers, I owe to Mary Gore Forrester. For that matter, I owe the teenagers themselves to her!

me, and if I intended to give you the best advice I could, I would have directed you in the way I now specify.[47] A similar account fits the case of the recalcitrant teenagers.

As for the promulgation of a law, the ultimate purpose in doing so is generally not that people understand but that they obey. To be sure, people must understand before they can be expected to obey, but the same is generally true for all deontic utterances. They surely have a meaning, and to understand that meaning is the first step toward acting as the speaker wishes. Informing is then only a subsidiary aim to influencing behavior.[48]

One cannot so easily apply counterfactual analysis to the first-person informative oughts. Why do I tell someone what I ought to do? Sometimes, it is an indirect way of specifying the duties of my listener. I might be boasting or complaining. I could be getting the other person to press me to do what I should do, or I might be hoping that he will convince me that I have no such duty. Of course, I could be just adding to the other person's store of information. Perhaps my listener is a social scientist, taking a survey of what people believe they should and should not do.

Some of these cases are clearly directive. I am getting myself or the person to whom I am speaking to do something, although not necessarily what I say I ought to do.[49] Similar remarks apply to the boaster and the complainer: they are surely seeking some reaction other than mere understanding from the listener.

However, the case of the social scientist's target does seem to offer a genuinely informative use of deontic language, which cannot be understood on the basis of a directive aim. But when informing another of what I understand to be my duties, with no aim of influen-

---

47. For a case in which the power relation is reversed, see the Argument to Book 5 of *Paradise Lost:* "God, to render Man inexcusable, sends Raphael to admonish him of his obedience. . . ." Raphael, in telling Adam how he should behave, gives the advice he would give if it could influence Adam.

48. I must remind the reader yet again that my theme is not the meaning of deontic language but the purposes for which that language is used. To understand a promulgator of a law to have the people's obedience as his chief purpose is not to presuppose some nondescriptivist account of the meaning of deontic talk.

49. As one reader noted, one could employ this criterion to argue that all speech is to some extent used directively. Any differences between the directive uses of deontic and of nondeontic language would be worth knowing; but I can find no such general differences.

cing anyone's actions, am I really *using* deontic language? Suppose the social scientist had asked instead what questions I had asked in the past thirty minutes, and I responded by repeating those questions. In repeating them word for word and even inflection for inflection, I am nevertheless no longer asking questions. Likewise, in listing my duties, I am not really using deontic speech. There is a formal mode/ material mode confusion built into this kind of case. I think we should consider the scientist to be asking, "What first-person deontic statements are you prepared to assent to?" Those statements, if listed, should have quotation marks around them. What the respondent says, then, does not use deontic language: it mentions sentences that use that language.

It therefore seems likely that most informative uses of deontic language can be understood on the basis of the directive use. Where they cannot be so understood, they may not prove to be genuine uses of deontic language after all.

The same sort of analysis applies to the ironic use of deontic language: "You shouldn't worry about the fact that you haven't telephoned your poor lonely old mother once in the last three days." Normally, uttering such a sentence is a fairly transparent attempt to bring about a particular action.

One could have more exotic reasons for using deontic language. One might use "You ought to eat your spinach" as a signal by which one spy recognizes another, for example.[50] But there is little point to dwelling on such exotic uses. I don't expect to find a theory that accounts for every single use of deontic language, only one that takes care of the great majority of cases.   And that I think I have done.

There is one type of deontic speech that I have so far done scant justice to: the language of permission.[51] I have discussed how we use the forms, "S ought . . . " and "S may not," not how we use "S may . . . " or "It is not the case that S ought. . . . " The language of permission might seem to resist the type of analysis I provided for the language of obligation. For when I issue a statement of permission to S, I am usually not directing S to do anything. Rather, I am specifically

---

50. Here, again, there might be a use-mention confusion lurking.

51. I am grateful to a reader for pointing this out. At the same time, I am somewhat embarrassed that he needed to do so. For the same point, as applied to the negations of performatives, is clearly made by Mary Gore Forrester in "An Argument for Descriptivism," *Journal of Philosophy* 71, no. 20 (1974): 759–69, 764–65.

refraining from directing S to act or to fail to act in a given way, and to refrain from giving direction is not to give direction.[52] I believe that these considerations decisively refute the supposition that a prescriptive component is built into the meaning of all deontic expressions. Even if the meaning of "S ought . . . " and "S may not . . . " could reasonably be understood as directive, the meaning of "S ought not . . . " and "S may . . . " cannot be. And the latter expressions are just as deontic as the former. But once again, my interest in this book is not in the *meaning* of deontic expressions but in their *use*. And I think we may, after all, take the directive use of the language of permission to be central, just as we did with the language of obligation.

For people usually issue statements of permission for one of two reasons. In giving permission, I might be putting forward my intent not to interfere with the permitted action, or I might be directing others not to interfere with that action.[53] In either case, I am saying what another may do, but my purpose is either to put forward what I myself will not do or to direct others.[54]

In directing others not to interfere, I am clearly using language directively. But in putting forward what I myself will not do, I am using the language of permission as I would normally use first-person oughts: to express intent. Now, as I indicated in discussing first-person oughts, one might express one's intent for a number of reasons. But at least the great majority of these reasons, I suggested, may be understood on a directive basis, although one can hardly suppose that the use of first-person oughts is somehow really directive.[55]

I therefore suggest that, although statements of permission are

52. But as G. H. von Wright points out, some permissions include what he calls "commands to enable." Such commands make an act possible for an agent to perform. (G. H. von Wright, *Norm and Action* [New York, 1963], 89.) Von Wright's example is the positive right to a job, construed as giving the would-be worker a claim against his society. Such permissions would involve direction; but von Wright's own language, "If a permission to do something is combined with a *command to enable* . . . ," suggests that the permission, as a permission, can be separated from the directive portion of the speech act.

53. These two purposes roughly correspond to what von Wright calls "tolerations" and "prohibitions to hinder or prevent" (von Wright, ibid.). But von Wright sees these as different sorts of permissions rather than different purposes for which statements of permission can be made.

54. I am using the words 'put forward' for lack of a more neutral term. It is worth noting that, on my view, there is nothing illogical in saying, "You may do that, but I'll stop you if you try." Rather, there is no clear point in issuing such a statement.

55. See pp. 40–42.

not themselves directive, their *use* may be understood as directive. Fitting them into the directive model involves some stretching, to be sure, but the stretch is not clearly greater than in the first-person oughts discussed earlier.

In the remainder of this book, then, I shall take as my working hypothesis that the central purpose for using deontic speech is directive: to cause people to act or to refrain from acting in certain ways.

My working hypothesis might strike readers as strongly resembling doctrines put forward by R. M. Hare.[56] But I believe there are at least three important differences. A look at these differences should clarify what I have asserted in this chapter.

1. Hare, in both *The Language of Morals* and *Freedom and Reason*, speaks of the prescriptive meaning (as opposed to the descriptive meaning) of judgments. This talk of meaning is consistent with Hare's regarding the relation between 'ought' and 'can' as presupposition, a matter of "the logical properties of the words used—not mere misleadingness or inappropriateness."[57] What I have called 'directive oughts' have, for Hare, their directive character built into their semantics.

    I am claiming that the directive character is a feature of the *use,* not the meaning, of 'ought' and 'may'. As a result, I regard the relation between 'ought' and 'can' as the pragmatic relation of implicature, not the semantic relation of presupposition.

2. Hare says that such terms as 'good', 'right', and 'ought' are evaluative terms as typically used. As such, he argues, they carry prescriptive meaning.[58] I claim only that 'ought' is *often* used directively, and that we can understand *most* nondirective uses on the basis of the directive use plus counterfactuals.

    I am not arguing that there is something natural and correct about my taking the directive use as primary,[59] but only that,

---

56. As it struck a reader for Brown University Press. I am grateful to this reader for insisting that I think hard about the relation between my position and Hare's. Hare's positions are set out in his books *The Language of Morals* (Oxford, 1952) and *Freedom and Reason* (Oxford, 1963).

57. *Freedom and Reason,* p. 59.

58. *Freedom and Reason,* p. 27. In light of Hare's insistence that prescriptivity is built into the *meaning* of such terms, his qualifier "as typically used" is a bit puzzling. He presumably believes that, in an atypical situation, the term does not carry the same meaning as in the typical situation.

59. How could we understand a claim that all uses of 'ought' are somehow really directive at bottom? That thesis would surely not be about the *intentions* of all issuers of judgmental oughts.

by doing so, I have been able to derive a single set of rules that can serve as a pragmatics for deontic speech. For all I know, someone might come up with a better set of rules by taking the judgmental use as primary, or one might do best by working out separate sets of rules for each main use. But no one has done either of these alternative projects, and I can't compare the system I have developed with ones that exist only in conjecture. My emphasis on directive uses is therefore not intended as beautiful and natural.[60] It is justified, if at all, only by the virtues of the system that results.

3. I do not claim that all nondirective uses of 'ought' can be understood on the basis of the directive. Odd uses, such as the recognition signal between spies, resist such treatment. Moreover, as I have noted, the counterfactuals I used in working with judgmental oughts are by no means free from difficulty, and the treatment of first-person cases leaves much to be desired. For these reasons, I would never claim to have found a universal, underlying directive use for deontic language, analogous to Hare's prescriptive meaning.

For these reasons, the similarity of my enterprise to Hare's is only a surface matter. It does not go deep.

Deontic speech is not the only kind of utterance that can be used directively. I might try to cause you to act in a certain way by making a declarative statement, by asking a question ("Wouldn't you like to . . . "), by issuing a command, and doubtless by using still other types of speech. The maxims that cover the pragmatics of deontic speech apply as well to a directive use of these other utterances. After all, one would expect no real difference in the pragmatics of two laws, one that begins "You should not . . ." and the other that begins "Do not . . .", but that continue with identical texts.

One might even conduct a careful study of the pragmatics of directive swearing, as expounded by Mr. Chucks the boatswain:

"The life of a boatswain is a life of 'mergency, and therefore I swear."
"I still cannot allow it to be requisite, and certainly it is sinful."
"Excuse me, my dear sir; it is absolutely requisite, and not at all sinful. There is one language for the pulpit, and another for on board ship, and, in either situation, a man must make sure use of those terms most likely to produce the necessary effect upon his listeners. . . . It is not here as in

---

60. Readers of Berke Breathed's popular comic strip "Bloom County" will carefully note the difference between directive oughts and penguin lust in this respect.

the Scriptures, 'Do this, and he doeth it' (by the bye, that chap must have had his soldiers in tight order); but it is, 'Do this, d——n your eyes,' and then it is done directly." [61]

It might be an interesting exercise to try to discover the extent to which my discussion throughout this book applies to directive uses of nondeontic speech. But although the directive use is not confined to deontic speech, I will confine my attention to that type of utterance from now on. The subject is more than big enough.

Given that we know the purpose of making a deontic speech, how best can we insure that we achieve that purpose? How can we have the best chance of success in using deontic speech to direct? If there are rules that spell out how one can best use deontic speech directively, those rules would constitute the pragmatics of deontic speech. That there are such rules is the burden of the second part of this book.

It is, then, time to turn to the specific rules of deontic pragmatics. We are done with "Why." It is time for "What."

61. Frederick Marryat, *Peter Simple* (London, 1888), chap. 14, p. 83. The expurgated oath is in the original. Quoted by Robert Graves, " 'Lars Porsena,' or the Future of Swearing and Improper Language," in his *Occupation: Writer* (New York, 1950), 26–27.

II | WHAT

4 The Structure of Deontic Pragmatics

In this chapter, I introduce the maxims of deontic pragmatics. I give here only a brief word of explanation for each and no hint of justification for any of them. Detailed explanations and justifications are the task of the following six chapters. I hope my discussion of Kant's Principle will have aroused sufficient appetite that the reader can make it through these seven chapters, which I have collectively labeled "What," to reach the third section of the book, termed "How." The seven chapters that form this second part are the heart of the book.

The most enjoyable part of my enterprise is apt to be, for most readers, not the presentation, explanation, or justification of a set of rules, but seeing those rules applied to actual cases. The applications occur mainly in part 3. Kant somewhere compares a long, arid stretch of his own prose to the Great Arabian Desert. I can hardly hope to vie with Kant in profundity, but I hope not to match his aridity, either. With becoming modesty, then, I call the six chapters ahead the Small Arabian Desert. And let the reader determined to push his camels through this desert be assured—there will be an oasis!

I ended the last chapter with a question: Given that the goal of deontic speech can be taken as directive, are there any rules for maximizing our chances of success in reaching that goal? Are there maxims of deontic pragmatics?

I believe there are eighteen such maxims. But one point needs to be clear at the outset: each of the eighteen maxims applies in many different types of contexts but might not apply in every type. For example, many of the maxims have little or no application when a person is legislating for himself. Nor do maxims dealing with particular cases always clearly apply to the formulation of rules. A maxim has general, but not universal, applicability.

When I speak of a maxim of deontic pragmatics, I shall capitalize the name of that maxim; when I speak of underlying principles, I shall use lower case. For instance, many philosophers have discussed universalizability, but Universalizability makes its first appearance in this book.

To introduce the maxims, I divide the uses of deontic speech into two types. First, a speaker might wish to establish, discover, or ascertain *general rules* of obligation and permission. Second, the speaker might wish to determine or judge the outcome of *particular cases*.

General rules apply in principle to more than a single act but need not hold for more than one person,[62] If Jones decides that in the future he will be bound by an obligation to telephone his mother every week, then I shall say that Jones is establishing a general rule. The legislative body that lays down laws for the populace, the writer on etiquette who tells us which fork to use, and the religious

---

62. As a reader of this book pointed out, this commonplace distinction presupposes an ability to count acts, and the establishment of identity criteria for acts is very much a live philosophical issue. I have nothing to contribute to the analysis of act individuation. But people do manage to count acts and so to distinguish in a rough and ready way between the particular and the general. Since I here distinguish the two only for the sake of the reader's convenience, rough and ready should be good enough.

leader who urges us to desist from our wicked ways all use deontic language to make or find general rules. I shall say that uses of deontic speech which establish or set forth general rules employ the *legislative mode* of deontic speech.

The use of deontic language in particular cases might be intended to have some effect on action or to have none. For example, I decide that I may pass up reading Putman tonight in favor of *Playboy,* that you should pay me the gambling debt you owe me, and that Caesar should never have passed the Rubicon. I shall say that a deontic speaker concerned with particular cases employs the *judicial mode* of deontic speech.

The division into legislative and judicial rules, like my further distinction between rules of matter and rules of manner, is merely a way to organize a mass of material. It is not a display of some deep and important structural principle. The homely fact is that a single chapter with eighteen subheadings would be unwieldy.

Three of the maxims of deontic pragmatics are common to both modes. These maxims are the chief subprinciples of deontic pragmatics:

1. Straightforwardness: Have as the goal of deontic speech that people behave in accordance with what your utterances say they ought, ought not, may, or may not do.
2. Consequences: In determining whether to make a deontic utterance, take into account the consequences of making that or any other deontic utterance.
3. Minimalism: Reserve deontic utterances for occasions when the goal is pressing, the likelihood of achievement high, and the availability of suitable alternatives for reaching the goal limited.

The rule of Straightforwardness may be taken as the basis for all the rules of manner, both legislative and judicial. For if a legislating body does not act regularly, publicly, and with openness, how can legislators expect people to follow their directives? If, on the other hand, one does not use rules to decide particular cases or have an equitable procedure to apply when rules fail, one's decisions are much less likely to gain their intended effect. Regularity, publicity, openness, use of rules, and equity are then all important considerations in determining the manner of our deontic speech, and all might be regarded as consequences of stating the aims of one's deontic speech straightforwardly.

The rule of Straightforwardness applies to all sorts of cases, even (as we shall see in the next chapter) those in which persons make rules for themselves. Exceptions to this principle are few, but they do exist.

The rule of Consequences is so obvious that one might easily overlook it. A speech act is an act, and it will have consequences. In particular, attempting to influence someone's conduct will most surely have consequences, from obedience to resentment to rebellion. One should normally weigh the probable consequences before determining whether to make a deontic utterance.

To be sure, the consequences of one deontic utterance might differ from those of another, just as the consequences of making the same utterance can vary widely from circumstance to circumstance. The rule of Consequences tells us to consider the likely outcome not only of making any deontic utterance at all but also of making a particular deontic utterance.

The rule of Minimalism is a partner to that of Consequences. The rule of Minimalism presupposes that to attempt to get people to act in accordance with one's wishes is generally a risky business. From the purely pragmatic point of view, whatever the moral aspects of the situation, one should not engage in deontic speech without ample justification. The risks are too great.

One example of the application of the rule of Minimalism is the old legal saw, *de minimis non curat lex,* that the law does not take account of trifling matters. Indeed, the law should not do so, especially if those matters are not considered trifling by everybody. For the good that can be done is small and is easily outweighed by the harm that might result.

In considering rules in the legislative mode, I distinguish between the *manner* of legislating and the *matter* of the legislation. As one might expect, rules dealing with the manner have no clear parallels with rules of the judicial mode, but rules dealing with the matter do.

I find three rules that cover the manner of legislating:

1. Regularity: Have a standard method of legislative procedure, and follow that method in this legislation.
2. Publicity: Provide methods by which those who are to be bound by the legislation can know of its contents and, where practicable, of its justification.
3. Openness: Provide a method by which new legislation can be

developed when cases are insufficiently or improperly determined by present legislation.

These three rules are not difficult to explain, and their justification will prove equally easy. Consider first the rule of Regularity. Certainly a legislative process that fails to work in an orderly manner is not likely to be effective. Even if a person makes rules only for himself, to do so haphazardly is rarely the best way. We are all familiar with the sad results that usually obtain from our New Year's resolutions.

Publicity is as obvious a need as Regularity. If I want people to follow the practice I announced in my legislation, it is normally best that those people know what my legislation says. There are exceptions—most notably when one is violating the rule of Straightforwardness—but it is most often best to adhere to the rule of Publicity.

Openness is perhaps not as obvious a requirement as the last two, but no legislator can think of every future contingency and write his legislation to meet whatever might befall. If legislators attempt to lock people into a way of behaving that becomes irrelevant or perhaps counterproductive, their legislation will be ignored, actively violated, or enforced at a heavy cost. The prudent legislator builds in some mechanism for change.

The judicial rules of manner are also relatively easy to explain and justify. These maxims are:

1. Use of General Rules: Decide the case under consideration, if possible, by subsuming it under properly determined general rules.
2. Equity: Provide a method for solving conflicts, in case general rules appear to give conflicting advice or prove insufficient in particular situations.

These two judicial rules of manner raise a number of questions. When does a case fit under general rules? How does one decide if rules are properly determined? Just what are the conditions under which rules genuinely conflict or do not suffice? These are important questions, which I shall address in chapter 8.

Not everyone is as enamored of general rules as are moral philosophers and etiquette experts. Some people see mere rigidity and harshness in my injunction to decide a case, if one can, by subsuming it under a rule. We are free people: down with the dead hand of rules! Perhaps so. But as I shall argue in chapter 8, following this rule of judicial manner has enormous practical value: one then has a rational justification for one's action. And the highest maxim of deontic pragmatics will turn out to be that one should impute, impose, and accept obligations in accordance with a rationally defensible structure.

Although it is ordinarily useful to follow general rules in framing one's particular deontic utterances, it is equally important not to be at a loss when rules fail to determine the nature of those utterances. Equity is therefore a necessary complement to the use of general rules.

The rules of matter are perhaps the most controversial, for they are harder to justify than the rules of manner. Moreover, I think many will find these maxims less obvious than the others. My examination of these rules, and particularly the legislative rules of matter, will consequently be more detailed than my look at the other maxims.

I find six legislative rules of matter:

1. Theoretical Virtue: Adopt only rules that are consistent with one another, clear, applicable, simple, and modest.
2. Universalizability: Adopt only rules that treat like cases alike.
3. Factuality: Do not adopt rules that depend crucially upon false statements about the way the world is.
4. Proportionality: Let the strength of obligations and the severity of sanctions be roughly proportional to the strength of the justification provided.
5. Economy: Adopt only rules the performance of which will meet your legislative ends at the least cost to those for whom you legislate.
6. Distribution: Provide a method for the distribution of goods and services, benefits and sanctions.

The rule of Theoretical Virtue is obviously something of a catchall. Since a piece of deontic legislation is not a theory, there is no *a priori* reason for such legislation to partake of the virtues of good theories; but we shall find that, on the whole, legislation that is consistent, clear, and the like is more likely to succeed in its aims. One virtue of a good theory is conspicuously absent from the list: completeness. There is no reason to think that a set of deontic rules should be complete. Certainly, there seems no point to fitting the whole world of actions into a tight-fitting structure of obligations, even if the task could in fact be done. For that matter, even if we stick only to morally significant actions, obligations are far from being the only part of ethics.

Universalizability hardly needs introduction to most people. I shall therefore concentrate on showing that it is a rule of deontic pragmatics, not part of the logic of deontic speech. The maxim of Factuality, when violated, leads even the most hardened relativist to doubt the worth of the offending system of legislation. When one's important deontic provisions depend crucially on misreading the way of the world, something is surely wrong.

Proportionality is enjoying something of a constitutional vogue in the United States, but no one is quite clear about the exact nature of the demands proportionality places on legislators. If one's object all sublime is to make the punishment fit the crime, how, outside the world of W. S. Gilbert, is this end to be achieved? Or is the Mikado's goal a distortion of Proportionality? Here are more questions in need of discussion.

The rule of Economy is an economist's version of rationality applied to deontic legislation. All such legislation is presumably going to achieve its ends only at some cost. The rule of Economy asks the legislator to count the likely costs and to choose one's legislation so as to minimize them.

The rule of Distribution states only that there should be some sort of regulation covering the way one distributes goods and services, benefits and sanctions. Presumably any such regulation should accord with other maxims for deontic legislative speech, but the present rule does not address that issue.

Not all of the six legislative rules of matter apply to every situation. For example, in legislating for myself, I probably have no goods or sanctions to distribute. Or I might not build any crucial assumptions about the world into my legislation, thus rendering the requirement of Factuality moot.

The rules for judicial matter are the following:

1. Judicial Factuality: Decide cases in ways consistent with the facts about the world.

2. Judicial Economy: Decide cases in a way that will carry out the legislative aim at least cost to the actors.

3. Judicial Publicity: Impute obligations only to people who knew or should have known that the obligations in question applied to them when they performed the acts in question.

4. Judicial Review of General Rules: Impute or accept particular obligations only when those obligations are imposed in accordance

with general rules that are consistent, clear, applicable, simple, modest, universalizable, and proportional.

I regard the judicial mode counterparts of the rules of Theoretical Virtue, Universalizability, and Proportionality as mere subrules for the judicial rules of matter. For a properly determined general rule is, among other things, consistent, clear, applicable, simple, modest, universalizable, and proportional, and the principle of Judicial Review of General Rules asks that one apply to particular cases only legislation that possesses these virtues.

In addition, factuality and economy are surely requirements for a properly determined general rule. But, as we shall see, decisions based on Judicial Factuality and Judicial Economy do not merely check whether the laws governing the case conform to the legislative rules of Factuality and Economy. The rules of Judicial Factuality and Judicial Economy must therefore be maxims in their own right. The rule of Judicial Publicity, however, is a close counterpart of the corresponding legislative rule of manner, an indication that my distinction between rules of matter and rules of manner is only for convenience in setting out the system.

These eighteen rules form the content of a single supermaxim of Deontic Rationality:

Deontic Rationality: Impose, accept, and impute obligations only in accordance with a rationally defensible structure.

The rule of Deontic Rationality is much broader than an economist's notion of rationality, as captured in the two subrules of Economy. It is also broader than the version of rationality put forward by many philosophers, such as Hume. But if a person is going to defend his deontic pronouncements, whether these concern general or particular obligations, there is more than one basis for doing so. The eighteen maxims all may be and have been invoked to help justify a decision.

I believe that the rule of Deontic Rationality and its eighteen submaxims constitute deontic pragmatics. It will be the task of the next five chapters to justify that belief. In chapters 5 through 9, I will take up the eighteen submaxims in turn, with the purpose of showing both how each is applied in deontic speech, and why each is a rule of pragmatics rather than of meaning or logic. Then in chapter 10, I shall argue that there are no fundamental rules of deontic pragmatics other than those I have given.

My method of argument in the next five chapters will parallel that of chapter 2. For each maxim, I shall look at a number of cases. These cases are intended to demonstrate both that using the maxim in deontic speech is normally helpful in achieving one's directive goal, and that on occasion use of the maxim is detrimental to one's chances of achieving that goal. A maxim that normally holds is indeed a principle; a maxim that doesn't always hold is a principle of pragmatics.

It might not be obvious why the existence of exceptions should prove that a maxim belongs to pragmatics. We can understand the point by looking at rules that admit of no exceptions. When a person utters a sentence, what that sentence means and what it logically implies are independent of the context of utterance.[63] If someone says, "All men are mortal and Socrates is a man," it doesn't matter who or what is speaking, when, where, to whom, or for what purpose: what was said implies that Socrates is mortal. To genuine rules of logic and meaning, there are no exceptions—that is, there are no contexts in which the rules fail to apply. You might not intend your words to have the implications they do, but those implications are there regardless.

But utterances often give rise to what Grice has called *implicatures,* and these clearly do depend on the context of utterance. There is nothing in the meaning of, "This is a charming day. The wind I fancy must be southerly," that implies "I would like you to stop discussing the love life of Romantic poets." Yet, in a certain context—chapter 7 of Jane Austen's *Sanditon*—the message conveyed by the first utterance is unmistakably the second. In another context, no such conclusion would be available.

No implicature of which I am aware is present for every single context of utterance of a proposition.[64] For there seems no limit on the ways propositions can be used. "Where the devil are my slippers?" spoken at the end of *My Fair Lady,* seems to be a marriage proposal. "All the enlisted men are here," when used as a recognition signal

---

63. Of course, as a reader pointed out, the same set of words can have different meanings in different contexts, through use of indexical or ambiguous expressions perhaps. Consider, "I have a yen for food," as uttered by two people, only one of whom is in Japan. But then, is it clear that in such a case the same sentence is being uttered? Certainly what is uttered expresses a different proposition on the first occasion from on the second.

64. A reader suggested that a person, by the mere fact of saying something, always implicates that what he is saying is relevant in the context. This suggestion is intriguing, but I am not sure it is correct. The notion of 'relevance' is surely strained, for example, when we suppose that an actor, in saying his lines on stage, is implicating the relevance of those remarks.

between two spies, should not lead anyone to conclude that some enlisted men are present. Hence, for every rule that gives rise to an implicature, there are contexts to which the rule applies but in which the implicature is not present. The possibility of such contexts is therefore a criterion that lets us distinguish between the rules that bring about implications and those that bring about implicatures.

Now the principles that give rise to implicatures are the rules of pragmatics, which stem from the purposes for which utterances are made. The rules of deontic pragmatics, in particular, are those maxims that, if properly applied in deontic speech, normally help to carry out the speaker's purpose in making that speech. But none of these rules helps achieve that purpose in every context; in some cases, a rule might even hamper such achievement. The rules of deontic pragmatics must therefore have exceptions. They give rise to implicatures, not implications.

Kant's Principle is an example. In chapter 2 I argued that in some contexts, one cannot derive "X can" from "X ought." Kant's Principle therefore is not a meaning-rule for 'ought' or a rule of deontic logic. Yet it does seem to hold in most contexts, and those institutions that do not subscribe to it behave in a pointless way. Hence, "X ought" *implicates,* rather than implies, "X can." If I can show how using Kant's Principle furthers the purposes of one's deontic speech, I will have proved that principle to be part of deontic pragmatics—although not necessarily a fundamental maxim.

My strategy in the next five chapters should now be clear. To justify my calling each of the eighteen submaxims a rule of deontic pragmatics, I must do two things. First, I must demonstrate how employment of a given submaxim usually furthers the speaker's purpose. I will do that by setting out what seem to be paradigmatic cases. Second, I need to present cases in which the submaxim does not apply because it fails to further the purposes for which the deontic speech is made. These procedures are even more closely related than one might suppose. For the best way to clarify any rule of pragmatics is to give circumstances under which the rule is, for some reason or another, not followed.

My method of proceeding is not peculiar to the pragmatics of deontic speech. Consider H. P. Grice's submaxim that in a conversation we usually try to say no less than we know, as long as saying what we know is relevant and useful.[65] We can best understand this rule by

---

65. H. P. Grice, "Logic and Conversation," p. 67.

looking at cases in which a person deliberately conceals the extent of his relevant and useful knowledge—for purposes of irony, perhaps.

My procedure involves an inescapable lack of precision. I can cite exceptions, but I cannot give a rule for deriving exceptional cases. The result is inescapable vagueness. But one cannot expect more precision than the subject matter allows, as Aristotle noted. And since there seems neither any limit to the number of ways in which purposes can be carried out or frustrated, nor any method of structuring those ways, imprecision is unavoidable.

Enough of what I will say. It is time to say it.

5 | The Three Principal Submaxims

In this and the succeeding four chapters, I shall look more closely at the eighteen submaxims that make up the structure of deontic pragmatics. I intend to clarify the use of each rule by giving examples, to show how the rule furthers the primary purpose of deontic speech, to present and analyze exceptions, and to consider possible objections.[66] My discussions of the maxims of deontic pragmatics will vary considerably in length. Some of these rules require more care and more caution than others; some, such as that old chest-

---

66. For a brief discussion of this procedure, please see chapter 4, pp. 57–59. I have more to say in chapter 13 about my method.

nut, universalizability, have been written about so extensively that I can concentrate on establishing the rule's pragmatic status and not worry too much about explaining it or justifying its acceptance.

In this chapter, I look at the three principal submaxims: Straightforwardness, Consequences, and Minimalism.

Straightforwardness: Have as the goal of deontic speech that people behave in accordance with what your utterances say they ought, ought not, may, or may not do.

The maxim of Straightforwardness, as a rule for legislation, holds that any legislative body intend that the people for whom they are legislating actually behave in accordance with the stated laws.[67]

Normally the straightforward way with legislation is the most practical. If Congress requires state legislatures to raise the legal drinking age on pain of losing highway funds, state officials would do well to assume that Congress means just what it says. For surely it does.

After all, with a straightforward agenda transparently present in the law, the normal machinery of enforcement should be available. But if the legislators' aim is not transparent, enforcement usually requires that members of the executive branch as well as judges be let in on the secret. And then one wonders how long the secret is likely to remain one!

The alternative to informing nonlegislators about a hidden agenda is to devise matters so cunningly that even the judges and members of the executive branch will be fooled.[68] They will enforce legislative goals even though they are mistaken about what goals they are

---

67. My use of 'legislative body' is parallel to my use of 'legislative mode'. One person who tells himself how he should behave in general would be, in my sense, a legislative body.

68. The term 'hidden agenda' has caused readers some difficulties. I do not intend to suggest that a speaker with a hidden agenda always has in mind that some definite kind of action be taken, different from the action his words suggest. I am suggesting only that the violator of Straightforwardness appears to be directing persons toward taking some action, but in fact does not intend that they do so. (In this way, his speech is not necessarily directive in the primary sense discussed in chapter 3. Rather, it may be directive in the secondary sense discussed in that chapter: a refraining from directing. See above, pp. 42–44.)

enforcing. I suggest that such a state of affairs, although possible, is thoroughly improbable; it is the legislative analogue of Gettier cases in epistemology! The rule of Straightforwardness, then, clearly applies to most legislative situations.

Even in legislation covering a single individual, straightforwardness seems in most cases to be the best policy. Consider the sad case of Sadie. Sadie announces that she will quit smoking. She instructs her roommate in this fashion: each time Sadie takes another cigarette, the roommate should whip her. What the roommate does not yet realize is that Sadie wants to be whipped. She has every intention of smoking up a storm in the future, to get more of that delicious pain.

Here Sadie is being anything but straightforward. Since only she and her roommate are involved, it might well seem that her indirection stands a good chance of success. Nonetheless, I suggest that Sadie's methods are not likely to prove effective. If her roommate has no objection to whipping Sadie, then Sadie would do better to ask the roommate directly. If the roommate does have an objection, Sadie's devious methods are likely to make the roommate feel used.[69] In either case, Sadie will probably end up as that most pitiful creature, the unsuccessful Machiavellian.

Even if we remove the roommate from the picture and let Sadie whip herself, straightforwardness still seems the best policy. If Sadie wishes to be whipped, and if she invents an obligation to stop smoking only as a pretext for whipping herself, her procedure is cumbersome and apt to misfire. Also, the practice of using obligation statements as mere pretexts may well be harmful to Sadie in the long run, if she ever needs to issue genuine obligation statements to herself. So if Sadie wants to whip herself, let her do so and leave smoking out of it!

Removing Sadie's roommate from the example makes little difference, it seems. That suggests that Straightforwardness is as much a practical virtue for those making rules only for themselves as for those making rules for others. Indirection in both cases is only rarely preferable to straightforwardness.

Nevertheless, we can come up with cases in which indirection is indeed the best way to proceed. We considered one example in chapter

---

69. I am assuming, to be sure, that Sadie will be unable to hide from her roommate her delight in being whipped. This assumption need not be true, of course: Sadie may be a consummate actress, or the roommate may be completely lacking in what I have heard termed 'sociological imagination'. But the likelihood is surely that the roommate will eventually stumble onto the truth. Once again, pragmatic rules, which usually but not always apply, for that reason deal with likely situations.

2: the Augustinian God, who demands the impossible. He does not intend that people do what He says they should, for nobody is able to fulfill that requirement. One reading of His purpose, I suggested, is the Pauline suggestion that He means to shut up all men under sin.[70] According to this construal, God is legislating with a hidden agenda. His unstated purpose in telling people how they should behave is to provide rules that must be broken. And when, inevitably, those rules are broken, God is thought to be justified in exacting retribution.

Hidden agendas also occur among human legislators, who sometimes vote for laws they think will prove impracticable, unnecessary, or downright onerous. Their reasons for doing so vary. Sometimes a legislature lets a popular movement have its way, in hopes that the eventual reaction will remove that movement as an effective political force. That purpose might explain why some congressmen, otherwise rational, voted for Prohibition. Or the legislator might support a bill solely to enhance her prospects of reelection. This action is not necessarily venal, although it may well involve a certain degree of self-deception. More than one legislator has said to herself, "If I vote for this bad, but popular, bill, I will be reelected and can provide my wisdom in the formulation of far more important legislation."

When one creates deontic legislation, therefore, there are times when it is practical and not particularly evil to violate Straightforwardness. Indirection is sometimes best.

It might seem that people *must* be straightforward in legislating for themselves, unless they fall victims to self-deception. Usually, people have no easy time concealing their own goals from themselves. Nevertheless, even when you know what you are after, you might choose to be less than straightforward, as the case of Joan indicates.

Joan's doctor convinces her that she should lose fifteen pounds and limits her to 1200 calories per day. From long experience, Joan knows that she is unable to keep within any limit. But she knows that she has enough will power not to exceed a set limit by too much. She therefore resolves to limit herself to 1050 calories per day. That way, she figures, she should be able to stay under the 1200-calorie ceiling.

Joan is certainly not deceiving herself, as Sadie did. Joan is well aware that her new rule is made to be broken. She is like a legislator who argues for adopting the 55-mile-per-hour speed limit on the grounds that fewer drivers will then exceed 65 m.p.h. The rule has an effect, all right, but the effect is somewhat different from what the

70. See pp. 36, n. 32.

rule, on its face, mandates. Both Joan and the legislator distinguish the rule's genuine effect from its stated intent, and both know they are after the former.

There is an odd flavor about Joan's case, although people have been known to make such resolutions. Does she intend to keep to the 1050-calorie limit or not? If she does not, what is the point of making the rule? But how, on the other hand, could she intend to do what she knows she will not do? At least this much seems true: Joan intends to try to keep to the 1050-calorie limit. For if she did not at least try to keep to that limit, her dieting would not have its intended effect of staying under the doctor's ceiling. There is nothing absurd in intending to try to do something, knowing that one will fail. Cavafy's poem on Thermopylae provides a good example. The Spartans heroically defend the pass, fully aware that eventually the Persians will find a way around, and the defense will fail.

Although one need not be straightforward in one's self-directed deontic statements, cases such as Joan's are clearly the exception. Normally, as in the case of Sadie without the roommate, it is foolish to have a less than straightforward aim in legislating for one's self.

One problem with a hidden agenda in general legislation is that people, being the complex creatures they are, might not act in accordance with that agenda. The congressman who voted for Prohibition in a "let the fever work its way out" mood might have been surprised and horrified at how long the Noble Experiment lasted, to say nothing of the side effects. Hidden agendas have a way of remaining all too hidden!

Machiavellian maneuvers have a tendency to resemble Rube Goldberg contraptions. Too many parts must function just right if the whole is to succeed, and it takes little foresight to prophesy a breakdown. The 55-m.p.h. speed limit may indeed effectively place the average highway speed at 62 m.p.h., whereas a 65-m.p.h. speed limit leads to an average speed of, say, 67 m.p.h. But a legislator who votes for the lower limit on this basis could be in for some unpleasant surprises. Perhaps people who know they are more than five miles over the speed limit drive in a more erratic manner than those who keep close to the limit.

The same holds true when people legislate for themselves. Joan is more than likely to act in some surprising ways if she follows her devious diet plan. She may find herself taking the 1050-calorie limit seriously, so that, because she is constantly exceeding that limit, she decides to give up the diet altogether. Or she might feel guilt at exceeding her limit, so she treats herself to a few banana splits in compensation.

Failure to be straightforward, to make the actual agenda agree with the face intent of the legislation, may, then, bring about some unexpected and undesirable side effects. One of the most common and important side effects is a diminution in respect for rules. Here, the 55-m.p.h. speed limit is the obvious example. In the area of the United States where I live, drivers who keep to a 55-m.p.h. speed limit are about as rare as black-footed ferrets. A few of each kind have been spotted in the last few years, and there have been rumors of a few others, but the species seems close to extinction. Except in a few notorious speed traps, nobody pays attention to the 55-m.p.h. limit. The rule is not merely broken on a wide scale. Rather, it is ignored, treated as if it did not exist.

One outcome I have observed is that more people now treat any speed limit as no more than a vague nuisance. Those who habitually exceed the limit on the highway tend, I believe, to exceed the limit by about as much in town, in school zones, and the like. They have learned, correctly or not, that the law does not mean what it says and can be ignored (or, at any rate, not taken literally). A person stopped by the police for going 40 m.p.h. in a 30-m.p.h. zone is consequently surprised and angry.

The same phenomenon of increased disrespect or disregard for the law was a notorious outcome of the Noble Experiment—Prohibition. Any legislator who voted for Prohibition just to let the fever run its course was very short-sighted, in light of the harm that disrespect for law can do to the body politic. More than one commentator has observed that when the people of a community obey its laws only out of fear of punishment, the community is in deep trouble.

The unfortunate side effect of increasing disrespect for law also occurs when a person serves as his own legislator. I have noticed that those who make unrealistic New Year's resolutions sooner or later stop making resolutions at all, or they make them only as a sort of joke or exercise in wistfulness. Likewise, if Joan sets herself a limit of 1050 calories and really means to try to keep to that limit, then failure might make her less able to set effective rules for herself. If she does not really mean to try to keep to 1050 calories, she has learned to disregard her own rules and could find it harder in the future to legislate effectively for herself.

When people learn that a law does not mean what it says, they tend to disregard not only that law but also other laws as well. This result surely defeats the purpose of legislation, if that purpose is to get people to behave in accordance with the laws.

For these reasons, there is a strong presumption against legislating with a hidden agenda. This presumption may be overcome in particular instances, when the good the hidden agenda promises appears to outweigh the evils I have called attention to. But overindulgence in hidden agendas defeats the purpose of legislation.

Not every violation of Straightforwardness arises from a hidden agenda. A legislator might have no hidden agenda because he has no agenda at all. Perhaps he votes for a bill because he likes its sponsor or (more likely) because he wants the support of a powerful interest group. But he has no desire that the people affected by the law behave in any particular way.

On unimportant bills, such behavior probably makes very little difference, but on important ones, the legislator had better act as if he thinks the interest group has reason on its side. If not even the legislators can find grounds for backing a successful piece of legislation, the result will rarely be a law that people willingly obey, if they obey it at all. Once more, the rule of Straightforwardness indicates the best legislative path to follow.

The rule of Straightforwardness, then, is justified as a maxim of the pragmatics of deontic speech in the legislative mode. For failure to keep the rule tends to destroy the purpose of legislating, whether for one's self or for others. The more widespread that failure, the less effective one's legislation is likely to be. But there is nothing impossible or illogical in a legislator's breaking this rule. It is not, then, a rule of deontic logic.

Legislators who fail to be straightforward are still acting as legislators, but they have chosen a usually poor means of achieving their legislative aims. It is that notion of fulfilling the purpose of a given mode of speech that stamps Straightforwardness as a rule of pragmatics for deontic legislative speech.

The same considerations largely apply when we turn to the judicial mode of speech, and many of the same cases we have already looked at can be adapted to fit this mode. We can envision Sadie seeking a particular whipping, for example. I see no need to go over the same ground again; I shall mention only those few circumstances where the judicial mode differs from the legislative with respect to straightforwardness.

A person who makes a deontic utterance in the judicial mode attempts to bring about particular actions, not to set down general rules. As with legislation, the advantages of direct announcement over indirection in the judicial mode are normally compelling.

We do sometimes find a use for indirect methods in making particular deontic utterances. If I want to make sure that my son mows the grass in the front yard, I could find it expedient to remind him of his obligation to mow both front and back. I know from experience that this reminder is likely to get him to do half the job, and he always does start with the front yard. The pitfalls of using such indirection, though, especially if indirection is one's standard mode of operation, are too obvious to need much rehearsing. When people find themselves wondering just what you are trying to get them to do, you might begin to see the value of being straightforward. If my son learns, as he will, that "You should mow the grass today" is code for "You should mow the front yard today," and if he retains a disposition not to do all that he is asked, I will soon find the front yard no better than half mowed.

With judicial straightforwardness, the issue of respect for rules does not arise, but there is a parallel consideration: respect for position. If my particular deontic utterances conceal their purposes, people will not know how to respond to what I say. If so, no one will probably even try to carry out the obligations my speech seems to place upon him. Even though this failure on their part may fulfill my hidden agenda, I pay a price for my success. For people learn that they do not have to pay heed to what I say. My position as an issuer of particular obligations erodes.

Straightforwardness, then, is valuable for most, but not all, instances of deontic speech, both legislative and judicial. Employing this principle is usually important if one wishes to achieve the ends for which one engages in deontic speech. The rule of Straightforwardness is therefore a general principle of deontic pragmatics.

Consequences: **In determining whether to make a deontic utterance, take into account the consequences of making that or any other deontic utterance.**

The rule of Consequences seems so obvious that it may seem that it can have no exceptions. It is compatible with all sorts of behavior. One person might put so little weight on consequences that an observer might conclude he is ignoring the consequences altogether. Another person might be so governed by anticipated results that she predicates any decision whether to make a given deontic speech entirely on those anticipated consequences. Despite their radical differences in behavior, both persons may be following the rule of Consequences.

Does anyone then ever disobey the rule of Consequences? Certainly. People often decide to make deontic utterances without paying any heed to anticipated consequences. Some proceed out of habit, some from ignorance, and some from deliberate policy. As we shall see, each of these three circumstances yields occasions when it is not only possible but practical for a deontic speaker to ignore the rule of Consequences.

Habit is, I expect, the most common of the three conditions. When a person commonly aims similar deontic utterances, in similar circumstances, at similar targets, he may well fail on the five-millionth repetition even to think about consequences. A boss may unthinkingly repeat a long series of ought-statements every working day, not because such repetition helps people remember or because of policy, but simply because of habit. One need not sing the praises of habit in the fashion of a William James to see how such an unthinking routine can be valuable. If the work to be done is intricate and the workers none too bright, the boss might do well to repeat her deontic remarks often, without any variation in wording or manner. And the boss is more likely to make such verbatim repetitions if she doesn't think about their purpose or consequences.

In addition, to question the purpose of making deontic statements might, within a highly rigid command structure, be a first step toward questioning the structure itself. For the smooth functioning of the machine, habit is better than reflection. Therefore, a habitual issuer of deontic statements might be better off not thinking about the effect of making that sort of utterance, even though she does take into account the effects of making a particular ought-statement.

Such situations are not the usual ones. Where the making of deontic utterances is normal, a bit of reflection about the effect of a particular deontic utterance will often prove valuable in achieving one's goal. In any case, reflection is rarely downright harmful. Likewise, the person who is blind to the effects her deontic utterances have on her underlings, who is oblivious to growing boredom or incipient revolution, is rarely to be envied. Habitual, unthinking use of deontic language, without regard for probable consequences, is rarely the best course.

Much the same can be said about cases of ignorance. People can fail to take the consequences of their deontic speech into account because they are unaware of what those consequences might be. And it is sometimes better for them to remain unaware. Take the case of a leader of a desperate wartime mission, a person with a genuine liking for his men. The leader is about to assign duties to members of his mission. If he knows that some of the troops, in carrying out their assignments, face certain death, the leader might find himself unable to give those men their assignments. Or he might not be able to do so without giving away what he knows, thus endangering the success of the mission. In such a case, the leader's ignorance might not be blissful, but it serves his purpose in assigning duties.

Perhaps the leader does not even know the purpose of the assignments he makes. A lieutenant of the Light Brigade at Balaclava, for instance, might be well served by not knowing that someone had blundered. Or both leader and follower could be pawns in a Machiavellian plot whose success depends on their ignorance. (More than one spy novel has such a plot.) In such cases, the person making assignments does not know the purpose of his deontic speech, even though he is fully aware of his own purpose in making that speech. It is the former, not the latter, that is important here.

But as with habit, ignorance is rarely the best policy when making deontic utterances. The leader of a desperate mission might be better off not knowing certain things, but most often his ignorance of crucial aspects of what lies ahead will hurt, rather than help. When both the assigner of duties and the person to whom duties are assigned remain ignorant of the probable consequences, success is rarely to be expected. And people who assign duties without even knowing the true purposes for which they do so are unlikely to succeed. The career of such a devious plotter as Louis XI, "Louis the Spider," contained failure enough to make any moralist happy.

Finally, people occasionally decide not to consider probable consequences in making deontic utterances. Experience might have taught them that the pale cast of thought inhibits people from acting effectively. And that brings to mind the title character of *Hamlet*. In act 5, scene 2, Hamlet informs Horatio that he has forged a request from Claudius to the English king "That, on the view and knowing of these contents, without debatement further, more or less, he should the bearers [*read* Rosencrantz and Guildenstern] put to sudden death, not shriving-time allow'd" (5. 2. 43–46). From the ensuing conversation one can gather that Hamlet was well aware of the probable effect of this deontic utterance. But one can imagine a somewhat different Hamlet, the Hamlet some critics have found incapable, through overindulgence in thought, of taking premeditated yet decisive action.

Such a Hamlet might still have forged the letter to the English king, but he could do so only by shutting his mind to the probable effect.

A person might have other reasons for deliberately ignoring probable consequences. Experience might have taught him that his unpremeditated efforts generally have better results than those he thought out at length. If Milton could boast of his unpremeditated verse, another might have reason to be proud of his spontaneous deontic utterances.

But these cases are once more the exceptions, not the rule. Individuals who shut their minds to probable consequences are likely to achieve their goals only by pure luck, if they reach them at all. Even if Hamlet thinks too much to act effectively, his deliberate resolve to think less probably won't help.

The rule of Consequences is not then a necessary feature of deontic talk. It seems almost a truism, a tautology, but it does in fact have content. In some instances, people do fail to follow the rule in their deontic speeches, and in a few cases, such failure provides the best way to accomplish the purpose of their deontic utterances. But in the great majority of cases, attention to probable consequences is clearly important in using deontic speech to get people to act as one wishes. The rule of Consequences is therefore part of the pragmatics of deontic speech.

Minimalism: **Reserve deontic utterances for occasions when the goal is pressing, the likelihood of achievement high, and the availability of suitable alternatives for reaching the goal limited.**

The rule of Minimalism is more controversial than the previous two principles of deontic pragmatics. Minimalism tells us not to make a deontic utterance unless we have a pressing goal, a good chance of success, and no suitable alternatives. It thereby regards as a pragmatic maxim the old conservative motto, "When in doubt, don't."

Am I then trying to elevate my conservatism of temper or of political belief to the status of a general principle? To such a charge, I plead not guilty.[71] For if the rule of Minimalism embodies conservatism, all of us are to some extent conservatives. In introducing Minimalism in

---

71. But it is only fair to admit that the idea for this section began with a reading of Friedrich Hayek's classic, *The Road to Serfdom*.

the preceding chapter, I mentioned as an application the old principle that the law takes no regard for trifles. One person's trifle is another's weighty concern, but most people uphold the legal maxim even if they disagree about its applications.

As an example, consider the issue of prayer in the public schools of the United States. Public, government-sanctioned prayer in the schools has been for a number of years ruled out by the United States Supreme Court. Every few years, these arises a clamor to reverse this decision and "put God back in the schools."

Now I am old enough to have been subjected to daily public prayer from first grade through high school. The prayer in question was specifically Christian: the Lord's Prayer. In addition to school prayer we had Bible reading. We children would take turns choosing and reading a fitting selection. I remember taking great care finding suitable passages, such as, "Cursed be every man that pisseth against a wall." Nice, gory passages depicting the violent deaths of opponents of Israel were fun to read, as were explicit remarks on the proper contents of belief or the nasty results of unbelief.

But if I remember correctly, the care I took in choosing passages was unusual. Most of the others paid little attention to what they were reading, and their audience paid even less. The same was true of the prayer, which we mumbled through. I know of nobody who treated those opening exercises, as they were called, as an occasion for a genuinely religious experience. They were a boring bit of time-wasting, something to get out of the way before the business of the day began.

With such memories, I was neither thrilled nor appalled when the Supreme Court struck down state-sanctioned prayer in the schools. The social legislation of the Warren Court, whether one approves of it or not, was of vast importance in changing this country, but the Court's school prayer decision was only a sideshow. School prayer, I think, is a trifle about which the law should not care.

Many people, however, disagree violently with my estimate of the importance of school prayer.[72] The result has been a long and continuing series of attacks on the Supreme Court, its members, and its decisions. I suspect, although I cannot prove this, that the net result has been to lower the Court's prestige and to detract from the force of its pronouncements on other matters. The slogan used

---

72. When I urged this point on an old school friend, who was raised a Catholic, his retort was: "You didn't resent those opening exercises because you were a Protestant!"

to be that the Warren Court "took God out of our schools and let the blacks in." Integration, as we all know, has been a long, slow process. If integration was also a moral necessity, as I believe it was, then the Court was ill advised to provide opponents of integration with any weapon that might serve to slow the process down even further. Pronouncing on a trifle, school prayer, gave opponents a useful weapon.

One need not accept my low opinion of the importance of school prayer to perceive that when the law stoops to trifles, it can do itself no good and may do itself harm. It is almost as though an authority has a limited store of good will and obedience to draw upon in making controversial decisions. To fritter away that store on unimportant matters is not intelligent policy.

Suppose that I am teaching a rubber bridge player how to play duplicate. I give her a long list of "Thou shalt nots." These include important rules ("You shouldn't try to fix an error yourself but should always call the director"), unimportant rules ("You should never deal cards into more than four piles"), important pieces of strategy, and unimportant pieces of strategy. I tell her nothing at all about the nature or relative importance of my utterances.

This example shows that the case for Minimalism does not rest on the resentment or resistance its violations often cause.[73] I should not have mixed important points with unimportant ones, if for no other reason than that doing so confuses my student and frustrates my own end in teaching her. If my procedure does not kill my pupil's interest in duplicate altogether, it will certainly leave her unprepared to play the game. By putting equal stress on trifles and on more weighty matters, I dissipate the force behind teaching what is important. As with the Supreme Court on school prayer, there is a sort of deontic Gresham's Law at work: bad deontic utterances drive out good.

The same deontic Gresham's Law applies as well if a person's goal is worthwhile but his deontic utterance has little chance of achieving that goal. Imagine a legislator, earlier in this century, about to vote on the question of prohibiting the sale of alcoholic beverages throughout the country. The legislator, we will suppose, genuinely and fervently believes that alcohol has caused massive social evils. But the legislator also foresees that laws prohibiting the sale and use of alcoholic beverages will be almost unenforceable, resulting in a widespread loss of

---

73. As a reader pointed out, if it did so I would not have argued successfully for Minimalism in either past tense or third-person cases.

respect and regard for the law. In the absence of further considerations, I believe that for the legislator to vote his conscience and favor Prohibition would be improper.

Sometimes, no doubt, a goal is so important that it justifies taking the risk of almost certain failure, but there is usually no duty to be ineffective. If one's aims are straightforwardly revealed in one's deontic utterances, to put on a brave but useless show is rarely the best means toward achieving those aims.

Often, deontic speech is not the only way to get people to behave as one wishes. One can give suggestions or examples or look for ways to make the task attractive. Of course, one can always resort to threats or to force. Deontic speech is often more practical than these last two alternatives, I suppose, but on the whole, where nondeontic means will do the job as well as deontic speech, it is best to choose the nondeontic alternative.

Here again I have in mind a quasi-economic model, similar to my deontic Gresham's Law. If one continually tells people what they should or should not do, they tend to grow resentful. If the deontic speaker's authority is not fully established, resentment can grow into rebellion. This principle seems to be a kind of law of diminishing deontic returns.[74]

Suppose that a mass of government regulations in a certain area helps to accomplish some worthwhile goals. If so, the set of regulations, no matter how complex and difficult to follow, may be justified. But if other means, such as a liberal use of incentives, would accomplish the same ends about as well, the rule of Minimalism gives a presumption in favor of the alternative in directing deontic legislation.

Naturally, if I may steal a simile from William James, in the great boardinghouse of government, the cakes and the syrup are rarely so well apportioned as that. The choice is usually not between two equal means of reaching the same goal, but among a number of possible courses, all aimed at somewhat different goals, with varying and undetermined chances of success. In such instances, the rule of Minimalism still affords a presumption in favor of nondeontic alternatives, but that factor is only one in a complex calculation. Nor it is clear how much weight one should give that presumption.

---

74. Compare George Orwell: "When human beings are governed by 'thou shalt not,' the individual can practice a certain amount of eccentricity: when they are supposedly governed by 'love' or 'reason,' he is under continuous pressure to make him behave and think in exactly the same way as everyone else" ("Politics vs. Literature: An Examination of 'Gulliver's Travels,' " in *The Orwell Reader* [New York, 1949], 293).

It seems at times as if the only real quarrel between today's economic liberals and economic conservatives concerns how much weight to give to the rule of Minimalism. The government's use of deontic regulation does achieve some ends better than available alternatives, but at a cost. Most conservatives will admit the achievement, most liberals the cost. The problem is to decide in each particular case whether the achievement outweighs the cost. Few people suppose that the same answer holds in every instance.

Some have argued, however, that to take matters case by case, as I have just recommended, causes one to overlook the baneful, overall effects of massive deontic legislation. Thus Alexis de Tocqueville said of the type of despotism a democracy might develop: "It covers the surface of society with a network of small complicated rules, minute and uniform, though which the most original minds and the most energetic characters cannot penetrate, to rise above the crowd. . . . [S]uch a power does not destroy, but it prevents existence; it does not tyrannize, but it compresses, enervates, extinguishes, and stupefies a people, till each nation is reduced to be nothing better than a flock of timid and industrious animals, of which the government is the shepherd."[75]

But to point to the evil effects of enacting a large mass of legislation is again only to add a factor to one's calculations. It lends further weight toward deciding against adopting any single regulation. Even if one agrees with Tocqueville's unpleasant prophecy, one may still decide on balance to put forward some piece of deontic regulation. "When in doubt, don't" is far from "Don't ever."

The presumption against deontic regulation applies in more situations than the governmental. I have found that constant nagging of teenagers to do their chores is a no-win course. They usually already know what they should do. I might get results by saying, "Don't forget that this is a garbage day;" but I will fail miserably with, "As a member of this family, enjoying its many benefits, you have a duty to take that garbage out this morning." There might be people who do not resent or resist deontic speech. But alternatives to the deontic, when available, should do no harm with such people, and with the rest of us they are likely to be more effective than a rehearsal of oughts.

Minimalism, then, seems reasonable as a general rule. But in some instances, adherence to Minimalism will not produce the best

75. Alexis de Tocqueville, *Democracy in America*, vol. 2, trans. Henry Reeve (New York, 1945), 319.

results. Obvious examples of such exceptions occur during a time of emergency. When something must be done quickly, we have no time to make sure that the goal is really important, the means reasonably assured of success, and the available alternatives inadequate.

Depression-era legislation comes to mind here. The New Deal introduced many procedures in a kind of "What do we have to lose?" spirit. Times were bad, and if the Administration failed to change the rules, the bad times looked to go on indefinitely. The New Deal had to appear to be doing something about the economy, even if no one was quite sure what should be done. The overall goal of revitalizing the economy was important, and to that extent, the New Deal complied with the rule of Minimalism. But the Administration had every reason under the circumstances not to scrutinize too carefully the ends of particular pieces of legislation, the probable success of the legislation in achieving those ends, or the availability of alternatives to deontic prescriptions.

Of course, ill-considered legislation often leads to trouble later on. Measures hastily enacted to cope with an emergency live on, perhaps to plague us, long after the emergency is over. But when the firemen are trying to keep a house from burning to the ground, it is no time to worry them about water damage.

Emergencies are not the only situations in which following the rule of Minimalism proves impractical. For example, an authority might find it best to impose obligations of little or no value. As a camp counselor many years ago, I once set my charges to digging a large hole, not because a hole was needed, but as a punishment that would work off a bit of their excess energy. I am now appalled at my action. I was a counselor, not a prison warden! But at the time, the very pointlessness of the procedure seemed the best reason to require it.

Sometimes the rule of Minimalism has no clear application to a situation. One might be unable to discover any good nondeontic alternatives, for instance, or one might have no method for assessing the likelihood of success. On some occasions all one can do is hope for the best. But even then, we do well first to try to apply Minimalism. One cannot always look before one leaps, but that is no argument for adopting a policy of leaping without looking.

The rule of Minimalism, if followed faithfully, will then usually but not always help in achieving one's deontic goals. It is therefore a part of deontic pragmatics, the last of the three principal submaxims.

6 The Legislative Rules of Manner

In this chapter, I shall look at the three legislative rules of manner, following once again the method of considering standard examples, exceptions, and objections.

Regularity: **Have a standard method of legislative procedure, and follow that method in this legislation.**

The principle of Regularity holds that legislation should be accomplished in accordance with a standard method of procedure. I shall first look at some cases where this rule might not be followed.

I remember the late Sam Rayburn, Speaker of the House of Representatives, conducting a session of a political convention. He held a vote on some matter in the following way: "All in favor say 'aye.' [Chorus of ayes.] There are no noes. The resolution passes." Speaker Rayburn was notoriously effective in getting the results he sought, and here he certainly departed from standard legislative procedure, if *Roberts' Rules of Order* are any guide. A convention delegate who wished to vote "no" might have been frustrated and angry, but the vote came out as the Speaker wished.

Of course, with an experienced leader such as Speaker Rayburn, highhandedness might well be the standard procedure. Members of the House had come to expect such methods. It was only the innocent television watcher who looked for a more formal (and fair) way of proceeding.

And that in itself suggests an obvious drawback to the Speaker's style: By acting in a way that seemed irregular, Speaker Rayburn gave at least one viewer a poor impression of the convention over which he was presiding. If the convention's main purpose was to attract votes for the party's candidates, the Speaker's methods undercut that purpose, which I am sure he shared.

Suppose I have been having some soreness in my back muscles recently, and my doctor prescribes a drug to deal with the problem. I am a bit apprehensive, for I happen to know that three horses have just been disqualified from this year's Kentucky Derby for taking that same drug. So I ask the doctor why I should take this drug. He might answer, "I have seen some recent literature on the subject. This drug has helped a number of people with symptoms such as yours, and there seem to be no likely side effects to contraindicate its use." I may still be apprehensive, but the chances are I will go ahead and take the medicine. (I am heartily impressed by his using the word 'contraindicate'.)

But suppose instead that he answers, "Well, I was reading about the Derby, and I thought it might be interesting to see what would happen if I prescribed this drug for a few humans. You are the fifth person I am trying it out on. The other four suffer from pneumonia, manic depression, chronic nosebleed, and syphilis, respectively. We need to find something that drug is good for!" The chances of my taking the drug are then zero, the chances of my finding a new doctor overwhelming!

With neither answer am I guaranteed that the medicine will be of any help. But if the doctor prescribes in accordance with his medical reading, he is following a standard procedure, and I am likely to take the drug. If his prescription seems mere caprice, he will have no success in getting me to take the medicine.

Now, any finite set of data can be fitted into an indefinite number of patterns. Whatever the actions of my doctor or of Speaker Rayburn, they accorded with some patterns of legislation. But that fact is insufficient to fulfill the demands of Regularity. The subjects of any piece of legislation must be aware that the legislators are not acting irregularly. For otherwise, the legislation is likely to fail of its goal.

Failure might not occur, however, if the legislators are not straightforward in their deontic utterances. Suppose that my doctor, in giving me a capricious account of his prescription, is actually doing a sociological survey to find out whether people will blindly obey a doctor's orders, no matter how lame the justification. In that case, he doesn't care whether I take the medicine or not—any outcome is grist for his statistical mill. However, when I report him to the local medical society, the self-defeating nature of his prescription will be clear enough.

It is hard to find a case in which a person follows the maxim of Regularity in making rules for himself, for we hardly ever keep to a standard mode of procedure in legislating for ourselves. Still, most people do not set rules for themselves impulsively. The least they will do is think the matter over first.

George usually gives a bit of thought to the rules he adopts. But, upon first seeing a flashy new car model advertised on television, George decides, "I've got to have that!" He then decides to save one-fifth of his salary every month until he can buy the new car. He has, up to this point, been in the habit of spending all or most of his salary.

What are the chances of George's resolution staying in effect until he has the money to buy a new car? Fairly slim, I think. The inspiration of the television commercial will fade as George faces the prospect of doing without certain things each month. I suspect he will convince himself fairly rapidly that the car model probably has a lot of defects, and that by the time he gets enough money together it will be obsolete and not worth buying. Spur-of-the-moment resolutions might work, but the odds are decidely against them.

On the other hand, if George has decided on a more settled way to save his money for the car—if, for example, he had checked to see if the model was as good as the commercial claimed, and if he had carefully checked his monthly budget to see where he might regularly save without working a hardship—then his resolution would have had a much better chance.

Thus even in the sphere of personal legislation, the advantage of a regular pattern of procedure in reaching a straightforward goal is obvious. However, we sometimes have good reason to violate the rule of Regularity. As with Minimalism, many examples arise during a time of emergency. Suppose, for example, that federal civil rights legislation has mandated good-faith attempts to integrate public schools, but those who do not wish to make such attempts have discovered a loophole in the legislation. It is summer, and if Congress does not quickly close the loophole, the integration program will be set back at least a year. Surely, those who support the integration program are justified in trying to close the loophole as quickly as possible, even if that entails a special session of Congress, suspension of normal rules of procedure, and other nonstandard, although legal, operating methods. Some people might not even require that the operating methods be strictly legal.

Or one might imagine a situation in which people are disgusted by the standard operating procedure of their legislative body. If legislators wish to pass what they think is an especially important piece of legislation, one they want everyone to obey, they might be well advised to avoid the usual procedure.

The goal can then, be sufficiently worthwhile in itself to overcome the presumption favoring a regular method of procedure. Regularity of method, therefore, is not part of the logic of deontic legislation but a principle of pragmatics, whose force comes from trying to meet one's goals in the most efficient manner. And it holds in most, but not all, deontic situations.

Publicity: **Provide methods by which those who are to be bound by the legislation can know of its contents and, where practicable, of its justification.**

An individual who is making rules for himself has little use for the principle of Publicity, unless we stretch that principle to include a ban on self-deception. Likewise, in the simple and straightforward situation where one person tells another what she ought to do, there is no need for invoking Publicity. If I tell Sarah she ought to stop smoking, my action is all the publicity my intended legislation requires.

The rule of Publicity comes into play only in more complex situations, where a legislative body tries to determine how another person or group, not present at the time, should or may act. A legislature that enacts the laws of the state, a writer on proper manners who has decided that one may indeed serve a cheap burgundy with fish, an insurance company that decides to accept premiums turned in no later than a month after the due date, all must take Publicity into account.

Publicity, in company with other rules of pragmatics, is sometimes applied out of habit or a sort of principle, even when neither publicity nor deontic speech itself has any point. An example comes from a work published in 1531, Chassenée's *De Excommunicatione Animalium Insectorum*: Certain insects have been eating up crops. Let us resolve the problem by excommunicating them! True, they are not communicants, for they cannot be members of the church. But excommunication is clearly a bad thing to visit upon anyone—so why not try it? After all, even caterpillars are "creatures obedient to the God who made them." But before anyone or anything can be excommunicated, formal notice and warning must be given. The insects must be informed, and they must be represented in a hearing. Only after the demands of Publicity have been met can these caterpillars be declared anathema.[76]

The maxim of Publicity requires only that people have a way to learn the legislation that binds them, not that they have found that way. Ignorance of the law is no excuse when a person is able to remedy that ignorance. When a person claims, "I didn't know that was the law," the reply in a proper legal system is, "You should have known."

The purpose of this maxim is clear. If a legislator's aim is straightforward, he is trying to get people to behave as his legislation mandates. But people if have no way of knowing what they should do, or why they should do it, the legislator's purpose is hardly likely to be furthered. Publicity, then, is a means to carrying out the straightforward intent of a legislator.

Of course, not every legislator's aim is straightforward. When it is not, the rule of Publicity might be of no help to him in reaching his goal. A tyrant who makes rules only to trip people up and put them in constant fear might find it useful to keep those rules hidden until people violate them. And a legislator who votes for a bill out of a desire to please an interest group might not care in the least whether anyone ever hears of the provisions of that bill afterwards.

For example, a certain odd religious sect becomes a power in the politics of a state, as did the group clustered around the late Jim Jones. Among this sect's dogmas is faith in the spiritual power of brussels sprouts. Sect leaders therefore push for legislation requiring

76. This example comes from G. C. Coulton, *Medieval Village, Manor, and Monastery* (Cambridge, 1925; reprint, New York, 1960), 268–69.

all citizens to eat brussels sprouts at least once a week. Some legislators might vote for this bill, in the fervent hope that nobody will ever hear of the matter, then or afterwards. Perhaps it will be enough for the sect just to know that its wishes are now law, or perhaps the matter will be quietly forgotten and the legislator can face his constituents with the sect's contribution in his pockets and no unpleasant questions from all those reasonable people who loathe brussels sprouts.

A legislative body can, however, have reason to follow the rule of Publicity even when its aims are not straightforward. The Augustinian God discussed in chapter 2 is an example. For if His purpose in putting forth the Law was to make all persons sinners, that purpose would be realized only if all persons can know the Law. That is why St. Paul insists that those who do not have the written Law have its precepts written in their hearts.[77] Similarly, when a human legislator has some devious purpose for his legislation, fulfilling that purpose usually requires that people know what the laws say. To vote for Prohibition in hope that the fever will run its course will accomplish nothing if people do not know that alcoholic beverages have indeed been prohibited.

There are not very many circumstances in which a legislator has a straightforward aim and does not need to make use of the rule of Publicity. I can only come up with rather fanciful examples, such as the following one. Its fanciful nature is proved by the fact that I have adapted it from a Woody Allen movie!

The absolute ruler of Azania announces to his privy council that all his subjects should become as proficient in Finnish as they are in their native language. Being clever, he realizes that if people come to know of this order, they will break out in fierce anti-Finnish riots. He therefore tells the council that they must work quietly and deviously to achieve his noble goal. Soon the country is filled with merchants, tax collectors, and soccer referees who speak only Finnish. The ordinary people of Azania find themselves picking up bits of Finnish in order to survive. (More likely, of course, the Finns learn some of the native language.)

The case is fanciful, but its point is not. To get people to act in a certain way is to initiate a causal process. There are many different ways of causing people to act as you wish, some more effective than others. To suppose is that the most effective means of gaining your way is always to tell people your wishes is romantic, at best. A legislator

---

77. Romans 2: 11–16.

might determine that the goal should be straightforward, but the means devious. In such a case, however, there is a major drawback to the legislative body's devious procedure. For one can no longer make honest or effective use of the counter, "You should have known what the law said!" An Azanian who refused to learn Finnish would have every reason to be surprised on being told that he had broken the law. The probable result would be, among other things, increased disrespect for any of the ruler's decrees. "Who knows what that so-and-so will want next? No use trying to figure it out."

A refusal to follow the maxim of Publicity, then, does not inevitably lead to bad results, but surely that is the tendency. And in the great majority of cases, following this maxim is the most effective means toward a straightforward legislative intent. It is therefore a rule of deontic pragmatics.

Openness: **Provide a method by which new legislation can be developed when cases are insufficiently or improperly determined by present legislation.**

The rule of Openness asks that a legislator provide a method for further legislation, to use when the existing deontic rules either do not apply to some important cases or settle important cases the wrong way. When I speak of a method, I include anything from an elaborate legislative procedure to a simple willingness to change one's mind. An example of the latter is the person who makes New Year's resolutions for himself in all sincerity, who means to keep to each of those resolutions, but who realizes that one or another of the resolutions might turn out to be impractical and is prepared to adjust his plans accordingly.

The reason for normally employing the rule of Openness is no mystery. Legislation is generally based on knowledge of the past but applies to the unknown future. Like induction, legislation is never a sure thing: the future might turn out to be very different from what we expect, and the legislation we have passed in anticipation of that future could be inadequate, useless, or even harmful. If legislators have no way of correcting their mistakes, their legislative aims will suffer.[78]

78. Thus James Madison, speaking of the United States Constitution, said, "That useful alterations will be suggested by experience, could not but be foreseen. It was requisite, therefore, that a mode for introducing them should be provided" ("Publius," *The Federalist* [New York, 1788], #43).

One might envision a writer on etiquette at the start of this century. She spends much of her book spelling out how one should behave to one's servants. She assumes that visits and letters are the only ways by which family news can be spread, and she therefore details the proper behavior for such eventualities. The writer announces that a woman, before she marries, should learn some elegant accomplishments, but after she marries, she is to manage the house and no more. These rules for good manners may have suited their time, but both they and the book in which they appear are useless today. If the writer did not keep her advice up to date as the century advanced, she failed more and more in her attempt to have people behave in accordance with her legislative aim.

But although there is good reason to remain open in one's legislation, at times a legislator will put openness aside. A legislator might think his goal worth pursuing, no matter what changes the future might bring. John Calvin, laying down laws for his theocratic state in Geneva, would not easily have been swayed by thoughts of an uncertain future.

Theorists have debated whether a lawmaking body can bind itself absolutely, but such a body can, at any rate, make legislative change very difficult. An obvious example is the cumbersome and difficult procedure for constitutional change in the United States. The history of efforts to amend the United States Constitution is, on the whole, a record of failure. One need only think of the many fruitless attempts to abolish the electoral college. Quite regularly we hear from distinguished people that the electoral college is an anachronism with a capacity for working some real mischief in thwarting the clear voting intent of the American people. Then come polls showing a majority of Americans favoring a more direct method of electing our president, followed by congressional attempts to find a better system. After that, silence. The impulse for reform has spent itself, at least until another close presidential election comes along.

The difficult procedure for amending the Constitution definitely serves a purpose.[79] It insulates the fundamental law of American society from momentary passions—which is to say, in the phrase made popular by John C. Calhoun, from "the tyranny of the majority." And one can well imagine a framer of the Constitution thinking this purpose important enough to attempt to foreclose a bit of the future.

79. See James Madison, *The Federalist*, #43: "[The method of amendment] guards equally against that extreme facility, which would render the Constitution too mutable; and that extreme difficulty, which might perpetuate its discovered faults."

The Constitution is not change proof, but it changes only in response to deeply felt needs that have proven themselves over a period of time.

Analogies occur when individuals set policies for themselves. Quite probably, almost all such individual legislation contains, explicitly or not, the capacity for being altered. But how likely that capacity is to become reality differs from case to case, even with the same person.

For instance, I decide that I ought to be more patient with students who need my help, and I therefore adopt a policy of greater patience. Various things might now lead me to reconsider my policy. Perhaps I work with a group of students considerably more irritating than most, or I come across studies that show that students do not respond well to patience, or I find that my patience is being interpreted as weakness, with results that are disastrous either personally or educationally. My policy might well survive some of these events, but surely it neither would nor should survive all of them. I doubt that I can have any clear idea in advance how adverse a future must be to cause me to alter my policy.

Openness, the willingness to alter one's legislation if the future demands such changes, is clearly, then, a matter of degree. How open one is depends primarily upon how important one thinks one's goal is and how ominous the future looks.

In some instances, openness can and perhaps should be suspended altogether. When a person makes a sincere religious commitment, he has no intention of letting any future events alter that commitment. And with some people, nothing that happens will alter a religious commitment. Perhaps nothing should do so.

The rule of Openness, to sum up, usually has great value in helping one achieve one's legislative purpose; but sometimes the rule is broken, and sometimes the rule has no practical value. It is therefore a maxim of deontic pragmatics.

The legislative rules of manner have proved relatively uncontroversial. But the legislative rules of matter should provide much more room for debate.

7 The Legislative Rules of Matter

There are five legislative rules of matter: Theoretical Virtue, Universalizability, Factuality, Proportionality, and Economy. I shall take up each in the order just given. These five, of all the eighteen maxims, are the most likely to play a dual role. They are maxims of deontic pragmatics, but often they also serve as moral precepts. In this chapter, I look only at the first role, saving any comments on the relationship between pragmatics and morals for chapter 14.

Theoretical Virtue: **Adopt rules that are consistent with one another, clear, applicable, simple, and modest.**

General rules of how people should and may behave are very different from theories of how people do behave. Deontic rules are not theories at all. Why, then, should a legislative body pay any attention to those virtues that make for good theories? The answer, as we shall see, is that legislation incorporating the virtues of a good theory is, by and large, well fitted to carry out the legislative end.

Neither analogy nor fetishism explain my belief that clarity, simplicity, and the rest are virtues of the deontic, as well as of the theoretical, realm.[80] If I were arguing merely from analogy, I would not have omitted completeness from the list of virtues befitting deontic legislation. But in fact, completeness does not serve the legislative end, for we have no reason to think that all behavior should be subject to deontic rules. And even when one is able to formulate deontic rules for a type of behavior, that course is not always best. Thus completeness in deontic matters is no virtue.

The virtues of clarity, applicability, simplicity, modesty, and consistency do, however, usually help to achieve legislative ends. A few examples will show why a legislator is well advised to practice these virtues.

Those who opposed the proposed Equal Rights Amendment to the United States Constitution often claimed that the amendment was vague and its effect unpredictable. At one hearing on the legislation, a proponent answered a long series of questions on specific effects of the amendment with a constant, "That will be for the courts to decide." Of course, the witness was right. In the United States, the courts do have the duty of interpreting the Constitution. But by not offering any grounds that a future court might, under the amendment, use in reaching decisions, this witness was harming his own cause. For few legislators will support legislation with so uncertain an effect that not even a proponent will chance an educated and rational guess as to how the courts will interpret it.

Likewise, where rules are inconsistent with one another, where one forbids what another permits, nobody knows what to do. The famous, so-called "Wicked Bible" is an example. Because of a misprint, this Bible issued the command: "Thou shalt commit adultery." A person who read the Wicked Bible and compared it with a Bible that prohibited adultery would be at a loss about how to act, at least with respect to adultery. No doubt, one of these Bibles has made a mistake,

---

80. Since the virtues of a theory form a cohesive whole, we have some reason to consider the maxim of Theoretical Virtue a single rule. But the chief reason for doing so is to avoid multiplying maxims beyond necessity.

but which? Those who have a legislative interest in minimizing the amount of adultery in the world are well advised to avoid such misprints, for the legislative aim is lost or at least harmed when inconsistency is present.

Modesty is a virtue of somewhat lesser value for deontic legislation than the others. A modest law is one that covers no more behavior than is necessary to fulfill the legislative end. Suppose I intend to be somewhat kinder and more patient with my family and friends. I might immodestly expand my intention by deciding that I should love all my fellow humans. The net result, given the relative unlovability of many persons, is that I will probably fail to meet not only my extravagant goal of universal love but even my original intent of better behavior toward those close to me. Extreme immodesty in deontic legislation, then, is likely to be ineffective, but lesser violations of the virtue of modesty will probably do little harm.

Finally, simplicity is a virtue strongly related to clarity. Every so often, I read in the newspapers an item comparing the number of words in the Gettysburg Address or the Declaration of Independence to the number of words in the latest Department of Agriculture decrees concerning hog farming. Needless to say, the government rulings are far more prolix. Such comparisons are more odious than most—it is always easier to be concise in announcing one's general policy than in giving highly specific regulations. But the complexity of many government edicts does seem more than a trifle unnecessary— like the fine print of insurance policies or software warranties, both of which employ a language bearing no visible resemblance to English. An unnecessarily complex bit of legislation frustrates a straightforward legislative end, through people's sheer inability to comprehend what is being asked of them.

The virtues of a theory can conflict with one another. For instance, the only way to achieve an adequate measure of simplicity might be to sacrifice clarity. We find similar conflicts of virtues in deontic legislation. The Equal Rights Amendment was, as its backers often pointed out, extremely simple. The operative language of the amendment was a single, short sentence. Opponents claimed that this extreme simplicity was bought at the high price of clarity and applicability.

When the virtues of deontic legislation conflict with one another, we should not expect to find any easily applicable, ready-made method of solution, as the case of the Equal Rights Amendment shows. Different people often put differing values on the competing virtues of simplicity and clarity, and two persons can have quite diverse ways of estimating the extent to which each of these virtues is present. What a lawyer regards as the simplest possible language for clarifying a legislative point might strike others as intolerable obscurantism.

Simplicity and clarity are not the only two virtues that can conflict. Indeed, there can be conflicts within a single virtue. For example, people sometimes differ widely about clarity—how important it is to be clear, how to measure clarity, the minimum amount of that virtue needed, and the degree to which a given piece of legislation embodies the virtue. Think of the many different ways philosophers such as Goodman and Kyburg have proposed for measuring the simplicity of theories. The simplicity of deontic legislation is no less likely a subject for disagreement.

No one has come up with a rational and agreed-upon method of settling clashes over measuring and evaluating the virtues of deontic legislation. So I see no merit in asserting that such a method exists, that in principle we can measure and weigh the various virtues in each case and thus decide conflicts. Schemes of weighting and measurement are available, of course, but we have no reason to prefer one over a host of others.

For imagine for a minute that the problem of measurement has been solved. Moreover, imagine that we can compare the measures of one virtue with those of all the others—an even less likely supposition! Somebody then offers a scheme that will supposedly let us enact all and only legislation that maximizes the total theoretical virtue. Before accepting that proposal, how should we assess it? The proposed scheme has obviously assigned a relative weight to each virtue, using a measurement scale analogous to that for temperature. On what principle did it assign those weights? The rule that each virtue counts as much as every other? I have already indicated that I consider modesty less important than clarity. The scheme therefore requires differential weighting, and I know of no rational principles that yield such a manner of weighting.

When virtues conflict, then, I know of no general scheme that tells us which to prefer in a given case. We neither have nor expect general agreement on how to measure the presence of a virtue, the scale of measurement to use, how to compare the scales for two different virtues, how to weight the merits of each virtue, or how to apply any virtue index to specific cases. Aside from that, there doesn't seem much of a problem.

I shall return to this issue later, when I consider what happens when rules conflict.[81] For now, it should be obvious that legislators who conscientiously try to maximize these theoretical virtues in their deontic legislation cannot do so with precision. They must use rules of thumb, and they must expect others to disagree with some of their assessments. To say that the rule of Theoretical Virtue cannot be applied with precision, of course, is hardly to say that it cannot or should not be applied at all.

I turn now to cases in which legislators, to fulfill their legislative aims, find it best to disregard one or more of the theoretical virtues.

It is easy to come up with cases in which legislators whose aims are not straightforward have reason to write obscurely or with unnecessary complexity. A secret anarchist, who hopes to throw the laws into contempt, might deliberately write inapplicable legislation. An insurance company might use a thicket of jargon to keep the awful truth from its policyholders.

But if the aim is straightforward, can legislators have reason to ignore or disobey any of the theoretical virtues? They certainly may ignore modesty. Decisions of the United States Supreme Court are not always marked by modesty. The *Bakke* decision, which I examine in detail in chapter 11, provides a good example. Five justices ignored the pleas of the other four and opted for a sweeping decision on constitutional grounds rather than a fairly narrow one based on civil rights legislation. My impression is that the five thought that a narrow-based decision would duck some important issues that needed to be faced. With respect to the immediate situation, then, the decision was a piece of immodest legislation, but five justices thought that the general principles they established justified any immodesty.

Simplicity may and sometimes should be ignored, usually in the interests of clarity. Legislation need not dot every 'i' and cross every 't', much less repeat itself several times over, but it can be more easily understood that way. Sometimes repetition is also useful in emphasizing legislation, even when that legislation is clear enough. One need only recall how various Biblical prohibitions were pounded in, repetition by repetition.

Clarity, like simplicity, may give way to emphasis. A deliberately obscure pronouncement might gain attention and obedience from its cloak of mystical authority. Consider the requirement that we not slander the Holy Spirit (Matthew 12:31). This piece of legislation,

81. See chapter 12: "When Rules Conflict."

because it combines obscurity with a drastic sanction, has gathered an enormous amount of attention from scholars and laymen. Now, consider a supposition totally without theological warrant: To slander the Holy Spirit one need only intend to do so, even without knowing what it means to slander the Holy Spirit. On this supposition, the very obscurity that brought this rule to public attention serves the legislative end.

Examples of a straightforward legislative end where consistency and applicability are unnecessary and their absence useful are less easy to find. One can perhaps sacrifice some degree of applicability, although one can hardly do so entirely.

Leaders who desire a certain kind of behavior from their followers sometimes want that behavior to come only with difficulty and after a period of testing. They therefore deliberately make the legislation hard to apply. For example, a religious cult leader who requires a sacrifice of two goats every month might demand that his disciples follow an involved procedure for choosing, transporting, and slaughtering the goats. He really cares nothing about such matters in themselves: he believes that if you've seen one sacrificial goat, you've seen them all. His goal in legislating is, however, to get two goats per worshipper per month. His true goal, then, supplements his legislative aim rather than replaces it.

I suspect that the price of giving up consistency is always too high. This suspicion is not just a philosopher's occupational prejudice. People do use inconsistency for emphasis, but doing so runs the risk of confusing others about what they should do. At best, when faced with an inconsistent pair of rules, a person can only guess at her duty. Merely apparent inconsistency does have a value, in that it provides work for those who make judicial decisions! Maybe that's why Supreme Court justices are always eager to find their wildest departures sanctioned by precedent.

In sum, the various theoretical virtues are normally worth incorporating into one's deontic legislation. But for each virtue, there are times when a legislator has reason not to be theoretically virtuous. Legislators can have reason to sacrifice any of the theoretical virtues, except perhaps consistency, even when they desire that people act in accordance with a piece of legislation. However, these cases are exceptional.

We discovered that the virtues can conflict, and we found no rational method for settling such conflicts. As a result, I can recommend to legislators nothing more specific than that they employ the blend of virtues that seems best for a particular piece of deontic legislation. The vagueness of this recommendation in no way detracts from the importance of theoretical virtue. For the theoretical virtues in most situations are conducive to the legislative end. Legislation that is consistent, simple, clear, modest, and applicable is usually more readily obeyed than legislation that lacks these virtues. Theoretical Virtue therefore belongs among the maxims of deontic pragmatics.

Universalizability: **Adopt only rules that treat like cases alike.**

A person should not treat himself as an exception to the rules, unless he has good reason to do so. What one person ought to do, so should every other person in the same situation. Since Kant, these and other formulations of the principle of universalizability have been familiar ethical principles. Why then do I need to go over such well-trodden ground once more?

First, I believe universalizability is not just a moral principle but a general deontic requirement. This claim will irritate a fanatical Kantian, who regards universalizability as the sole defining condition for morality. But I think it is not hard to see the value of adhering to universalizability when one's ought-statements are legal, prudential, or even claims of etiquette.

More important, I believe there are times when one does best not to universalize. We do in fact sometimes ignore this principle, and I believe that we should on occasion do so.

Both of these claims are necessary if I am to show that the principle of Universalizability is part of the pragmatics of deontic speech. I therefore concentrate in this section on those two claims. I do not try to show that, morally speaking, one normally ought so to act that the maxim of one's actions may serve as a universal law. Instead, I spend my time arguing that one should also universalize when making most nonmoral deontic statements, but that at times one is justified in not universalizing.

First, then, let us look at the scope of the principle of Universalizability, to see whether we can in fact apply it in nonmoral deontic situations.

Imagine a writer of etiquette books. She has fairly stringent rules governing how people with light-colored skin should behave, while her rules governing the conduct of those with darker-colored skin are much easier to obey. Further, let us suppose that we, her readers, are convinced that the color of a person's skin makes no difference in determining either how desirable or how possible it is for that person to conduct himself in accordance with a certain set of rules. The writer, we conclude, fails to treat like cases alike.

Is the writer's conduct immoral? I believe so, even though she might not realize how discriminatory her legislation is. But I have not argued for that belief.[82]

Nor shall I do so. For or not whether readers accept my belief that the writer should not regard skin color as relevant, I think we can all agree that there's something really foolish about her intended legislation. If the author really intends to get people to act as she suggests, she needs to justify her having two sets of rules. And any justification she provides will rely on skin color, which does not seem to have a bearing (nor does she show it to have a bearing) upon conduct. Immorality is not the sole nor even the major reason why this book is likely to fall stillborn from the presses. Foolishness is.

A second type of instance that should lead us to consider universalizability as more than a rule of ethics comes from the much-contested area of duties to one's self. Giving the principle of universalizability a general deontic status and not restricting it to the moral sphere might help with such vexing questions as whether, and how, one can literally have a duty to one's self.

Suppose that Jean is very anxious to do what she considers her religious duty. She adopts the motto, "I am third," meaning that in everything she does, God comes first and other persons come second. Unlike St. Martin of Tours, who divided his cloak with a beggar, Jean believes it her duty to give away the whole cloak, even if doing so reduces her to a state no better than that of the beggar.[83]

A strict Kantian must regard Jean's conduct as immoral, for she fails to treat like cases alike. In making an exception of herself, she does not perform her duty to at least one person: herself. A Kantian might add that, if everyone practiced constant self-sacrifice, opportunities for self-sacrifice would wither away, along with the self-sacrificers themselves. Jean has a moral duty to treat herself as she treats others: no better, to be sure, but also no worse.

82. This point was urged by a reader for Brown University Press.

83. Sancho Panza has given the definitive commentary on St. Martin's deed: "He must have been following the old proverb that says, to give and to keep has need of brains" (M. Cervantes, *Don Quixote*, vol. 2, trans. J. M. Cohen [Baltimore, 1950], Chap. 58, 839).

But this strict Kantianism seems almost paradoxical. Jean's conduct is quixotic, and it may well prove as ultimately futile as the actions of Don Quixote himself. For, as Aristotle noted, the practice of some virtues requires money and position. If Jean carries her principle to the extreme and gives up her own life to secure a minor incremental benefit for others, then she has surely sacrificed for insufficient return all chance of being of further help. Tilting at windmills is nothing to such conduct! But is it really immoral? Jean's actions might be foolish, but are they morally wrong? Only a Kantian could say that they are. Some people have adopted and tried to live up to Jean's motto, "I am third." Many people believe such conduct to be utterly admirable. When Jean does not universalize, her actions, far from being condemned by non-Kantians, might be thought of as morally praiseworthy, if a bit foolish. To say that Jean should treat herself as she treats others is therefore not obviously to lay down a moral rule.

Almost everyone since Kant agrees that the principle of universalizability is not enough to generate morality. By exercising very little ingenuity, one can find an acceptable general rule to cover the most despicable conduct. For example, Nero could justify sending his mother to sea in a collapsible boat on the grounds that she had been a good swimmer and that older people need exercise. The point is almost banal by now.

I believe there is a much more important way in which the principle of universalizability fails to generate moral rules, though: Often, one universalizes for the sake of prudence or of some other nonmoral type of goal. For example, suppose that I have just started a thousand-piece jigsaw puzzle. I begin by placing pieces with a straight edge in one pile and those without a straight edge in another. I then subdivide each group by color. When I come to piece 587, I find it no different in any relevant respect from those in the straight-edged, greenish pile. Should I put it in that pile, as I have done with other relevantly similar pieces? To do so would be prudent. If my goal is to complete the puzzle in the least amount of time, then I should certainly group 587 with the others. I am following a principle I have willed to be a universal law—but I am hardly morally bound to do so.

One might object to the puzzle-example on the grounds that the principle of universalizability has to do only with one's treatment of human beings. But to universalize can be prudent, rather than moral, even when one deals with humans. A drill instructor teaches some of his recruits to perform actions one way, others in another way. The result is hardly immoral, but it is certainly imprudent. If, for example, the instructor provides different procedures for the care of intricate weapons, confusion might be the least practical problem to arise. Teaching everyone the same drill is easier for the teacher, and it will surely be more conducive to his and the army's ends, but morality hardly enters into the matter.

I have been arguing that universalizability is not sufficient for generating moral rules. The principle of Universalizability, my examples suggest, often assists us in achieving reasonable goals, if not necessarily moral ones, in a reasonable way, if not necessarily in a moral way. And these goals are in turn the general goals shared by all deontic speech.[84] We must now consider whether at times it is best not to follow the rule of Universalizability. If so, I believe I will have shown this principle to be one of deontic pragmatics.

No one is likely to dispute the point that some laws do violate Universalizability, by showing favoritism toward a lucky few. Good examples are the Jim Crow laws formally on the books in the United States and the apartheid statutes in South Africa. Under such laws, blacks are forbidden to use certain facilities open to whites. The schools and train stations open to blacks are usually much inferior to those provided for whites. Clearly, the difference between two persons in the color of their skin is not relevant to their ability to be educated or their need for train travel. These laws are therefore not treating similar cases alike, and they dispense with universalizability.

Even those people who deliberately disobeyed Jim Crow laws to force a change did not deny that such statutes were the law. Lack of universalizability, I believe, makes Jim Crow statutes bad laws, vicious in their effects, but it does not make them nullities. Their existence suggests that a violation of Universalizability does not introduce a logical inconsistency.

I find it hard to imagine how Jim Crow legislation could be justified, except by arguing that racial differences are somehow relevant to education or waiting for trains. Some have argued exactly that, however, so I must find a case of legislation that clearly lacks universalizability but that is nevertheless clearly justified.

I am about to paint my house and would like my children, who are about the same age, to lend a hand. I have two jobs for the children to perform: to use the paint roller on the lowest part of the house and to use a brush on the storm windows. The first task is quick and easy and requires me to issue few instructions. The task of doing the storm

---

84. This last point was urged by a reader for Brown University Press.

windows is considerably more difficult, delicate, and time consuming. I prefer to have the same child do all the storm windows, since on-the-job training for both would lead to too many botched windows. Let one of them learn how to do it on an out-of-the-way window, and then maybe he can do the rest reasonably well. So, dreading the outcome a bit, I assign these unequal tasks. And then arises that cry every parent knows: "It isn't fair!" I quickly agree that it isn't. But there is no way I can be fair here and still get the jobs done well.

This example is not artificial, nor is its point confined to domestic matters only. At times a legislator will decide that different work calls for different hands, even though there is no good reason for assigning one particular set of tasks to one particular set of people. If I am feeling democratic, I might let my children fight it out among themselves to determine which tasks each is to perform, but such a fight might be drawn-out, figuratively bloody, and overwhelmingly counterproductive. Eventually, the democratic experiment is likely to fail, and I must step in and assign tasks after all. And in doing so, I deliberately do not employ Universalizability.

One could come up with a description of my action that portrays me as treating the two children alike. But then, one can always find some universalizable description of any action, however unfair. If Universalizability is to have any content, the description one universalizes must be either that provided by the legislator or some normal and reasonable account. As the legislator in this matter of painting the house, I consider that, by giving the children different jobs, I am not treating them alike. And I know of no normal and reasonable account of my assignment of jobs that would pass the test of universalizability.

We see then that sometimes the legislator has a goal or set of goals that can only be accomplished, or can best be accomplished, by deliberately assigning duties or permissions in a way that fails to treat like cases alike. When the legislator considers his goal of great importance, he is surely justified in disregarding universalizability.

Perhaps such considerations motivated the three justices who joined Justice Brennan is dissenting from the majority opinion in the celebrated *Bakke* case. Admissions procedures at the University of California at Davis Medical School gave Allan Bakke no chance of obtaining one of the sixteen places reserved for members of minority groups. Title Six of the 1964 Civil Rights Act appears on its face to forbid such discrimination. Although Justice Brennan argued that Bakke was not really damaged by Davis' refusal to admit him, this argument seems disingenuous. Justice Brennan's case would have been more compelling had he argued that efforts to rectify the evil effects of past discrimination in society justify a degree of unfairness to Bakke and other white males.

For I doubt that anyone thinks a legislative goal can never justify unfairness. The question in the *Bakke* case is whether the goal was indeed important and pressing enough to justify the particular degree of unfairness to Bakke. In this and other cases, unfairness amounts to a lack of universalizability in one's legislation. Therefore, the principle of Universalizability can and should be set aside in some cases.[85]

Universalizability normally does, however, play a large role in any worthwhile legislation. If the legislator wishes his product to be effective he will usually take care to treat like cases alike. A blatantly discriminatory law, unless those discriminated against are utterly powerless, is likely to raise objections strong enough to defeat the legislator's purpose. And even utter powerlessness does not last forever.

The person who legislates only for himself is no different in this respect from the person who legislates for others. If I decide as a general rule to discriminate against certain others, for no good reason, my actions are likely to cause difficulties. And if the person I discriminate against is myself, as was the case with Jean, frustration of my legislative end seems almost inevitable.

Universalizability, then, resembles the other legislative pragmatic principles in serving the legislative end. It provides in most instances the best and most efficient way of achieving a given goal. But there are times when the principle, if applied, does not serve the legislative end. In such cases, it can and should be dispensed with.[86]

Factuality: **Adopt rules that do not crucially depend upon false statements about the way the world is.**

There are at least two major ways in which legislation might depend upon claims about the world. First, the legislation can contain a 'whereas' or 'since' clause, overtly stated or tacitly understood. A law might begin: "Since people of this race are innately less capable than others of good citizenship, they should be treated in the following

---

85. I am not implying that Universalizability should have been disregarded in the *Bakke* case. See chapter 11 for further discussion of that case.

86. Of course, this 'should' is practical. Sometimes a legislator should, practically, do something he should, morally, not do.

manner. . . ." Here a supposed fact about the world provides justification for an assertion of how people should behave. The use of factual claims to justify deontic legislation in this way is common.

Second, the world might have to be in a certain condition for people to comply in a nonvacuous way with deontic legislation. For example, suppose that the state of Nevada, in trying to find a speed limit acceptable to local drivers, enacts legislation forbidding drivers to go faster than the speed of light on Interstate highways. Drivers have no choice except to obey this law, but their compliance is vacuous. The new Nevada speed limit thus depends on the world's being such that drivers can go faster than the speed of light.

When in either of these ways a piece of legislation depends on the world's being a certain way, one can lack reason or ability to comply with the legislation. Suppose that the leader of the newest religious sect obliges his followers to make a pilgrimage to Tahiti at least once. Most of the sect's members are able, by dint of careful saving, to scrape up the price of regular boat or air fare to Tahiti, but few are able to raise the amount needed to charter a boat or an airplane. Fulfillment of the deontic requirement therefore depends upon the existence of regular boat or air service to Tahiti, even if a few members of the sect do manage to get there in other ways. That these few sectaries do not need regular boat or air service to fulfill their obligation does not change the fact of dependence. These remarks should help clarify what it means to call dependence crucial.

Certainly, there is little practical problem most of the time in determining whether a supposedly factual justification for a bit of legislation is a major factor or not. As a former member of my university's Faculty Senate, I know that many 'whereas' clauses in legislation are pure window dressing. Consider the vote of commendation to a retiree: "Whereas Mr. Blank has given our University 40 years of faithful and diligent service, he deserves the hearty thanks of the Faculty and a shiny tin watch." The truth is that Mr. Blank was lazy, surly, and generally unavailable when needed. But that in no way cancels the operative part of the legislation, for the faculty is still expected to cough up money for a tin watch and to wish Mr. Blank well without gagging on the words. This case is one of noncrucial dependence.

It is also easy in most cases of deontic legislation to determine how crucial a factor the state of the world is for nonvacuous compliance. If the leader of my imagined religious sect calls for a pilgrimage not to Tahiti but to Elizabeth, New Jersey, and if his followers all live in New York City, the nonexistence of regular air or boat service to Elizabeth would rule out only improbable ways of fulfilling their religious obligations. There are any number of ways remaining, including the most likely ones: walking, bus, car, taxi, train.

It is therefore usually easy for a legislative body to determine when proposed legislation depends crucially on the truth of some assertion about the world. The theoretical question is thornier, raising long-standing issues about the relation of 'is' to 'ought'. Fortunately for me, I need not go into the theoretical question here. It is enough that a legislator be able most of the time to recognize crucial dependence.

I shall end these preliminary remarks by noting that legislators seldom make their legislation depend on claims they know to be false.[87] The rule of Factuality most often deters legislators from basing their laws on dubious claims about the world. For example, some people have claimed that statistical evidence supports the position that blacks, as a whole, are innately less capable in academic matters than whites, as a whole. Such claims have provoked outrage. They have also provoked a mass of of statistical evidence and explanations, all intended to show that there are no innate racial differences in academic ability. Any legislator who bases educational policy on a belief in innate differences in ability between whites and blacks is taking a huge risk. For if it should turn out, as it well might, that all important differences in academic achievement can be explained by cultural or socioeconomic factors, then the legislation flagrantly violates Factuality.

Why should a legislator worry about violating Factuality? When supposed facts are used to justify deontic legislation, there is an obvious danger if people learn that these crucial beliefs about the world are false. For people will then be far less prone to obey the legislation. But if people remain unaware that a critical 'whereas' clause is false, the legislation's violation of Factuality might make no practical difference.

For example, consider Ruth Benedict's remarks about the Dobu culture.[88] As she explains the matter, the behavior of the Dobu is predicated largely on the assumptions that people are constantly trying to harm one another by witchcraft and that such witchcraft is effective in gaining its ends. A Dobu setting policy for himself or others will

---

87. This is true only of important legislation. The harmless bill that puffs the virtues of one's constituents often departs widely from the truth in its factual claims, as the bill's sponsor well knows.

88. Ruth Benedict, "Anthropology and the Abnormal," *Journal of Genetic Psychology* 10 (1934): 59–82; excerpted in M. Mandelbaum, F. Gramlich, and A. R. Anderson, *Philosophic Problems: An Introductory Book of Readings* (New York, 1957), 341–48.

therefore use these assumptions to justify his legislation. As long as he has no reason to question whether witchcraft really works, he has no worries about violating Factuality. Nevertheless, his witchcraft is not in fact effective, and he is violating the principle of Factuality.[89]

But although it might be a bit romantic to claim that the truth will always out, still facts do come to public knowledge often enough. The attitude of the average educated European about the efficacy of witchcraft is far more factual than it was four centuries ago. On this subject, Queen Elizabeth II is far more enlightened than was King James I.

Therefore, a legislator has reason to try as best he can to obey the rule of Factuality. For the legislator cannot expect any public ignorance on this point to last. And when the public becomes enlightened, legislation based on the false statements becomes as dead as the laws (still on the books in some places) against witchcraft.

A legislative body has even stronger reason to avoid those breaches of Factuality that make nonvacuous compliance impossible. For when the public tries to fulfill the requirements set down in a piece of legislation, it will most certainly come to know of any crucial conditions for doing so. If I try to meet my religious obligations by going to Tahiti, or to Elizabeth for that matter, I will soon find myself considering ways of getting there. If all reasonable methods of travel are not open to me, I will soon find that out. When I do, I am unlikely to blame myself for any failure to fulfill my obligation, but I might begin to doubt the authority of my sect's leader, which would be unlikely to accord with that leader's legislative end.[90]

Keeping the rule of Factuality is therefore usually the best way of fulfilling one's legislative aim. If we can find some circumstances in which one does best to provide legislation that depends crucially on false statements about the world, we will have proved Factuality a rule of deontic pragmatics.

Under what circumstances can a legislative body have reason to override the presumption in favor of Factuality? One famous, or infamous, example is the "Noble Lie" in Plato's *Republic*. Plato's Socrates, in legislating for his ideal community, asks that each citizen be told that he was born from the earth. The metal in one's soul determines one's proper station in life. Socrates knows that this story

---

89. Belief in the power of witchcraft may well be effective, but that's an altogether different matter.

90. Although it might accord with the leader's goal. Perhaps the leader was using absurd deontic legislation to shock his followers into thinking for themselves.

is false, and he worries that the people of his ideal community will also realize its falsity. But he thinks the lie worth the telling.

For the point of the story, as Socrates sees it, is to provide a basis for the claim that everyone ought to be content with his station in life. Members of the merchant class should not act as soldiers, members of the ruling class should not seek money as merchants, and so on. Socrates bases this deontic legislation on what he explicitly calls a lie. He legislates contrary to the rule of Factuality, and he knows it.

The reason Socrates disregards Factuality is no mystery. He thinks the principle that each social group should do its own work is so important, so necessary to the success of his planned state, that any means whatsoever for establishing the principle in the state is acceptable. He is worried that the truth will come out and the strategy of the Noble Lie backfire, but on balance, he is willing to take the chance.

Perhaps Socrates would cite an overriding need to establish basic principles in his state as quickly as possible. If the first few generations born in the ideal community accept the Noble Lie, then the tradition that each class does its own work should be firmly enough entrenched to survive exposure of the Lie.

The same can be said of parents who pass on the story of Santa Claus to help improve the behavior of their children. The song, "Santa Claus Is Coming To Town," suggests that the jolly old elf has espionage methods Big Brother might envy. Its not-so-subtle burden is that goodness pays off with rich rewards, badness with unpleasant sanctions. Probably most parents who tell their children of Santa are not quite so crass, but the message is usually the same—with a bit more sugarcoating.

Parents realize their children will eventually see through the accounts of Santa Claus and construct or discover a better explanatory paradigm. What Socrates only feared might happen, parents know must occur: the subjects of the legislator will realize they have been fed a lie. Such parents, if they are at all rational, must believe that the short-term gain in pleasure for the children and in positive reinforcement for good behavior justifies the cost in eventual disillusionment. That belief is open to question. A child might well learn from the exposure of the Santa Claus story not to trust her parents. The telling of the legend might do more harm than good in the long run. But most American parents go ahead and tell it, whatever qualms they may have. I did.

Individuals can set for themselves policies based on claims they know to be utterly dubious. Usually, this occurs when their options have been narrowed so that they have no real choice. Bridge players are often advised: "If you're playing a hand, and things look bad for you, think what distribution, however unlikely, will enable you to make the contract. Then play as if that distribution actually holds." If I follow this advice, I might decide that I should play to squeeze my left-hand opponent. My play is based on the assumption that he has all the missing high cards. The probability that this assumption is true is, let's say 6.25 percent, but if my partner keeps putting me in these ridiculous slam contracts, what else can I do?

Rarely do people set policies for themselves based on what they already know to be false. There inevitably is some compelling motivation behind such a legislative end. For example, take Shakespeare's Sonnet 138:

When my love swears that she is made of truth
I do believe her, though I know she lies.

If we understand the author to be setting a policy for himself rather than simply reporting past actions, he is intentionally basing a policy on what he knows to be false. He thinks he should believe what his mistress says, even though he knows it to be false. When matters have come to such a pass, they are desperate indeed! Only an overwhelming desire to keep his mistress, at whatever cost, can explain the author's resolution.[91]

The rule of Factuality, then, can be set aside. It may and perhaps should be disregarded when the goal of the legislation (or the goal behind the legislation) is important or pressing enough that the legislator considers the lack of factuality justifiable. But in most of the examples we have looked at in this section, ignoring Factuality results in a high degree of uneasiness. Legislation that you base on what you believe false usually extracts a high price.

Proportionality: Let the strength of obligations and the severity of sanctions be proportional to the strength of the justification provided.

This maxim should not be interpreted as calling for more than an approximation to genuine proportionality. No Benthamite calculus

---

91. It is by no means obvious that the author can keep to this policy. The will (or, in this case, Will) to believe might not be able to swallow known absurdities.

is likely to give us the precise amount of fine an evildoer should pay or the exact length of time lawbreakers should spend in prison. Nor is there any precise way to measure the weight a legislative body should give to each justification. It is easy to justify laws against embezzlement, it is easy to justify laws against criminal negligence in food preparation, and it is hard to justify Sunday blue laws. Comparing justifications for these types of laws in point of weight seems almost impossible.

Despite the imprecision built into the notion of proportionality, legislators do generally attempt to apply the principle, and many have stated explicitly that doing so is important. A recent court decision provides a good example.

The United States Supreme Court held in 1983 that a person convicted of a series of nonviolent felonies did not deserve to be sentenced to life imprisonment under a habitual offender statute.[92] The majority was clearly applying a version of Proportionality. But the four dissenting justices held that the rule of Proportionality should not be judicially enforced in a noncapital case. All nine justices, then, agreed that there is a rule of Proportionality.

In the majority opinion, Justice Powell speaks continually of the need for proportionality. "In sum we hold as a matter of principle that a criminal sentence must be proportionate to the crime for which the defendant has been convicted.[93] Justice Powell traces proportionality back to Magna Carta. He finds it mandated by the Eighth Amendment to the United States Constitution. [94] The Court recognized disproportionality as a violation of the Eighth Amendment as early as 1910.[95] The principle, Justice Powell concludes, applies in the case of Helm. What this offender did simply does not call for the harsh sentence he received.

It might look as if I am equivocating on the matter of what the severity of sanctions should be proportional to. My rule of Proportionality calls for the severity of a sanction to be roughly proportional to the strength of the justification of the law in question. But Justice Powell argued that Helm's life sentence exhibited too great a disproportion between the sanction and the crime commmitted. The nature and viciousness of a crime, on the one hand, and the strength of

---

92. The case is *Solem* v *Helm*, #82–492, decided 28 June 1983. Like the *Bakke* case, this case was settled by a bare five to four majority.

93. *Solem* v *Helm*, p. 12.

94. Ibid., p. 6.

95. *Weems* v *United States*, 217 U.S. 349 (1910), pp. 367 and 372–73, cited by Justice Powell, ibid., p. 9.

a law's justification, on the other, seem to be quite separate matters. I don't think they are separate, however. We could add another consideration at this point: what the perpetrator of a crime deserves. What a criminal deserves normally depends on how heinous a crime he has committed. At least one generally valuable way of measuring the seriousness of a crime is to gauge how strong a justification society can muster for legislating against that crime. A law with little or no justification behind it is one that people tend to ignore, for they regard its violation as no crime at all. When they are punished, they think the law decidedly unfair. Laws with extremely strong justifications behind them, such as laws against murder and treason, impose the heaviest sanctions. Fulfillment of the obligations imposed by these laws is crucial to the maintenance of an organized society. No justification could be stronger, and as a result, people generally think severe punishments for murderers and traitors correct.

The seriousness we assign to a crime is therefore a function of the strength of our justification of the law governing that crime. Hence, when Justice Powell speaks of proportionality to the seriousness of a crime and I speak of proportionality to the strength of a justification, our positions fit together well.

We can apply these considerations briefly to the dispute in the United States over abortion. One difficulty with proposed legislation to outlaw most abortions is that there is no general agreement in our society on the strength of any justification for such laws, and hence on the seriousness of an offense against the laws. Those who think abortion to be murder find a strong justification, those who disagree find at most a much weaker justification. Therefore, even if abortion becomes a crime, we have no agreement on how serious a crime it is. One wonders then how a person convicted under proposed anti-abortion laws could rationally be sentenced.

There is, of course, a large body of literature on the topic of proportionality, justice, and fairness. As with Universalizability, therefore, I shall spend little time in trying to justify the claim that proportionality in deontic legislation is desirable. Instead, I shall concentrate on establishing Proportionality as a maxim of pragmatics. As before, to do so I must look at cases in which one does best to ignore Proportionality in one's deontic legislation.[96]

---

96. As a reader of this book pointed out, many of my cases deal with the application rather than the formulation of disproportionate sanctions. The entire discussion does seem to spill over from the legislative to the judicial area, but, at least in the nongovernmental cases, it is hard to draw a line between making and applying a disproportionate rule.

People sometimes violate Proportionality when the rewards and punishments attached to legislation are so lightly regarded that no one really cares how disproportionate the legislation is. For example, take rules of etiquette. One can easily justify etiquette as an institution in society, as a means of smoothing relations among persons. Some of the particular rules put forward by an etiquette manual are also fairly justifiable. A person should not talk with his mouth full of food, for those who talk with stuffed mouths are not easy to understand and thus throw sand in society's machinery. But I have no idea how one might justify rules for place settings at the table. Certainly, the rules we follow in American society cannot intelligently be claimed to result in the most convenient way of eating!

And yet, writers on etiquette have rarely made much of an effort to distinguish amply justified rules from those that have no special justification. Such writers are a highly deontic tribe, much given to flat "You should" and "You must not," with a very occasional "You may" thrown in. Conditions have improved a bit in recent years. A present-day writer, such as Miss Manners, does try to give a bit of justification for her deontic pronouncements when possible, but often her justifications consist of generalities or even witty irrelevancies.

One should expect this state of affairs to obtain in the etiquette industry, for American society attaches few rewards to impeccable manners and few punishments to the opposite. We do still tend to frown on total grossness, of course, unless the offender is a rock star or a professional athlete. But there seem to be few individual rules of manners, the violation of which will lead to any significant sanctions against the lout in question.

One does well to contrast American society with a society which etiquette played a vital role. Manners were crucial in the French court before 1789. The sanctions incurred by a failure to follow proper ceremonial procedures could be severe. And yet, officials of the court did not bother to give much justification for the minutiae of ceremony. How can that be?

One part of the explanation is surely that nobody expected Louis XIV to justify any part of his conduct. The very idea of such an expectation would have been *lèse majesté*. Many theorists did try to justify the institution of absolute monarchy and the need to obey each of the monarch's commands. More than one writer of the time commented on the value of having an elaborate court ceremonial, as a means of isolating the ruler from his subjects. But these efforts hardly amount to an attempt to justify the particular details of court etiquette.

Now that such courts are part of the dustbin of history, now that an intruder can make his way into the private apartments of the Queen of England without being instantly sent to the Tower and the block, any attempt to introduce an elaborate ceremonial procedure, with stiff sanctions for violators, is likely to prove futile. For such an attempt to have even a tiny chance of success nowadays, its proponents would need a far stronger justification than has ever been given. Proportionality has made its way into manners, if there remain any areas where specific manners really count.

One finds this out in a hurry while raising children. A parent does not often do well to emulate the Sun King. Children want to know why they should or should not do certain things. If a parent can justify "Don't talk with your mouth full" but not "Keep your elbows off the table," the former stands a far better chance of eventual grudging acceptance—in lip service, that is. Probably the only time my children will be careful not to talk with their mouths full of food is when they are admonishing their own children not to talk with their mouths full! Regardless, lip service is probably better than no service at all. Even a legislator on matters of etiquette, therefore, is well advised to justify her rules whenever possible, as the rule of Publicity suggests. When few make a major effort to import Proportionality into rules of etiquette, probably only few think the effort worthwhile. Such examples show that even in social and moral contexts, sanctions, although less well defined than in the law, are often present. When they are, they can be grossly out of proportion to an offense. Thus the rule of Proportionality is not restricted merely to the law.

Sometimes legislators find it best to disregard Proportionality when they think their aims override almost any other consideration. What happens on these occasions is the opposite of what we saw with rules of etiquette. For here the very importance of the legislators' goals convinces them to forgo Proportionality. For example, legislators might believe that a stiff sentence will provide an effective deterrent from a relatively unimportant type of criminal behavior. (Once again, an unimportant crime is one governed by a law for which there is no very strong justification.) If that criminal behavior is widespread enough, the legislators may well think that deterrence is an important goal even though the crime is relatively unimportant.

One way of protecting society against violent crime is to incarcerate those predicted to have a certain violence potential. As Andrew von Hirsch has argued, though, there is no present or likely future means of making such predictions without yielding a huge number of false positive cases.[97] That is, to put behind bars one person who actually would commit a violent crime during a specific period, we must imprison many who would not commit any such crime during that period. Now, suppose that a certain legislator must help make laws for a society in which violent crime is a major, and increasing, menace to huge numbers of law-abiding people. The legislator might well recognize that, because of the problem of false positives, there is no strong justification for jailing a person solely because someone predicted that person will commit a violent crime. But the legislator might, nevertheless, support and work for preventive detention laws. For he sees no other good way of accomplishing a goal that he believes to be of overriding importance.

Many people say that we have to do something about violent crime. Their attitude seems to be that, if the only effective way to prevent such crime requires doing significant injustice, so be it. Those who argue against punishment based on prediction will have success, I suspect, only if they convince the public that using the predictive model is not an effective way of stopping or hindering violent crime.

I have so far used examples that call on the deterrence and the protection-of-society models of punishment. The other prominent forward-looking model is the rehabilitative model. Here too, we can construct a case in which a legislator has reason to disregard Proportionality. Consider the treatment of youthful offenders tried as juveniles.[98] The purpose of removing such offenders from their homes is clear from the name of the institution in which they are placed: a reform school. Society's stated object is not to punish but to reform them.

If so, when should we consider a juvenile offender reformed? I know of no general answer to this question. Some might reform quickly, some never. But it is certain that the period needed for reform bears no clear relation to the seriousness of the crime. A juvenile who felt himself driven to murder to relieve an intolerable family situation might soon be considered reformed, while a person who committed a petty theft might prove incorrigible.

97. See Andrew von Hirsch, "Prediction of Criminal Conduct and Preventive Confinement of Convicted Persons," *Buffalo Law Review* 21 (1972): 717–58; reprinted in J. Feinberg and H. Gross, eds., *Philosophy of Law* (Encino and Belmont, Cal., 1975), 593–614, especially pp. 598–602.

98. Occasionally the courts decide to treat juveniles who commit major crimes as adults. In such cases, the rehabilitative model is, for good or ill, not used.

A legislator who took seriously the goal of reforming juvenile offenders would be unlikely to set a fixed limit to their period of confinement. Such a legislator would probably ask that the legal system treat each case individually: a juvenile should be confined until competent authorities have decided that she has reformed. Any legislator who thinks that giving indeterminate sentences is impolitic or unwise, will at least try to find out how long different types of youthful offenders normally take to reform, and will determine the lengths of sentences accordingly. But whatever the particular mode of sentencing, if the legislator's goal is the reform rather than the punishment of a juvenile offender, considerations of proportionality are irrelevant.

Yet, they cannot be set aside completely. The current tendency to treat serious juvenile offenders as adults shows that people object to a large-scale violation of proportionality. If a juvenile commits a serious enough crime, his youth does not prevent people from believing that his punishment should be correspondingly severe. Likewise, a juvenile who has committed a petty crime but who is declared unreformed after several years is usually let go, for otherwise too great a violation of proportionality occurs.

The Patuxent Institution in Maryland was an experiment in providing adult recidivists with treatment during the period of an indeterminate sentence. In theory, the criminals were let out when and only when they were declared cured by a board of medical personnel. According to the 17-year study of Patuxent, however, the theory was rarely followed. The great majority of those discharged from the institution were let go because of a court order, not because of a medically declared cure.[99] Even with adults who were three-time losers, apparently enough punishment was enough. That, after all, was what the Supreme Court decided in the case of Helm, the seven-time loser. The rehabilitative model, then, needs to be tempered with some degree of proportionality.

In times of extreme national emergency, authorities may waive Proportionality in favor of martial law, under which military courts may impose harsh sentences for seemingly minor offenses. Yet the price of nonproportional martial law is often forbiddingly high.

Clement Vallandigham was a candidate for the governorship of Ohio in 1863. A Democrat, he based his campaign on the premiss that Lincoln's administration was unwilling to make a desirable and pos-

99. "Maryland's Defective Delinquent Statute: A Progress Report," Patuxent Institution, 9 January 1973, pp. 22–23.

sible peace with the South because Lincoln wished to free blacks and enslave whites. Vallandigham, after a stump speech to this effect, was arrested by military officers, tried by a military court, and sentenced to prison—a sentence later commuted by Lincoln to banishment to the Confederate states. Needless to say, the government's behavior was, from start to finish, massively highhanded and unconstitutional. There was no proportionality, that is, between Vallandigham's exercise of free, if demagogic, speech and the punishment he suffered. The result was an uproar, even during a time of extreme national emergency. Only the emergency, the use of force, and Lincoln's adroit commutation of the sentence kept matters somewhat under control. Vallandigham in prison clearly did far more damage to the Union cause than would Vallandigham at large, or even Vallandigham as governor. It would have been much better to have maintained proportionality—but then, the military governor was General Ambrose Burnside, whose whiskers were apparently his most distinguished feature.

I conclude that a legislator is sometimes justified in setting aside Proportionality for the sake of some important goal, but only if there is no good alternative means of reaching that goal. Otherwise, at best proportionality will sneak back in—as it did in the behavior of courts toward the Patuxent Institution—and at worst, the law will be ignored, disregarded, or maintained only by brute force.

If we look at the normal state of legislative affairs, I think we will have no trouble determining that adherence to the rule of Proportionality is usually invaluable in serving the legislative end. In his opinion in *Solem* v *Helm*, Justice Powell documents a long history of the proportionality requirement in American law. But Americans are far from alone here. M. R. Glover mentions in an article an English ancestor who served on a jury trying a boy accused of stealing sheep. At that time, the penalty for stealing sheep was death. People in England were becoming more and more aware, however, of the disproportionality of this sentence to the severity of the crime committed. The net result, according to Glover, was that the jury simply refused to convict. It would rather let a thief go free than have him executed for so petty an offense. Thus, a Draconian law, because of its disregard of Proportionality, succeeded only in defeating its own purpose.[100]

Presumably, the English people for many years did not think death too severe a penalty for stealing sheep, for the death sentence had long been on the books. What changed was the public attitude toward

100. See M. R. Glover, "Mr. Mabbott on Punishment," *Mind* 48 (1939): 488–501; reprinted in J. Feinberg, ed., *Reason and Responsibility*, 5th ed. (Belmont, Cal., 1981), 446–49, especially p. 447.

that sentence. Similarly the great reforms in the English criminal law during the 19th century were not triggered by any recent increase in the severity of the law. Rather, the law had for centuries imposed harsh sentences for petty crimes. The reformers' work was possible only because people had begun to feel qualms.

Applications of the rule of Proportionality therefore depend at least in part upon two factors: the relative severity of other laws; and the severity of the law in question as presently perceived by influential sections of the public. No rule is intrinsically proportional or disproportional.

Justice Powell, in *Solem* v *Helm*, confirms this reading.[101] He invokes a three-part test, each section of which a given prison sentence must meet if it is to pass the test of proportionality. First, the court must look to "the gravity of the offense and the harshness of the penalty." Presumably, the two are roughly equivalent. Second, the court should compare how the state handling the case punishes other crimes. Third, the court should compare how the same crime is punished in other jurisdictions.[102] If proportionality were simply a matter of the nature of the crime and the nature of the sentence, Justice Powell's second and third criteria would be out of place. But they do not seem to be, which tells us much about proportionality.

It tells us most particularly that a legislator or a judge cannot use a numerical calculus to determine proportionality. Even if one can somehow equate the gravity of a sentence to the severity of a crime, one must take into account at least two other factors: the relative severity of other punishments, and the opinion of influential sections of the public—including future juries, as the sheep-stealing example shows. What is not considered cruel and unusual punishment at one time may well be thought so at another. Legislation calling for that punishment and legislation that later abolishes it might both be in accord with Proportionality.

Finally, the requirements of proportionality are often confused with those of universalizability. A law can, in a perfectly uniform and evenhanded way, hand out shockingly disproportionate penalties.[103]

---

101. He says explicitly, "But no penalty is per se constitutional" (op. cit., p. 12).

102. Ibid., pp. 12–14. Justice Powell, oddly enough, says on p. 13 only that courts *may* invoke the second and third parts of the test. But on p. 14, he says that all three parts *should* guide a court in determining whether a sentence is properly proportional.

103. Likewise, uneven application does not guarantee disproportionality. That non-whites have been more prone than whites to receive capital punishment offends against Universalizability but not, as far as I can see, against Proportionality.

Again, Origen castrated himself in accordance with the Biblical injunction that if a person's eye offend him, he should pluck it out.[104] Whatever the offenses that caused Origen to take his drastic action, the deed was surely a violation of Proportionality, at least as that rule applies to a particular case. But Origen's deed was not necessarily an offense against Universalizability. Far from it, I suspect: Origen was surely ready to suggest that others follow his lead and, in Gibbon's intriguing phrase, "disarm the tempter." To treat one's self more severely than is warranted does not necessarily mean that one will treat others with any less severity.

Proportionality is then an important principle in its own right. Sometimes legislators disregard Proportionality and occasionally they are justified in doing so, but most of the time they best serve their legislative ends by adhering to it. We may conclude that Proportionality is indeed a maxim of deontic pragmatics.

But Proportionality, like Universalizability, is not only a rule of pragmatics. It is also a principle of justice, and as such it has far more than pragmatic force behind it. Nothing I have said in this section is meant to deny its role in justice, only to confirm its importance as a maxim of deontic pragmatics.

Economy: **Adopt only rules the performance of which will meet your legislative ends at the least cost to those for whom you legislate.**

The rule of Economy, our next legislative rule of matter, presupposes that a legislative body can choose how people are to achieve the end of proposed legislation. The rule of Economy asks that legislators tailor the legislation so that people can comply at the least cost to themselves.

For example, Bob decides that he should lose thirty pounds. He resolves to do so. Now there are a number of diets available to him, along with surgical procedures (including the one discussed in *The Merchant of Venice*) and exercise regimens. If a number of these means will lead equally well to a loss of thirty pounds, the rule of Economy

---

104. Gibbon comments in one of his more memorable footnotes, "As it was [Origen's] general practice to allegorise Scripture, it seems unfortunate that, in this instance only, he should have adopted the literal sense" *(Decline and Fall of the Roman Empire*, vol. 1 [London, 1776–1788], chap. 15, n. 97).

dictates that Bob choose the one that seems likely to cost him the least. Under this rule, the Shylock diet will not be the chosen method. Like Proportionality, Economy asks only for rough measures. If the costs incurred under two alternatives appear to be about the same, legislators should not take an incremental difference in economy to be a good reason to prefer one piece of legislation over another. For the meaning of 'cost' here includes many different factors, and anyone who looks for a precise calculus of costs will have difficulty finding a satisfactory weighting scheme. In the diet example, Bob is likely to take into account the possibility of physical damage, temporary or permanent, the likelihood of pain and discomfort, monetary costs, and no doubt other considerations. Bob might even decide that the most economical means of achieving his goal cost more than that goal is worth, in which case he will probably abandon his resolution.

The point of the example does not change if, instead of Bob resolving to lose weight, Bob's doctor prescribes a 30-pound weight loss for Bob. Here, too, the doctor will, if conscientious, try to find the program that will meet the legislative end at least overall cost for Bob. There seems no essential difference where Economy is concerned whether one is legislating for one's self or for others.

For suppose Bob puts himself, or is put by his physician, on the new thirty-day Keokuk Wonder Diet: eat nothing but brussels sprouts and drink nothing but prune juice. For all I know, such a diet may indeed cause the desired weight loss, as well as the loss of a few other things, such as health. But surely there are better ways to lose 30 pounds! That is, there are ways that will achieve this end at far less cost to the dieter. If, then, Bob starts the Keokuk Wonder Diet, the chances are very good that he will not stick it out the full thirty days. More likely, he will never lose those 30 pounds. Failure to be economical in his or his physician's choice of means increased the likelihood of his abandoning or, at the least, sharply curtailing the end sought.

It is then usually a good idea for a legislator to prescribe the most economical means available, for in this way, the legislative end is most likely to be achieved. But this rule, like the others, has exceptions.

One range of exceptions occurs, as I have already indicated, when there is little significant difference in cost between several paths to the same legislative end.[105] In such a case, it makes sense for legislators

105. The notion of 'cost' here is so broad, however, that one need not consider cases of this kind to be violations of the maxim. I owe this point to a reader for Brown University Press.

to leave the means of fulfillment entirely up to the persons for whom they are legislating. If the choice of means is fairly unimportant to legislators, giving a degree of freedom is more likely to be productive than dictating that choice.

Of course, when legislators have a choice of means, economy is not their only concern. For instance, an American legislative body that prescribes means when there is little difference among alternatives might be taken as infringing on people's rights. But that is a substantive moral or political fact about some but not necessarily all political systems. The matter of practicality in seeking the legislative end, on the other hand, does seem to arise in every system. Like other principles of deontic pragmatics, then, Economy might well serve as a substantive rule for a particular political, moral, or social code, but its role in a particular code should not blind us to its universality.

Another range of instances in which a legislative body does best not to apply the rule of Economy occurs whenever the legislative end is not, for one reason or another, considered to be crucial or even very important.

When the President of the United States proclaims a National Day of Prayer, for example, the details for implementing this bit of executive legislation are usually left fairly vague. At most, the president will suggest that people go to a place of worship, denomination unspecified, and engage in some way in some sort of prayer to some sort of deity on behalf of this country—the one bit of specificity in the whole proclamation. To be sure, there are good constitutional reasons why the president dare not issue more specific instructions, but such reasons are not the entire story.

For imagine a president issuing a call for a National Day of Prayer during a time of genuine national peril. This president, we shall assume, is strongly convinced that his or her own religion is correct and that all must follow the prescriptions of that religion if the country is to be saved. Constitutional scruples would hardly deter such an American Khomeini from attempting to specify the means of compliance in great detail.

The fact is, I think, that our politicians usually leave open how and, for that matter, if we are to observe a National Day of Prayer because they just don't think the matter is very important. Ritual pieties are useful for placating certain constituents, and proclaiming those pieties hurts nobody except a few civil liberties types. A politician might even sincerely believe in such pieties. But when she fails to call for any particular means of compliance or to suggest even social penalties for nonobservance, she betrays her low estimate of the importance of observing the pieties.

Likewise, when I resolve to behave in a certain way (say, to cut down on calorie consumption) but do not specify any means for achieving that goal (say, skipping dessert four days a week), there is very little force behind my resolution. I might, like a good politician calling for a National Day of Prayer, proclaim my goal all-important, but my failure to specify means betrays my real lack of interest or motivation. The goal in such a case has so little appeal that it usually remains unachieved.

These seem to be the two types of cases in which the rule of Economy does not serve a legislator well: when there is no important legislative end, or when there is no clear difference in economy among different means to that end. But when the legislative end is important and when there clearly is a most economical means toward fulfilling that end, the principle of Economy seems to apply with great force.

One might regard a system of sanctions against criminal behavior as a society's attempt, by the most economical means open to it, to discourage conduct prejudicial to that society's continued existence or flourishing. If the system of sanctions appears not to be doing the job, or to be doing the job at excessive costs, or to be doing the job less efficiently then some alternative, one is always justified in calling for wholesale reform. A violation of Economy here is anything but practical.

The rule of Economy is therefore an important consideration in legislation. It is far more easily dispensed with than, for example, Proportionality, as long as no means is clearly most economical and no legislative goal is important. In any other situation, Economy, like Proportionality, is a valuable means toward achieving the legislative end. It is therefore a principle of deontic pragmatics.

Distribution: **Provide a method for the distribution of goods and services, benefits and sanctions.**

The rule of Distribution is the last of the legislative rules of matter and a principle importantly different from the rest. The other legislative rules do not require that there be any legislation; they mandate only that whatever deontic legislation there is must be of a certain kind or be put forward in a certain manner. The rule of Distribution, however, requires that there be deontic legislation of a certain kind. It is, so to speak, an existential rule whereas the others are universal.

In calling for legislation to govern the distribution of goods and services, benefits and sanctions, the rule of Distribution sets no limits on how this task should be accomplished. The legislation might be completely laissez faire: those who acquire goods within the law would be totally free to keep and enjoy those goods. Or the legislative body might set up a meritocratic, egalitarian, racist, or aristocratic distribution principle. Or the legislature might impose a complex distribution principle with elements from many schemes mingled together. The maxim of Distribution requires only that there be some method of distribution.

Of course, this is not to say that all distribution schemes are equally good. A racist plan that gives first-class goods to whites and only leftovers to blacks does not offend against Distribution, but it is surely offensive, nonetheless. Such a scheme is hard to square with the rule of Universalizability.

Since the maxim of Distribution mandates that there be a method but does not say what the method should be, what is the point of the maxim? There seems little purpose in calling for a method when almost anything will satisfy the call. But appearances are deceptive here: I can think of at least two reasons for finding the rule of Distribution valuable and important.

In the first place, when there is a settled mode of distribution, the dissemination of goods and sanctions within a society has a chance of taking place in an orderly manner. Even those who disapprove of their society's actual distribution scheme will be enabled through knowledge of that scheme to plan for the future in an intelligent way.

When one thinks about it, a person living in Hobbes' state of nature would not be in the worst possible human condition. At least he knows that he is living in a state of war of every man against every man. He knows that his neighbor is out to get him, and he can plan accordingly. A person who has no awareness of his neighbor's attitude would be even worse off. Even the crude distribution plan of the Hobbist state of nature, then, where a person has a natural right to all he can grab, is better than no distribution plan at all.

In the second place, a method of distribution enables people to give rational justifications for engaging in certain procedures and furnishes reasons for denouncing or punishing those who follow or advocate other procedures.

Which procedures are to be justified and which punished will obviously vary from society to society, depending on the particular method of distribution adopted. The activities of a Carnegie or a Rockefeller would reap very different responses in societies other than the one in which these men actually flourished. But a person who knows how goods are distributed in his society can give socially acceptable reasons for preferring some types of behavior to others.

When members of a society can both anticipate the future intelligently and give reasons for the reward or condemnation of behavior, the legislators of that society have a good chance, other things being equal, of achieving their legislative ends. When people do not know what goods and evils to expect from their actions, and when no one can say after the event why matters should have turned out as they did, I see little chance for effective legislation of any kind at all. The presence of some distributional scheme is therefore important, perhaps even necessary, for the success of legislation in general.

When I try to construct an example where a distribution rule is not useful, I come up only with cases in which some element present in other deontic contexts is missing. For example, one might think of a social group in which there are no goods or sanctions to be distributed. Whether this should even count as a genuine social group is a problem for the legislation of sociologists. But certainly one can form sets of individuals who have nothing to do with one another. No distribution rules are needed for the set consisting of me and the fourth tallest person in Tierra del Fuego.

A more plausible example of a state of affairs in which a method of distribution is unnecessary arises whenever individuals legislate for themselves. One might find even here a sort of distribution rule, something like an on-off switch: "I'll take these goods if such and such happens, but otherwise I won't." But not all of an individual's behavior has to do with goods and sanctions.

I can imagine a person who imposes no rules on himself with respect to goods and sanctions. Gerald reacts to these as they come, although even this response is not a deliberate policy. He does, however, have rules to govern other aspects of his conduct. Gerald might, say, formulate a policy never to tell lies, but he has no scheme for rewarding himself for telling the truth or for punishing himself for deliberate untruths. Gerald could get by without a method of distribution. But it is not clear that he is well advised to do so. With a coherent distribution policy, he would avoid a certain amount of chaos in his life and improve his overall chances of achieving his various goals.

The requirement that there be a method of distribution is therefore far from pointless. Rather, it is almost always a valuable maxim to follow.

Up to this point, my examples have dealt primarily with the distribution of goods. But the distribution of sanctions claims our attention as well.

Rarely will a government act utterly capriciously in providing sanctions for its populace. Probably the only examples of utterly capricious rule are cases of one-man rule, reasonably secure but newly established. The government must be reasonably secure so that the ruler can indulge his caprice instead of acting to strengthen his rule. It must be newly established, because older governments tend to have standard procedures and rules that a subject can to some degree anticipate.

Perhaps the best example of an utterly capricious regime is the Roman Empire under Caligula, although even he, in some more of his bizarre actions, seemed partially motivated by a desire for increased security. If Suetonius is to be believed, no subject of Caligula knew when or where the emperor's wrath might fall. "When the bridge across the sea at Puteoli was being blessed, he invited a number of spectators from the shore to inspect it; then abruptly tipped them into the water. Some clung to the ship's rudders, but he had them dislodged with boat-hooks and oars, and left to drown."[106] With Caligula, no one knew what to expect, and rational justification was hard to come by.

Perhaps such behavior might make sense if it were part of a deliberate campaign of *Schrecklichkeit*. But Caligula did not seem to be acting according to plan. His distribution of punishments did not appear aimed at effectively maintaining a reign of terror. He followed no policy but his caprice. And he didn't last long.[107]

It is then possible for a society to distribute sanctions in a capricious manner, but to do so will normally tend to frustrate that society's purposes. Even if Caligula's purpose was unlimited self-indulgence, Cassius Chaerea and the other plotters soon put a stop to it for fear of what Caligula might do to them. Caligulan caprice was pretty clearly self-defeating.

---

106. *The Twelve Caesars*, trans. Robert Graves (Penguin, 1957), 165.

107. I do not mean to suggest that Caligula's misdeeds can all be traced to a violation of the maxim of Distribution!

With sanctions, then, as with goods, it is almost always useful toward achieving one's legislative ends to have a rule of distribution. The maxim that there be such a rule seems clearly to be part of the pragmatics of deontic legislation.

This concludes my treatment of the various legislative rules. In the next chapter, I turn to the judicial rules of manner.

OASIS

We are now officially two-thirds of the way across what, following Kant, I have referred to as a desert. We have looked at twelve maxims in all: three general rules and nine legislative rules. The end is in sight.

Actually, it is closer than one might suppose. True, we have six judicial maxims left to consider, but they need less detailed consideration than the twelve we have already looked at. In fact, I shall give in each of the next two chapters a summary of the argument about each rule; and the reader is free to skim the summary and go on to the succeeding chapter.

Still, to have examined twelve maxims already, looking at both paradigmatic and exceptional cases, is to have ridden through a desert. Having made a desert (without calling it peace), I owe the reader something of a break. Hence, this short respite from the relentless march of maxims. We can rest the camels for a few minutes: we are at an oasis.

During this brief rest, I shall present the sad story of Gustav Lindberg.[108] The story, as one might expect, has a moral: that courts should consider more carefully the probable effects of their pronouncements.

Lindberg was a director of the Scandinavian American Bank of Tacoma, Washington.[109] In 1920, he set out to buy some timber land. The manager of the Scandinavian American Bank had previously arranged loans for Lindberg from eastern banking houses; when Lindberg asked the manager to arrange a loan for the purchase of the timber land, the manager did so. Apparently without Lindberg's knowledge, this loan came out of funds belonging to the Scandinavian American Bank itself.

Shortly afterward, the Scandinavian American Bank failed. State banking officers found Lindberg's note, and soon Lindberg found himself charged with violating the state banking act. The relevant provision reads:

> No bank or trust company shall, nor shall any officer or employee thereof on behalf of such corporation, directly or indirectly, loan any sum of money to any director, officer or employee of such corporation, unless a resolution authorizing the same and approved by a majority of the directors, at a meeting at which no director, officer or employee to whom the loan is to be made shall be present, shall be entered in the corporate minutes.[110]

The next clause makes it clear that any director who accepts such a loan is guilty of a felony.

No doubt the manager of the Scandinavian American Bank should have known this law, should have known that it applied to Lindberg, and should have gotten Lindberg's loan from another institution. But it seems unreasonable to expect Lindberg to have known better. He had every reason to think the loan was legal and aboveboard.

---

108. *State v Lindberg*, 125 Wash. 51, 215 Pac. 41 (1923). I first learned of this case from Richard Wasserstrom's article, "Strict Liability in the Criminal Law," *Stanford Law Review* 12 (July 1960): 731–45.

109. All details of the case come from the decision of the Washington Supreme Court cited in the previous footnote. Because the court was unanimous in rejecting Lindberg's appeal, there was only one opinion written: that of Justice Fullerton.

110. *State v Lindberg*, p. 43.

The trial court refused to allow a defense of nonculpable ignorance, however, and the Washington Supreme Court unanimously concurred. The supreme court noted, first, that the statute did not contain the word 'knowingly' or a synonym; second, that Lindberg's offense was *malum prohibitum*, and intent need not be shown for crimes that are not bad in themselves; third, that Lindberg acted voluntarily and hence at his peril; and fourth, that the statute was intended to prevent overborrowing of bank funds by bank officers, and "To be effective in this regard the statute of necessity must be more or less arbitrary."[111]

The fourth consideration, I believe, gives the game away. The court was thinking of how to make the statute effective. They were considering the pragmatics of the legislature's speech when they should have been considering the pragmatics of their own decision.

For what would be the effect of the *Lindberg* decision, aside from the effect on Gustav Lindberg himself? Would it be to stop bankers from making loans from their home banks? Hardly, for Lindberg did not realize he was doing so. Would it be to make bankers more cautious? But Lindberg was never shown to have lacked caution. In effect, the court's decision showed those about to engage on a banking career that a hidden reef existed, one that might wreck a career and brand the banker a felon, but one that could not be foreseen and avoided by unlucky bankers.

Of course, a banker might avoid the hidden reef simply by refusing to borrow money. But that would provide a penalty merely for engaging in the practice of banking. The banker might also decide to arrange all his loans himself, without trusting any subordinate to do the job—one more penalty for being a banker.

Richard Wasserstrom is then right to conclude that the effects of the court's decision "might conceivably make banking a less attractive occupation, although they would probably not cause the disappearance of banking as an institution in society."[112] On the whole, society has an interest in there being both banks and bankers and therefore in having banking remain attractive.

Wasserstrom suggests that the court's decision to regard the banking statutes as strict liability provisions, not requiring guilty intent as a part of the felony violation, did not excuse the court from doing a bit of projecting. If they were trying to regulate the conduct of bankers, they should have done so in a way more likely to produce the desired

111. *State* v *Lindberg*, pp. 45-47. I have omitted a long train of citations.
112. Wasserstrom, *op. cit.* p. 737.

results.[113] The *Lindberg* decision seems admirably suited to produce only undesired and undesirable results.

Back in the desert, members of our caravan might have gotten a little tired of the pragmatics of deontic speech. But at least one banker-turned-felon could have testified eloquently to the importance of the maxims. The oasis thus confirms the value of the desert.[114]

113. Ibid., p. 738.

114. Is it appropriate to suggest that readers who have made it this far have gotten their just deserts?

8

Judicial Rules of Manner

INTRODUCTION TO THE JUDICIAL RULES

In this and the following chapter we will be looking at the judicial rules of deontic pragmatics. The legislative maxims apply to those deontic utterances that attempt to set general policy, whereas the judicial maxims apply to deontic utterances dealing with particular cases.

Not every utterance a person makes is deontic, and not every decision on whether and what to speak requires us to take into account what we ought to do, or are permitted to do. If a person does decide on deontic speech, the maxims of deontic pragmatics are usually not the only major factors in determining what to say. They may not even weigh heavily at all in making a decision. This is especially true with the judicial rules.

If it is late at night and I want to read a bit before going to bed, I do not worry about whether I ought to read carefully the latest issue of *Nous*. Any such duty weighs very little, even if it is in accordance with all the rules of deontic pragmatics. Unless there's an article in *Nous* that I really want to read, I'm far more likely to decide on a magazine or book that is far less demanding. And if I end up reading Jane Austen or a professional football magazine, I have no reason afterward to think my decision a bad one.

A decision about what to read does not usually involve making a particular deontic utterance, of course. I might decide to tell myself, "You should read *Nous*," but I need not. But when I do decide to make a particular deontic utterance, often the goal of bringing about a certain behavior from people is no more than a subsidiary target.

Consequently, only when a person decides primarily or largely on deontic grounds to engage in particular deontic speech is she likely to take these judicial rules into account. In choosing what I should read at bedtime, I do not decide the matter by subsuming it under properly determined general rules. Why should I?

The judicial maxims are very different in this respect from the legislative maxims we have already considered. For in setting policies, one's primary goal is almost always to get people to act in a certain way. As a result, the legislative maxims of deontic pragmatics usually play a major role when one determines general policies.

The limited role the judicial maxims play in our deontic utterances, however, should not prevent us from examining those maxims. As I argued in chapter 3, even though one's aim in deontic speech is often not to bring about behavior of a certain type, we can usually understand other aims on the basis of that one. To the extent that one's speech is genuinely deontic, these judicial maxims should play a role in our understanding of that speech, even if they don't weigh strongly in the speaker's decision to make that utterance.

The reader might object that I seem to be falling into the fashionable habit of overstressing deontic factors. It is true enough that new duties and new rights seem to spring up like dandelions on the political landscape, and the result is often counterproductive. I think it a good and prudent thing to treat my cat with kindness, but upon being told I must respect the cat's rights I might get nasty. But this matter lies beyond the scope of this book. My topic is the use of deontic language, not when to make our language deontic. No doubt many people overuse the words 'ought', 'duty', and 'obligation', but that is irrelevant to a discussion of the rules they should follow when using those words.

Let us then turn to the judicial rules of manner.

Summary of the Judicial Rules of Manner

There are two judicial rules of manner: Use of General Rules, and Equity. The principle of Use of General Rules asserts that a person should make particular deontic decisions, wherever possible, in accordance with general rules. Normally, obeying this principle makes a person's particular deontic utterances more effective. A parent who can answer the question "Why?" with a general policy is more likely to succeed than one who has no better answer than "Because I told you to."

However, there are cases in which spontaneity is so valuable that it outweighs the need for following general rules, other cases in which more than one rule is available and attractive, and still more cases in which no available rule looks attractive. The principle of Use of General Rules then holds in most but not all cases, as one should expect of a maxim of deontic pragmatics.

The maxim of Equity asks for a way of determining the proper deontic speech when general rules give either conflicting advice or no advice at all. In general, this maxim presupposes that any deontic judgment is better than no deontic judgment. That certainly seems true in formalized situations such as the civil courts. Even with individuals, one rarely does well by refusing to make deontic judgments, whereas those who do decide what they should do have at least some chance of success.

However, when the consequences of a wrong judgment are serious enough, it might well be that no deontic judgment is the best deontic judgment. For example, if the president has incomplete evidence about a possible nuclear attack, he does well to postpone any irrevocable determination until the last possible moment. Thus again, the rule of Equity holds in most but not all cases.

Use of General Rules: Decide the case under consideration, if possible, by subsuming it under properly determined general rules.

One might not always be able to subsume a particular case under general rules. The case might display some crucial peculiarities that make no existing rule a reasonable fit, or legislation might be insufficiently developed at the time the case arises. It is not unknown for a judge to lecture a defendant for evildoing and then reluctantly release the culprit on the grounds that no law has been violated.

Again, the law sometimes becomes so detailed in its considerations, so determined to anticipate any situation that might arise, that many cases prove to be lacking in a crucial detail. The disposition of such cases rarely satisfies anyone: the man was clearly guilty; how could he go free on a mere technicality?

If enough people are angered, the law might be rewritten, becoming even more Byzantine in its complexities and less likely to apply to a future case. Perhaps, instead, an imaginative prosecutor stretches things a bit. I remember the case of an accused racketeer, alleged to have killed a rival and thrown his body into the Ohio River. When the suspect was found not guilty of murder, the disgusted prosecutor announced plans to press charges of illegal dumping and pollution of a waterway!

It rarely happens that no rule applies to a given case. Far more often, several rules apply, each one mandating actions the others forbid. As I drive down a curving, two-lane highway, I should obey the speed limit. But if I do, I will be driving slower than others wish to go on this busy road. Drivers will back up behind me, unable to pass safely. In frustration, they will take chances that might well lead to accidents. So I decide I should drive faster and not impede traffic flow. My problem here is not that there aren't enough rules to cover the situation, but that I can obey only one of those that do.

Where more than one rule applies, the maxim of Use of General Rules does not help determine which rule to follow. The maxim says only that one should judge in accordance with a rule. Only the substantive principles of a particular society can point out the proper rule to follow, and even they might give no answer.

But the maxim of Use of General Rules has more value than the preceding paragraph indicates. In a developed society, for any likely deontic judgment there is usually some rule that accords with it, however reprehensible that judgment might be. But mere accordance is not enough to satisfy Use of General Rules. That maxim asks that a person's judgment be made by subsuming the particular case under a general rule. A judgment can be in accordance with a rule without the decider's knowing it, but that would not fulfill the maxim of Use of General Rules.

Hence, what the maxim forbids is that a person make his particular deontic judgments at random—by the feel of things, perhaps. A judge who has presided over so many witch trials that he has gotten a "nose for witches" should not take his "nose" for evidence. Even Monty Python's Sir Bedivere at least reasons out his decision in the case of an accused witch, although his reasoning could serve as a nice textbook on informal fallacies.

Why should someone obey the maxim of Use of General Rules? The clear practical reason is that making particular deontic judgments in accordance with rules is usually important in making those judgments effective. (As always, I do not deny that there might also be moral reasons for complying with one of my maxims, but they are irrelevant to my concerns.) If I assert that I ought to take the last slice of pie for my breakfast, I expect to have to justify my assertion to the rest of my family—and if not to them, to myself. If I cannot fall back on some sort of rule, my act of assertion will be in danger of being ineffective. Only force can save it, and force has its limits. How much better it would be to say, "Well, we should share the pie equally, and I missed out on my share last night."

In the preceding example, my goal in applying deontic language to a specific situation was to bring about action or inaction of a certain kind. The maxim of Use of General Rules also applies when I tell a person what she shouldn't have done in order to affect her future behavior. If I tell my daughter, "You shouldn't have stayed out so late last night" with the intention of getting her to keep more reasonable hours in the future, I need to be able to point to a rule, or at least an accepted policy, if I hope to be obeyed.

The same is true of other types of deontic statements. I can employ the language of permission to affect a person's behavior. I am waxing a floor, and somebody looks as if he wants to cross the floor but is hesitant. My saying "You may go ahead and cross" is intended to remove his hesitation. Similarly, if I inform my son that my daughter has a right to read a certain trashy book, I am trying to affect his behavior by getting him not to interfere with her miserable choice of reading matter. In both cases, my judgment is more likely to be effective, other things being equal, if I can appeal to some sort of principle.

An example we have looked at in chapter 2—the student who faced the agonizing choice between fighting for a free France and staying with his mother, who needed his help—is pertinent here. Suppose the student unthinkingly decided to go off to England to fight. He did not judge the case by subsuming it under any rule, but acted instinctively, in accordance with a feeling about what he ought to do. Such a judgment would probably prove far more unstable than a principled one. If the pressure of events keeps the student from changing his assessment of what he should have done, I think him more likely to regret and feel guilt over his course of action than he would had he thought the matter out.[115]

These cases all indicate that under normal circumstances, it is usually the practical course to make one's deontic judgments by subsuming particular cases under general rules. This is certainly true when making a certain deontic utterance with the intention of bringing about action; when this is not one's intention, the analysis of chapter 3 suggests that the maxim helps at least in understanding the utterance.

Let us now turn to cases in which general rules are available, but subsuming the particular circumstances under those rules is impractical.

Jane is a woman who prizes spontaneity. Her chief abhorrence is a canned action, one that has been mulled over long in advance. Tom has a strong desire to act in ways that will please Jane. He is therefore trying hard to curb his usual tendency to make deontic utterances that betray study and thoughtfulness. Tom and Jane are walking together one evening when a beggar, probably a wino, approaches and asks for a handout. If Tom stops and thinks for a bit, then explains carefully why he should or should not give the handout, Jane will be disgusted. If Tom must give a deontic speech, he had better do it immediately and without explanation.

Suppose this scene is played out many times, and each time Tom

---

115. This example looks, as one reader of this book suggested, like armchair psychologizing. I regard it instead as a generalization from behavior I have observed. People who make important decisions on the feelings of the moment do have a tendency to regret their choices, in my experience. But since I have no reason to think that my experience is representative of that of the human race, one might well call my generalization a piece of armchair sociologizing.

immediately responds that he shouldn't give money to the beggar. Jane is likely to suspect him of acting in accordance with a settled and, God forbid, rational policy! Anticipating her disapproval, Tom decides to change his strategy. Fortunately, he has a good memory for numbers; he knows the decimal expansion of *pi* to one hundred places. Hence, for each beggar who approaches, Tom goes one place further in that expansion: if the digit is even, he announces immediately that he should give the money, and does so. If the digit is odd, he announces immediately that he shouldn't give the money, and does not do so. If either Jane or a beggar asks why Tom gives or doesn't give the money in a particular case, Tom is totally unable to give a justification. This pleases Jane immensely. Tom is, to be sure, continuing to decide in accordance with a rule, but at least he is finally giving the *appearance* of spontaneity.

This scenario is far-fetched, but it makes a point of some importance. Philosophers who stress the value of being reasonable in one's decision making sometimes forget that not everyone agrees. There are people who think that reasonable decisions betray a cold, calculating spirit, perhaps even the makings of an Eichmann. Such people might have too narrow a view of reasoning, perhaps thinking of it solely as economic or game-theoretic calculation, but that is irrelevant. For better or worse, quite a few people do prefer genuinely spontaneous and intuitive decisions to rational ones. When dealing with such people, occasions can arise when any unreasoned decision is preferable to any reasoned one. And the maxim of Use of General Rules does no good in such circumstances.

One might also be justified in refusing to make a decision by subsumption under rules when the circumstances are radically different from any in one's experience. In such a case, one might think, the rules one knows are likely to be irrelevant. Better to play the whole thing by ear.

Supppose I am about to give my very first sit-down supper for a group of extraterrestrial aliens. The problem is one of arranging place settings.[116] These aliens look quite different from humans, so perhaps I should proceed by analogy—that is, if they look like tarantulas, I should use the mode of place setting most convenient for giant spiders. But perhaps I should simply make an uninformed guess on the principle that what works for earthly spiders is most unlikely to work for the vastly different aliens. When I have occasion to suspect the viabil-

---

116. I suppose we can think of place settings as a sort of "symbolic speech," to use a term much in vogue with the Supreme Court at one time.

ity of any relevant rules, it might be better not to try to follow those rules.

Here too, the fanciful nature of the example should not lead anyone to think that the type of occasion it illustrates will never arise. Sometimes we embark on deontic speech with little knowledge of the particular circumstances, and on occasion our spontaneous remarks achieve the best results.

But even though many people might claim to prize spontaneity, probably few are consistent enough to approve all spontaneous decisions, whatever their nature. It is probably best to follow rules in dealing with such people, although you should not stress that you are doing so. Likewise, deciding spontaneously when you are ignorant of important circumstances can turn out better than deciding in accordance with the wrong rules. But in the long run, spontaneity is unlikely to be the best course.

We can conclude, therefore, that if you are going to issue a particular deontic utterance, you usually do best to subsume the case under a general rule. That is, Use of General Rules is a principle of deontic pragmatics.

Equity: **Provide a method for solving conflicts, in case general rules appear to give conflicting advice or prove insufficient in particular situations.**

The rule of Equity is an obvious complement to the maxim of Use of General Rules. When we cannot determine a particular deontic utterance by subsumption under a rule, equity comes into its own.

As I noted in the previous section, subsumption can be inadequate to form a deontic judgment in either of two quite different circumstances: No relevant general rule might adequately cover the peculiarities of the situation, or two or more conflicting rules might apply. In either case, the rule of Equity mandates that people have some way of judging what their deontic speech should be (and perhaps even whether they ought to employ deontic speech at all).

How to make a deontic judgment differs, as I indicated in the last section, from person to person and from society to society. One person or social group might have a well-defined structure of rules, such that for any likely situation one could determine which rule overrides the others. Another person or group might base all deontic judgments on a single principle—perhaps that of estimated utility in the long run.

Yet another might flip a coin or simply follow instincts. All of these methods are countenanced by the rule of Equity. The important thing under that rule is that the judgment be formed somehow.

The rule of Equity presupposes, then, that, by and large, any deontic judgment is better than no deontic judgment at all. Where one can use rules, one should; but where one cannot use rules, one still needs some way to determine what to do. We need first to look at this presupposition.

Certainly in a formal setting, such as a civil court, there is great value in making deontic judgments. The intricacies of a libel suit, for example, are such that general laws are rarely sufficient to determine specific damages. The constraints are usually fairly vague: was there actual damage? If so, how much? Was the article written after a good-faith effort to determine its truth? Is the plaintiff a public figure? These considerations all apply but are rarely sufficient to determine what, if anything, a plaintiff in a libel suit should recover from the defendant.

It would be possible, I suppose, for juries and judges in a typical libel suit to announce that, since subsumption under a rule does not yield answers to important questions, they will simply make no judgment about what, if anything, the plaintiff ought to receive. They might keep the case open until someone comes up with a rule that determines the judgment. In that event, the plaintiff might as well forget about any chance of winning the suit. But if the state has an interest in minimizing libel, as it surely does, then the state has an interest in having judges and juries determine their judgment in such cases. It does seem generally true in the civil law that any deontic judgment is better than no judgment.

The same seems to hold in the criminal law. One might regard the old Scots verdict of "Not Proven" as a refusal to reach a judgment of guilt or innocence. But whatever its purpose, that verdict is hard to justify. Those who committed the crimes in question are not suitably punished, while the innocent receive a totally undeserved social stigma.

Much the same unsatisfactory result occurs in the United States when a grand jury conducts a wide-ranging investigation of the sort known as a "fishing expedition." Thanks to a publicity-conscious district attorney, the public learns that the grand jury is investigating a number of suspected racketeers. The jury continues its investigation for quite a while, and then it quietly adjourns, issuing no indictments. This course of events is both common and reprehensible. The grand jury has cast a cloud of suspicion. It should either issue indictments or dispel the cloud by announcing that there is no evidence to warrant further action. Reaching no judgment is surely worse than reaching any judgment in this case; definite charges can at least be refuted.

To be sure, a faulty deontic judgment is sometimes so bad that we might conclude afterwards that no judgment at all would have been preferable. If the grand jury issues indictments that will never stand up in court and that will serve only as nuisances and slanders, we might prefer even the cloud of suspicion to such an outcome. The legal preference for any deontic judgment at all over no judgment is only a *prima facie* one. A method that determines many important cases badly is usually worse than no method at all. But other things being equal, it does seem in the law's interests to be able to settle cases.

When there are lesser or no penalties or rewards involved in the matter, we often feel less of a need to determine what we ought to do. As a result, we might have good reason to disregard the maxim of Equity in such situations. For example, suppose that a historian is trying to decide whether Pericles should have tried harder to make a lasting peace with Sparta. Unless for some reason her professional status or future requires her to reach some clear-cut conclusion, there is no shame in her leaving the matter open. Indeed, she might well decide on the evidence that one cannot safely determine what Pericles should have done, in which case refusal to judge is the historian's duty. However, if the historian is serving as an adviser to a national leader, and if she considers the example of Pericles relevant to a crucial decision the leader must make, then the historian might well find that any judgment is better than none.

Similar remarks hold for many of our practical judgments about deontic speech. If there is no harm in failing to make a deontic judgment, and there often is not, it rarely happens that any such judgment is better than none at all. Even so, one might argue that individuals who continually fail to judge what they (or others) ought to do will harm themselves in the long run.

Sometimes the consequences of making a particular judgment are so grave that a person must be quite sure before deciding how to act. For example, the radar screen shows a large number of unidentified objects that might be nuclear missiles from an unfriendly nation. Should the president order our planes and missiles to retaliate? He does well to wait as long as he can in the hope of further information.

But in such circumstances, although it can hardly be said that any deontic judgment is better than no judgment, there is still a good reason to follow the rule of Equity. If the president's options are so important, he had better consider in advance how he will react to the further information he might receive in the next few minutes. That is, even if he thinks it best not to judge on present information, he should have a method available for using future information to reach a judgment.

The same is true in less drastic situations. A college student is unsure of the field she should major in. For the first year or so of her college career, she need make no judgment, but it is in her interest to think about the matter and at the very least consider how she will ultimately reach an answer. Leaving the matter to last-minute hunches is probably a bad idea, for her choice of major is too important to her entire future.

Both the president and the college student must eventually determine what they should do. But even in cases where one need never make a deontic judgment, as long as the possible outcomes of any choice are important enough it seems to be in one's interest to provide a method for making an eventual judgment. If general rules don't settle the question of what choice is best, other means should be sought. Here again, an example makes the point.

I decide to leave a certain amount of money to two charities when I die. I consider that I ought to leave most of the money to the more deserving of the two charities, but I do not know which of the two fits that description. If I die before determining which is more deserving, the two charities will split the money evenly. If my health is reasonably good, I am under no particular pressure to judge which charity is more deserving, either now or in the near future. But I should at the very least seek to determine the manner in which I will eventually judge the question. Otherwise, I might find myself dying, unable to make an intelligent investigation or judgment, and hence forced to give up my resolve to leave the bulk of my money to the more deserving charity.

I conclude that in questions of obligation and permission, it is generally of great practical importance to provide a way to judge what ought to be done. If the case can be decided by fitting it under a general rule, it is usually best to do so. Where this is not possible, one should look for some other method. The two judicial rules of manner are pragmatically reasonable. They are part of deontic pragmatics.

9 | Judicial Rules of Matter

SUMMARY OF THE THE JUDICIAL RULES OF MATTER

The final four rules are the judicial rules of matter: Judicial Factuality, Judicial Economy, Judicial Publicity, and Judicial Review of General Rules. I shall take them up in that order.

Judicial Factuality asks us to make particular deontic statements that conform to facts about the world. An act of permission, for example, requires a certain stage setting; if that setting is not as expected, the act of permission usually misfires. But sometimes it seems reasonable to act as if the facts are one way, even though one knows them to be quite otherwise.

The rule of Judicial Economy asks people to judge cases in such a way as to carry out the legislative aim at the least cost. Judges who issue sentences designed to deter, to rehabilitate, or to protect the public especially need to follow this rule, for uneconomical sentences have led to public outrage. But sometimes it is useful not to specify any means toward a given goal, and sometimes other considerations make it reasonable to choose a means other than the most efficient.

The rule of Judicial Publicity asks that we impute particular obligations only to those who realize or should realize that they are obligated. If a person has no way of knowing either that a law is in force or that it applies to him, there seems no point in blaming or punishing him for violating that law. But when the legislative end is not particularly important, or when it is overridden by more important concerns, Judicial Publicity seems inapplicable.

Finally, Judicial Review of General Rules is something of an *omnium gatherum*: It tells us to impute or accept only those particular obligations that accord with rules that are consistent, clear, applicable, simple, modest, universalizable, and proportional. Under this principle, the response "That's the law" is never sufficient, for one should always consider the nature of the law in question. But sometimes, as in cases of national emergency, the evil consequences of breaking bad laws might far outweigh the evil consequences of obeying them, leading us not to apply the principle of Judicial Review of General Rules.

We thus have good reason to think that all four of the principles discussed in this section hold in most but not all cases, and that they are therefore principles of deontic pragmatics.

Judicial Factuality: Decide cases in ways consistent with the facts about the world.

I am talking informally with a group of people when, quite without preparation, I say, "You may go now." My tone shows neither sarcasm nor exasperation. Instead, it sounds as if I am simply giving them permission to leave. Yet my permission was not sought, nor do I have any reason to think it was desired. For there is no reason whatsoever why these people should require my permission before leaving.[117]

---

117. I heard this example in a lecture many years ago. I have forgotten the lecturer's point or even who the lecturer was, but the example has stuck with me. I apologize to the unknown speaker for being unable to acknowledge the authorship properly.

The net result is surely puzzlement. What was the point of my saying what I did? If I am asked to explain, there is little I can say other than: "Well, I thought I'd give you permission to leave." If I had really meant to accomplish anything by uttering my original statement of permission—to direct others not to interfere with their leaving or to announce my own intent not to interfere—I have little chance of success. For there was no prospect of their leaving just then, and so there was nothing to interfere with.[118]

What went wrong? An obvious answer is that the act of giving permission, like many other verbal acts, presupposes a certain stage setting to be effective. When I said, "You may go now," the stage setting was lacking. But even more went wrong with my statement of permission. I should have been aware that the necessary stage setting was missing, and the others knew it. If I had had any reason to think I was in authority over the others in the group, my attempt at giving permission would not have seemed so grotesque.

We can characterize the example by saying that I violated the rule of Judicial Factuality. I made a particular deontic speech in a way that accorded poorly with the facts about the world. Since I should have known better, my speech seems utterly pointless.

Let's change the example somewhat. It is the first day of a new semester, and I face a new class. Because I have, unfortunately, failed to prepare, I tell the class that they are excused: They should check their names on the class roster as they leave and expect their first working session of Philosophy 301D next Wednesday. At this, they look confused, and it turns out that none of them is listed on the roster. There now arrives a red-faced and puffing professor of economics, who apologizes for being late. I went to the wrong room and tried to excuse the wrong class!

In this amended example, my words are equally ineffective, and there is still some puzzlement, at least until the professor of economics arrives. The difference from the earlier example is that here I am unaware that the stage setting is not what is needed to make my statement of permission effective. I really thought and had some reason to think that I am in a position to dismiss that class, although in fact I'm not. My actions can be explained, whereas in the earlier example they cannot be. I am embarrassed, of course, and I resolve to double-check the room number for each new class in the future.

---

118. See in this connection the discussion of the use of permission statements in chapter 3, pp. 42–44.

Sometimes the university does make last-minute room switches, and one cannot be too careful.

Puzzlement and, in some cases, blame do then depend in part on whether the deontic speaker should have known if the actual stage setting accords with his words. But the effectiveness of that speech depends only on what the facts are, not on what the speaker should have known. Even a speaker who has no way of knowing what the true stage setting is can still violate the rule of Judicial Factuality.

In the preceding examples, a violation of Judicial Factuality consisted of a stage setting in which the deontic utterance was grotesquely out of place. Sometimes, however, the stage setting renders an utterance ineffective but not grotesque.

For example, an employer with old-fashioned economic views announces that, for the good of all concerned, he ought to pay each of his workers no more than a subsistence wage. He also states he ought to bargain individually with each worker on that wage. If any employee refuses to work for mere subsistence, the employer claims he should have the right to hire someone else. But the employer is living and working in late twentieth-century America, where minimum wage laws, unions, and a finite pool of available workers negate any chance that his oughts will be put into effect. Unless the employer is only indulging in nostalgia for the good old days of capitalism, his deontic utterances are a waste of breath. What he says ought to happen can't happen, and there is no point in violating Kant's Principle. But when this employer issues his deontic speeches, I doubt that people are puzzled. We can understand the capitalist's views and why he expresses them, as we could not understand the permission to leave.

Violations of the rule of Judicial Factuality do then occur, and they usually lead to pointless, although not always absurd, deontic speech.[119] But, as we have seen with the other rules of deontic pragmatics, one sometimes has reason to set aside the maxim of Judicial Factuality, often in the interests of some overriding goal.

My son, who has recently learned to drive, asks if he may try his hand at maneuvering along a busy Southern California freeway during our vacation. To say that he may suggests that I have a high degree of confidence in his driving ability. Alas, I don't have that confidence: I'm scared! But I reflect that he probably won't make a fatal mistake and that he has to learn how to drive freeways sooner or later. So

---

119. If the employer *is* only being nostalgic, then his remarks have some point, but they are surely useless as directives to his employees.

I tighten my seat belt, grit my teeth, and with the best grace I can muster tell him, "Sure you may." Surely sainthood has been granted on lesser grounds.

In the interests of giving my son the needed driving experience and building his confidence, I have deliberately spoken as if I had no qualms about his freeway driving skills. In fact, then, my granting him permission conflicts with my beliefs concerning his ability.[120] And those beliefs, even should they ultimately prove to be unjustified, are themselves facts about the world. Of course, I made the speech because of what I take to be a more important fact about the world—my son's need to learn to drive freeways—but that does not wipe out the conflict with facts.

In granting him permission, then, I have made a deontic speech that conflicts with my beliefs, which are facts about the world. As long as we don't crash, I think I am justified in breaking the rule of Judicial Factuality. Even if we do crash, I will probably keep to that opinion.

For a more melodramatic example, consider a jury's decision to find a man who deliberately murdered his wife's lover guilty of involuntary manslaughter. The effect of their verdict is to dictate to the judge that the defendant should not receive a very severe punishment. But the verdict of involuntary manslaughter contradicts all sorts of facts about the case: there is ample evidence of premeditation, there is no question of mistaken identity, and so on. Yet the jurors opt for that verdict, as jurors have been known to do. For they think it a powerful extenuating circumstance that the murdered man was the lover of the murderer's (or rather, the manslaughterer's) wife, even if the law does not recognize it as such.

Because the law sets up punishments for types of cases and not for particular instances, crimes will occur for which a jury thinks the

120. As a reviewer of this book pointed out, this case seems importantly different from the previously discussed cases of misplaced permission. Presumably, if a professor knew he was in the wrong classroom, he would not attempt to issue permission statements to the class. But in the freeway-driving case, I am presumably aware that I lack the confidence that my giving of permission implicates—yet I give permission anyway. (I am using 'implicates' in Grice's sense, explained in chapter 2.)

Despite this difference, I think the sense of 'conflict' is the same in both cases. In the classroom example, if the professor recognized that the stage setting for his speech was wrong, he would normally (although not always) have no reason to attempt to give permission. In the freeway-driving example, the stage setting is once again wrong; I do not feel the confidence my speech implicates. The difference is not in the type of conflict but in my having, in the driving example, a separate reason for giving the speech despite the conflict.

prescribed penalty too severe. The jurors will then often find a lesser charge on which to convict the defendant, even though the facts of the case plainly contradict the verdict. Consistency with the facts is often sacrificed to the goal of a more appropriate punishment.

A judge who suspects the goal of the legislator to be less than straightforwardly expressed in a law but who nevertheless applies that law to a particular case is engaged in a charade. Such a judge has little reason to obey the maxim of Judicial Factuality. If Dante is right, the judge's supernatural punishment might be slightly different if he adds cooked facts to bad law. Simple fraud differs from complex fraud, but the smell of fraud is just about the same in either case.

A similar situation arises when one suspects some sort of defect in the manner or the matter of the legislation one is supposed to apply to a particular case. If I am unsure whether Miss Manners is an authority on table manners, it will not concern me very much if she disapproves of my recommendations on the number of forks you should set at each place at your dinner party. The conflict between her general rules and my specific advice is a fact, but it is a fact I can blithely ignore.

I will summarize this section by saying that adherence to the maxim of Judicial Factuality is, on the whole, an important factor in making deontic speech successful, but at times we have good reason to put this maxim aside. It seems reasonable, then, to rank Judicial Factuality as one more principle of deontic pragmatics.

Judicial Economy: **Decide cases in a way that will carry out the legislative aim at least cost to the actors.**

Like the principles of Judicial Factuality and Judicial Publicity, the maxim of Judicial Economy is the counterpart of a legislative rule. Judicial Economy requires us to judge cases in a way that will carry out the legislative aim at the least cost to the participants in the matter.

A judge who must sentence a convicted felon usually has quite a bit of latitude. Judge Roe may impose any sentence from probation to five years in prison on the embezzler before her. How is a conscientious judge to decide which sentence is appropriate?

Almost everyone would agree that Judge Roe should take into account the reason she is sentencing this embezzler. Why did the legislators forbid felonies in general and embezzlement in particular? How well does this particular criminal fit the legislative projection? Unless Judge Roe considers such questions, she has little rationale for any sentence she imposes. The judge, therefore, has good reason to follow the maxim of Judicial Economy.

In a recent case, a teenaged boy was tried as an adult for killing his father. Evidence strongly suggested that the father had been a brutal bully to his children. The trial aroused strong feelings, which were intensified when the boy was convicted and sentenced to the state penitentiary. The prospect of the boy's serving time among hardened adult criminals angered many people.

In announcing the boy's sentence, the trial judge leaned heavily on the concept of punishment as deterrence. Other teenagers, according to the judge, would be less likely to kill abusive parents when they knew such a sentence awaited them. The judge's decision might have been legally above reproach, but as an exercise in convincing the public, it was a flat failure.[121] The usual reaction was one of outrage: the boy did not deserve such a harsh sentence.

I believe that the judge, by considering only the fact of the crime and the general utility of deterrence, failed to appreciate the value of Judicial Economy. He did not consider how best to carry out the legislative end at least cost to the boy (and, for that matter, to society as a whole). By insufficiently utilizing the rule of Judicial Economy, the judge was unable to justify his sentence to the public. And when people find no justification for a particular sentence, the structure of criminal justice is harmed.

A different example makes a similar point. A couple comes to a marriage counselor. Both husband and wife recount the various difficulties that have arisen between them. The counselor listens carefully, thinks things over, and then issues his advice: the husband should do certain things and refrain from doing others; so should the wife. If the couple follows this advice, the counselor thinks the marriage will endure and prosper.

Here the counselor clearly has an end in view: to preserve and improve the marriage. This end was, in effect, legislated by the couple by their act of consulting the counselor. His job is, if possible, to achieve that goal. But to succeed, the counselor needs to choose an appropriate means to the end sought. If he counsels a course of action

---

121. The sentence was eventually eased after the governor's intervention.

that is unnecessarily difficult or imposes major and unwanted changes on husband or wife, his advice is likely to be ineffective—even though, were it taken, it would lead to the goal.

For example, suppose the husband spends all his free evenings at a local bar, drinking beer with his (male) friends. The counselor might recommend that the husband make an abrupt and immediate break with those friends, abstain completely from alcohol, and include his wife in all his social activities. Such recommendations will probably have no effect. The husband is not likely to change so drastically and so suddenly, even if a drastic change is in every way desirable. A more tempered reform of the husband's habits would help the marriage at less cost.

These examples show the value of utilizing Judicial Economy in one's deontic pronouncements. But, as with the other rules of deontic pragmatics, on some occasions this maxim is best disregarded. First, it rarely happens that more than one means will lead to exactly the same goal. A person's choice of means helps determine the goal he seeks. Although Means A might be slightly more cost-effective than Means B, Goal B might be slightly more desirable than the marginally different Goal A. The greater the difference in the two goals, the less important the role Judicial Economy should play in the decision.

For an example, let us return to the marriage counselor. Many possible goals are consistent with the general plan of preserving and improving the couple's marriage. The rule of Judicial Economy will help the counselor find the best means for reaching any of these goals, but it will not tell him which of the goals is most desirable and which most attainable. If the counselor knows independently which goals are desirable and attainable, he can balance these factors against the economy of various means. But it might turn out that the choice of means plays very little part in determing the nature of the counselor's advice.

Thus, the marriage counselor might say to the husband: "The important thing is that you ought to socialize more with your wife and less with your buddies. I don't care how you do this: the two of you will have to work that out. But it's something you need to work toward if your marriage is to get any better." In this case, the marriage counselor is trying to make more precise the vague plan of improving the marriage. By deliberately failing to specify any means of reaching the goal he recommends, the counselor is almost entirely forgoing considerations of Judicial Economy. The means in this example are much less important than the end.

One also does best not to apply the rule of Judicial Economy whenever a goal different from the legislative aim overrides that aim and dictates a means that, from the standpoint of the legislative aim, is uneconomical.

For example, a criminal sometimes, for reasons of public safety, receives a more severe sentence than is needed to fulfill the aim embodied in the criminal code. One might look at examples of recidivism in this way. The fact that a person has committed a certain crime for the third time, rather than for the first, has no clear bearing on the nature of that crime. It therefore has no obvious and necessary bearing on the legislative intent in providing punishments for the crime. But a judge obviously considers when sentencing whether this is a first offense or a third, and properly so. For the judge's goal in this particular case is not merely to fulfill the legislative end but also to protect the public from further repetitions of the same offense by the same offender.

Likewise, the marriage counselor might have other goals in mind than the legislative aim. In counseling the husband to get a job instead of spending his days as well as his evenings at the local tavern, the counselor might well be trying to save the marriage, but it would be surprising if he was not also giving some thought to the payment of counseling fees! The presence of other goals might lead the counselor to set aside considerations of strict Judicial Economy.

The legislative end then sometimes splinters into different goals, attainable by separate means; at other times the deontic speaker has important goals other than those intended by the legislative body. In either event, the deontic speaker might have good reason to minimize or even disregard the rule of Judicial Economy.

The pattern we have seen in all the other rules of deontic pragmatics thus repeats itself with Judicial Economy. The maxim is normally a valuable way of making one's deontic speech effective, but in a number of instances it can and should be set aside. Judicial Economy therefore seems part of the pragmatics of deontic speech.

Judicial Publicity: **Impute obligations only to people who knew or should have known that the obligations in question applied to them when they performed the acts in question.**

The maxim of Judicial Publicity presupposes the successful application of Legislative Publicity. For agents to know that a rule applies to them, the legislative body must have made that rule available for those agents to know. But just as there is more to judging a case than knowing a rule, so there is more to Judicial Publicity than ascertaining that a rule has been adequately publicized. It is one thing to be aware of a rule and quite another to be aware of that rule's application to a given case.

A person moves into a new state one autumn. The next spring, he decides to buy a fishing license. He is aware that nonresident licenses cost much more than resident licenses. Since his new state has some excellent fishing, he is happy he is now eligible for a resident license. Unfortunately, he finds out some time after he has received his license that to count as a resident for licensing purposes, he must have lived in the state for a full year. He faces a fine and revocation of his license. The would-be fisherman knew the relevant law about resident and nonresident licenses, he knew he needed to get the appropriate license before he went fishing; but he did not know which license was appropriate for him. Granted, when the authorities find out, they will tell him that he should have known, but perhaps there was some failure of publicity.

This case is not fictional: it occurred in my state some years ago. The issuer of a fishing license is supposed to tell candidates of the length-of-residency requirement, but in this instance he did not. The fisherman only found this out some time later, by accident. He saved himself a larger fine by reporting himself to the authorities. The fisherman both knew and should have known what the relevant law was, but he did not know how that law applied to him. In view of the failure of Judicial Publicity, it is an open question whether he should have known how the law applied.

Sometimes, of course, a law provides clear-cut conditions for its own application, so that to know the law is to know the sort of person to whom it applies. The law governing fishing licenses might be of this sort. But as Aristotle showed, to know the sort of person to whom a law applies is not necessarily to know, or even to be able to know, that any given individual, including one's self, is within that group. What Aristotle called particular ignorance, ignorance of relevant facts, does occur.

For example, the law forbids a person to carry a concealed weapon. It also spells out, in many jurisdictions, the types of potential weapons that may not be concealed. In at least one jurisdiction, people are not allowed to carry concealed spray cans of Mace. Linda keeps such a can in her apartment, but she knows the law and does not carry it around with her. Then one day she picks it up and puts it into her purse by mistake. She was in a hurry, and the Mace can looked like her hair spray. Should she have known as she walked out that she was breaking the law? Perhaps she should have been more careful, but it is easy enough to make such a mistake. At any rate, even if Linda cannot be fully excused, one cannot blame the friend who accepts Linda's invitation to take home and try her new brand of hair spray.

As Aristotle says, there are many details of a situation that a person can be ignorant of, and this ignorance is not always culpable. Whenever those details are crucial to the application of a rule, whether that rule be one of law, morals, prudence or etiquette, it need not be true that the ignorant person should have known that the law applied to him.[122]

The cases so far are instances of ordinary ignorance. We can draw the same conclusion with far more confidence in cases where particular ignorance results from mental disease or defect. A man is convinced that he is the intended victim of a giant conspiracy. To protect himself, he shoots an ominous-looking stranger, who turns out to be a meter reader from the gas company. Is it reasonable to say that the gunman should have known that the moral prohibition against murder applied to him? His delusion caused him to misread relevant particulars.

Again, consider the odd case of Edith Hough. On May 30, 1957, a gentleman caller, Zurab Abdusheli, came to Miss Hough's door to express his sympathy upon the recent death of her father. Miss Hough "said later that Abdusheli became 'psychologically aggressive,' so [*sic!*] she wrapped her pistol in a towel and shot him several times. As he lay moaning on the day bed where he had fallen, [Miss Hough] placed the pistol close to his temple and shot again, 'to put him out of his misery.' Then she telephoned the police."[123]

There seems little point in searching for rational motives for Miss Hough's actions. At her trial, a number of psychiatrists, including one

122. The Aristotle reference is to *Nicomachean Ethics*, Book 3, chap. 1, especially 1110b27 ff.

123. The quotation is from the opinion of Circuit Judge Wilbur K. Miller (*Hough* v *United States*, 271 F.2d 458 [1959], p. 463) well after the events described. Miss Hough had been found not guilty by reason of insanity of murdering Abdusheli and had been committed to St. Elizabeth's Hospital. When the medical staff of the hospital later sought her conditional release, the district court denied it. She appealed to the U.S. Court of Appeals for the District of Columbia Circuit. Judge Miller's words are from his dissent to that court's decision. Thomas Szasz discusses this case in his *Law, Liberty, and Psychiatry* (New York, 1968), 139–42.

Dr. Karpman, testified that Miss Hough was an aggressive paranoid schizophrenic. In fact, Dr. Karpman, a friend of Miss Hough's late father, had urged the father fourteen years earlier to hospitalize her: "I told him personally, that we never can tell what measures or what a person of this type of psychosis might do."[124] Miss Hough was apparently an aggressive psychotic of long standing. If her psychosis had led her to be genuinely ignorant of why her caller was there, I doubt there is any way of making intelligible a claim that she should have known better.

These cases, by showing that the maxim of Judicial Publicity requires a deontic speaker to do more than merely ascertain whether a person knew or should have known the rule in question, give us a clue as to the value of the maxim. For suppose that Jack's mental disease leaves him ignorant of a crucial factor in applying a law. It is then false that Jack should have known in a particular situation that the law applied to him. What, then, is the point of enforcing the law in Jack's situation? Kant's Principle is at work here as a rule of deontic pragmatics. If Jack simply cannot know a crucial factor, there is no point in saying that he should have known it. If Edith Hough's ignorance of her caller's true mission was invincible, it is useless to convict her of murder.[125]

The rule of Judicial Publicity thus receives a similar justification to the one I provided for the maxim of Legislative Publicity. If people have no opportunity to know the law, it is at best useless and at worst counterproductive to convict them of violating that law.[126] Likewise, it is no better than useless to convict people who neither know nor should have known that a law applied to them.

I do not mean to claim that people should always be excused from responsibility under the law whenever their acts are the product of mental disease or defect. But when mental disease or defect causes a person to be ignorant of certain facts crucial to the applicability of a law, that person can hardly be accounted legally responsible

---

124 *Hough* v *United States* p. 468. The late Mr. Hough had also been a psychiatrist, a fact that might help explain Miss Hough's reference to Abdusheli's becoming "psychologically aggressive."

125. Conviction is useless according to a retributive view of punishment, that is. If one considers the protection of society, the chances of rehabilitation, or the likelihood of deterring others from crime, one could well find a point in conviction. This was noted by a reader for Brown University Press.

126. Again, when I say "at best" and "at worst," I am speaking from a pragmatic perspective. The question of injustice is quite another matter.

for any resulting misdeeds. After all, the law has always recognized nonculpable particular ignorance as an excuse.

So far, then, it appears that Judicial Publicity is a maxim in itself, not just a pale reflection of the rule of Legislative Publicity. However, the cases to this point have been primarily about judicial publicity in the law. In other deontic contexts, such as those of morals or of etiquette, rules might not be as clear cut. Is the requirement of judicial publicity any different in those contexts?

I do not think so. If moral rules are vaguer than their counterparts in the law, that argues only that we should show more charity when determining that people should know if a moral rule applies to them. No matter how strongly one believes that it is immoral to covet a neighbor's wife, one can have difficulty determing just which of one's acts constitutes the forbidden coveting. But if we have determined that the coveter should have realized that the rule against coveting did apply to certain of his acts, and if we then proceed to impute to him the obligation not to covet his neighbor's wife, Judicial Publicity is satisfied.

Judicial Publicity is then a maxim and an important maxim, but I have yet to show that it is a maxim of pragmatics. We must therefore now consider whether there are occasions when the rule of Judicial Publicity should be set aside. As we have seen so often before, the presence of some overriding goal might well give us ample reason to disregard a principle of deontic pragmatics. Even people who cannot reasonably be expected to know that the law against treason applies to their actions might receive harsh treatment in the interest of the public welfare.

During the American Civil War, Northern editors were jailed for writing disloyal editorials, and at least one newsboy who sold issues of disloyal newspapers also ended up briefly in a military prison. Measures against the so-called Copperheads were certainly unfair, to say nothing of being unconstitutional. What mattered at the time, however, was whether they were effective.

An overriding external goal is not the only circumstance that leads people to abandon Judicial Publicity. The same result can occur when the legislative end is not considered very important.

For example, I tell a seven-year old how he should hold his fork at the dinner table. I am not presupposing that he should have known the rules of etiquette in advance, or that his way of holding the fork was a violation of such rules. I am simply giving him information on the proper way to do things. Now if I attach some punishment to his failure to hold a fork properly, then I had better be assuming that he should have know better. That assumption serves my interest as well as his if I wish to change his behavior for the better. But as long as no reward or punishment enters in, Judicial and Legislative Publicity seem unnecessary. After all, there's a first time to learn anything.

My conclusion is then that there are specifiable circumstances for which Judicial Publicity is not and should not be invoked. But, on the whole, to follow this rule is a valuable means toward attaining one's legislative end. Judicial Publicity is therefore a rule of deontic pragmatics.

Judicial Review of General Rules: **Impute or accept particular obligations only when those obligations are imposed in accordance with general rules that are consistent, clear, applicable, simple, modest, universalizable, and proportional.**

The three previously examined judicial rules of matter ask people to make their particular decisions in accordance with rules that embody one of the legislative virtues, but they do more than simply invoke Legislative Factuality, Economy, and Publicity. Judicial Factuality asks that one take into account relevant particulars, Judicial Economy requires us to consider the costs in a particular case, and Judicial Publicity requires not merely that people be able to know the law but that they be able to apply it. Hence, Judicial Factuality, Judicial Economy, and Judicial Publicity count as rules of deontic pragmatics.

However, I see no need for seven separate maxims prescribing that particular obligations accord with rules embodying the legislative virtues of consistency, clarity, applicability, simplicity, modesty, universalizability, and proportionality. For such maxims do not add to the considerations I discussed when examining the corresponding legislative principles. Consequently I have lumped together those seven virtues into a single judicial principle, Judicial Review of General Rules. The maxim of Judicial Review, as I shall call it for short, is then something of a grab bag. It corresponds in a way to the principle of Use of General Rules. For the latter tells a person to decide cases by subsuming them under properly determined general rules—that is, rules formulated in the proper manner—while Judicial Review asks that the decision maker subsume the case under laws that, from a pragmatic perspective, have the proper matter.

Judicial Review thus provides at retail a number of virtues that were up to this point available only wholesale. The importance of this maxim clearly depends on the importance of the legislative virtues it retails. If it is usually important to us that we adopt only rules that apply equally to everybody, it should be of equal importance that we decide particular cases by subsuming them under universalizable rules.

Let us suppose that a law, based on no relevant differences between races, openly treats black persons worse than white persons. Such a law is clearly an offense against the principle of Universalizability, as I have noted before. Because it offends against that principle of pragmatics, the discriminatory law probably will poorly serve its legislators' purposes. The sit-ins in the American South during the 1950s and 1960s were aimed at just such discriminatory laws. Let us reflect on the trial of a black person arrested for sitting at a lunch counter reserved for whites. Should a conscientious juror vote to convict under a discriminatory statute?

The question is not an easy one, nor is the answer obvious. On the one hand, the law is the law, and the protester did break the law. However reprehensible the statute in question might be, it was properly framed and promulgated. Failure to convict would strike a blow against the efficacy of law in general.

On the other hand, a conscientious juror recognizes that a statute that demands differential treatment for no relevant reason simply cannot be justified. Although the manner in which the statute was framed is perfectly all right, its matter is, from the standpoint of pragmatics, defective.[127] The principle of Judicial Review then leads the juror to look for some better basis for a decision.

I do not know which decision a conscientious juror should reach. From the pragmatic perspective, the juror appears caught in a dilemma: Use of General Rules pulls one way, Judicial Review pulls the other. I believe that this dilemma often arises in such cases. The best course of action is not well defined, and any theory that makes it seem well defined is at best questionable. Jurors who are conscientious and free of prejudice will be pulled in both directions, and it is most unlikely that the theory of deontic pragmatics will dictate which way they should incline.

In any case, we do have good *prima facie* reason to decide such cases in accordance with laws that have pragmatically acceptable

---

127. The statute is also, of course, morally vicious, but the morality of any legislation is not our present concern.

matter. The principle that provides that reason is Judicial Review of General Rules. Judicial Review is therefore an important principle with widespread application to particular instances.

We must expect to find circumstances in which we have good reason to disregard the principle of Judicial Review, just as we found such circumstances for each of the corresponding legislative virtues. If emergency legislation prospers from ignoring a certain virtue, for instance, one would expect the same to hold true for emergency judicial decisions. I argued in discussing the maxim of Proportionality that considerations of public safety can override the requirement that a legal statute conform to that principle. If so, in a time of danger to the public safety, a judge has good reason to utilize a disproportional statute.

One such time of danger was certainly the American Civil War. I mentioned earlier the case of Clement Vallandigham. The legal history of this and of a later, parallel case make a nice illustration for my point.

While the war was still on, Vallandigham appealed for a writ of habeas corpus from his arbitrary arrest by General Burnside. The U.S. Circuit Court in Cincinnati denied the appeal, Judge Leavitt commenting that the president had suspended the writ under his wartime powers and that "the President is guided solely by his own judgment and discretion."[128] The U.S. Supreme Court denied the review, claiming it had no powers of certiorari in the matter.[129] The war was on, and Vallandigham was legally out of luck.

But the war finally ended. In 1866 the Supreme Court handed down its famous decision in *ex parte Milligan*. Milligan, like Vallandigham, was a civilian convicted by a military court of sedition. Milligan also had appealed to a federal circuit court for a writ of habeas corpus, had been refused, and had taken the case to the Supreme Court. But here his story diverges from that of Vallandigham. The Court held unanimously that Milligan should go free. A majority of the Supreme Court went so far as to claim that, as long as the regular courts remained open, nobody at any time should order the military trial of civilians.[130]

The difference between what the Court decided in 1863 and what it decided in 1866 is striking. It is hard to deny that the major factor

128. Quoted by Bruce Catton in *Never Call Retreat* (New York, 1965), 166. He lists as his source, *Appleton's American Annual Cyclopedia* for 1863, p. 473.

129. Robert McCloskey, *The American Supreme Court* (Chicago, 1960), 107.

130. Ibid., pp. 108–10.

in the Court's shift was the fact that the war ended in 1865. In a time of clear and massive danger to the public safety, the Court was willing to allow the fullest possible scope to the disproportionate and unfair procedures of martial law. When that danger was removed, the Court not only reduced that scope to zero but even went so far as to issue a "never again" message, perhaps as a sort of apology for its earlier spinelessness.

The Vallandigham decision, therefore, used a piece of disproportionate legislation as its guide. When the condition that justified overriding legislative proportionality ended, so did the occasion for such a decision. Emergencies may thus bring about decisions in particular cases that do not accord with the maxim of Judicial Review.

Another situation where the principle of Judicial Review is best ignored occurs when, as a result of new and usually unforeseen circumstances, it is foolish to apply a certain law, even though from the perspective of deontic pragmatics the legislative matter is perfectly sound. On occasion, "if the law says that, the law is a ass!" Many rules of good manners prevalent at the turn of the century, although perfectly reasonable at the time, were rendered obsolete by changes in the world. To enforce rules about leaving calling cards in an age of telecommunications would be absurd. It would likewise be fatuous for a highway patrolman to try to enforce the 55-m.p.h. speed limit in a narrow canyon with flood waters rising dangerously. No matter how proper that law might be, there are occasions when it is folly to apply it. And, of course, nobody would do so.

Circumstances alter cases, and no legislator can foresee every eventuality. No matter how proper a statute might be, one cannot count on its not becoming grotesque in a particular circumstance. We should therefore expect the maxim of Judicial Review not to apply under every condition.

I conclude that we sometimes have good reason to disregard the principle of Judicial Review. On occasion, there are other and better means to the legislative end or to some end that overrides the legislative. However, in most instances we have seen the importance of adhering to the maxim of Judicial Review of General Rules. It is therefore one more rule of deontic pragmatics—the final one.

10   Is That All There Is?

We have now looked in detail at the eighteen principles that make up the substance of the supermaxim of Deontic Rationality. I have tried to justify my claim that each of these eighteen is indeed a maxim of deontic pragmatics. But are there other maxims, perhaps even other important maxims, still waiting to be discovered?

The short and simple answer is that I do not know. In a earlier draft of this book, there were only sixteen maxims. In the paper from which the book sprang, I had fewer still. Perhaps the discovery of new principles of deontic pragmatics will become a new and vibrant growth industry.

What I really need is a Transcendental Deduction of the Eighteen Maxims, to allow me to demonstrate that, thanks to the eternal and immutable nature of the universe, that's all there is and there ain't no more. I need a Transcendental Deduction, but I don't have one. H. P. Grice gives an architectonic for his conversational rules by modeling them on Kant's categories, but I suspect his tongue remains securely in his cheek. I doubt that he means to rest any evidential weight on this fanciful architectonic. But whatever Grice's intent, I cannot even imitate his imitation of Kant.

When I was an undergraduate, a friend of mine was given an oral examination on Aristotle. The rather vicious question asked him was, "Why are there only four causes?" It took me a long time to come up with what I think Aristotle's answer would have been: "Well, if you have any candidates for a fifth type of cause, let's put them to the test. Chance, you say? No, that won't work, because . . . "

That's the only sort of answer I can give to the question, "Is that all there is?" I need to examine each of the promising candidates, and add any maxim that survives the examination to the list of eighteen. Of course, I cannot be sure I have looked at all the promising candidates that might be offered, but I retain some faith in induction.

I begin by looking once more at Kant's Principle, that 'ought' implies 'can'. I argued in chapter 2 that this principle is one of pragmatics. Why should it not be added to the list of eighteen?

We don't need to add Kant's Principle to the list because it is already there, implied by other maxims. In particular, the rules of Straightforwardness and of Legislative and Judicial Economy are enough to ensure that 'ought' implicates 'can'. For suppose you wish to make a general deontic speech. You are probably trying to get people to behave as your legislation prescribes. To be successful, you would be well advised to look for those means that cost the actors the least.

Now if one knowingly prescribes what people cannot do, one's purpose is by definition not straightforward. And if one unknowingly prescribes the impossible, it will soon be obvious that there is no economical way of fulfilling the prescription. Under normal conditions, then, an 'ought' without a 'can' either will not be prescribed or, if prescribed, will not be enforced.

The same holds true for a particular deontic speech. If your aim is straightforward, you can recommend the impossible only out of ignorance. And you will not remain ignorant for long since you will soon find that there is no economical means (because there is no means at all) of fulfilling your aim.

Conversely, if one's purpose in speaking deontically is not straightforward, there seems little room for Kant's Principle. The Augustinian God, whose intent is to shut up all men under sin, and the depraved Roman emperor, whose intent is to find an excuse for executing a person, do not accept Kant's Principle precisely because their aims are anything but straightforward.

Failure to follow Kant's Principle might also stem from indifference to economy. A legislator who cares nothing about the economy of the means his legislation prescribes might shrug off failures to keep to such statutes. So might a judicial authority indifferent to matters of economy. Both might claim that if people don't do what is prescribed, so much the worse for them. A legislator or judge unconcerned with means could well overlook the fact that, with a rule that defies Kant's Principle generally or when applied to a particular case, no means of fulfilling the rule are possible.

Therefore, if the point of deontic speech is to get people to act in certain ways, then speech that violates Kant's Principle is rendered pointless by the principles of Straightforwardness and Economy. 'Ought' implies 'can', but we need no special rule to justify that claim.

We might look for new maxims of deontic pragmatics by considering the nature of the legislative end itself. I have argued that this end should be straightforwardly expressed, minimal, capable of fulfillment, and possessed of various virtues. But surely these are not the only limits that can be placed on the purposes of legislation! And, of course, they are not. But any other limits that people put on legislative aims derive, I believe, from particular deontic realms: the moral, the practical, the constitutional, and so forth. There is no good reason to think that such limits are inherent in the very purpose of deontic speech.[131]

Take for instance a society in which legislation mandates the death penalty for those who commit certain crimes. This legislation is not out of keeping with the opinions of most people in the society. It is not applied capriciously. It is not applied only to members of a subgroup whose definition is irrelevant to the legislation, such as a racial or ethnic minority. But nevertheless, many thoughtful people

---

131. I do not mean by these remarks to suggest that each of my eighteen maxims is applicable in every deontic context. Where there are no goods to distribute, for example, the maxim of Distribution has no place. But each of the eighteen maxims does seem applicable to many different sorts of contexts, and I can find no other maxims that seem so generally applicable.

in the society argue against the propriety of capital punishment even under these circumstances.

What arguments might the opponents of capital punishment in this society use? They have quite a bit of latitude in their choice. Some arguments might be moral, based on the wrongfulness of deliberately taking a human life or on the impossibility of making good the evil done by executing the wrong man. Some arguments might be practical, taking into account statistics on the deterrent value (or lack thereof) of the death penalty. Others might try to find constitutional language, such as the prohibition against cruel punishment, to serve as the basis of opposition.

The practical arguments make use of our eighteen maxims as they stand. For such arguments try to show that the legislative purpose in mandating the death penalty is simply not being carried out or is not being carried out economically. Similarly, any constitutional arguments, in so far as they are not mere appeals to the printed page, use the eighteen maxims. Such arguments therefore do not require us to expand our list of eighteen principles.

Moral arguments can also make use of some of the eighteen maxims such as Universalizability and Proportionality. But these then appear as moral principles rather than pragmatic maxims. People who attack capital punishment on moral grounds do not intend to show the impracticability of the legislative end. The moral arguments are therefore not directly dependent on nor part of the pragmatics of deontic talk.

To the extent that arguments against the death penalty use principles derived from the purpose of deontic speech, then, they seem to rest on the set of eighteen maxims. And to the extent that they do not rest on those maxims, they seem to result from moral considerations rather than general deontic principles.

What we have seen from this quick look at arguments against capital punishment seems generally true. Of course, there are many constraints we choose to put upon legislative ends, and there are many constraints we believe we should put upon such ends. But not all of these constraints result from the pragmatics of deontic speech, or even from the pragmatics of a particular kind of deontic speech (such as moral deontic speech). Any genuinely pragmatic constraints seem to embody one or more of our eighteen principles, and all other types of constraints are irrelevant to our present purpose. However important and worthwhile moral, nonpragmatic constraints might be, we have no reason to add them to our list of eighteen.

After all, people will occasionally choose legislative ends that are morally vicious. It is sheer romanticism to suppose that all vicious ends will in the end prove impractical, much less self-defeating. Although it is surely practical to have moral principles, it is fatuous to suppose that each principle of one's moral code is defensible on pragmatic grounds.

In a way, we have returned to a consideration first mentioned in chapter 1. A moral code is made up of more than threshold principles. Even though the threshold principles represent the contents of the pragmatics of deontic speech in general, we should not expect every part of a given moral code to be justifiable on pragmatic grounds. And someone who does have this expectation is easy game for relativist or even nihilist objections.

This consideration, however, suggests a new source for maxims. Suppose we should discover that an utterly abominable moral code is consistent with my eighteen maxims. Such a code not only allows for but positively fosters bad judicial or legislative decisions. I would immediately search for a nineteenth maxim that would screen out the detestable code. I would have no guarantee of finding such a maxim, but I would be well motivated to make the search.

But is there any reason to think that such an abominable moral code can actually be consistent with the eighteen maxims? Those maxims succeed, I have shown, in ruling out codes based on racism, caprice, willful cruelty, and the like. In fact, the eighteen maxims screen out all the abominable moral codes I can think of. Until someone raises a specific example of an unscreened but detestable code, I think we should stick with our list.

In general, then, although there are many principles that can serve to circumscribe the legislative end, I see no likelihood of finding further pragmatic maxims among them. The list of eighteen appears sound.

A further source of possible new maxims is the constraints we frequently impose upon the means by which one may seek a given end. These constraints are not always merely an application of Economy, Publicity, and other established maxims of deontic pragmatics. We quite often agree that however good the end might be, certain means are simple unacceptable. But what makes them unacceptable is usually not their failure to embody the aims of deontic speech. More often, those means infringe upon rights or adversely affect the public welfare.

For an illustration, let us reconsider the death penalty. Many people who do not oppose the death penalty as such are strongly opposed to using any but the least painful available means for imposing that penalty. Montaigne was such a person, and I am another. But it is not the impracticality of using the electric chair when lethal injection is available that causes my objection to electrocuting criminals.[132] It is, I believe, wrong to execute in a needlessly cruel manner; but I am in no position to assert that a cruel method of execution will prove either inefficient or self-defeating. My argument against electrocution is therefore not pragmatic, so we should not look for new principles of deontic pragmatics there. Someone else could conceivably come up with a pragmatic argument against cruel execution, but I think such an argument could only depend on such principles as Proportionality and Economy, which are already on the list of eighteen.

One area in which we might find more maxims is the realm of meta-principles. By a meta-principle, I mean a rule that tells us when to apply one or another of the eighteen maxims or when to take a maxim as overriding and when to take it as only *prima facie*. I shall look at meta-principles in chapter 12. But even if we can formulate a coherent set of meta-principles, I think it best not to mix them in with the principles of deontic pragmatics. Principles of deontic speech are different from principles governing the use of principles of deontic speech.

I am therefore aware of no general method by which someone might supplement my list of eighteen maxims. Of course, for all I can tell, somebody will be able to flesh out my list with particular rules I have simply not thought of. Here is where a Transcendental Deduction would be most comforting. But none exists.

Our deontic speech is, of course, subject to other pragmatic rules than those specific to deontic pragmatics. To the extent that deontic speech is conversation, it is subject to Grice's Conversational Principle and its various submaxims. To the extent that it is social, it is subject to Lakoff's rules of politeness. But is our deontic speech subject to more rules of deontic pragmatics than the eighteen maxims? If so, I cannot think of what those rules might be. I could, of course, have a rather large beam in my eye.

Is that, then, all there is? Maybe. I might even be so daring as to say: Probably.

---

132. I understand, though, that some prison officials favor lethal injection because it is comparatively inexpensive.

III   HOW

11 An Extended Example: Pragmatics and the Bakke Decision

INTRODUCTION TO THE *BAKKE* DECISION

In this chapter, I shall trace how the eighteen maxims of deontic pragmatics can be found, often in conflict with one another, in an extensive, famous, and controversial decision of the United States Supreme Court: *Regents of the University of California* v *Bakke*.[133] My major purpose is to

133. No. 76–811, decided 28 June 1978. Page references to this decision will hereafter be in parentheses.

show how the pragmatic principles actually function together in an extended piece of deontic speech.[134]

Allan Bakke, a white male, was twice denied entrance to the medical school at the University of California at Davis. His test scores and other credentials were better than those of most of the minority students admitted to the Davis program under an affirmative action plan, which set aside sixteen seats per year exclusively for members of disadvantaged minorities. Davis, like most American universities, receives federal money; hence, the provisions of Title Six of the 1964 Civil Rights Act, which forbids discrimination by federally funded institutions, apply to Davis. Bakke therefore brought suit, claiming that his exclusion from the Davis facility was in violation of Title Six, of the Californian state constitution, and of the Equal Protection Clause of the Fourteenth Amendment to the United States Constitution.[135] Bakke contended that he had been illegally barred, by reason of race alone, from competing for one of the sixteen reserved seats.

A bitterly divided United States Supreme Court expressed its conclusions in no fewer than six separate opinions. Justice Powell's opinion expressed the decision of the Court, yet no other justice fully concurred with the views Justice Powell set forth. Four members of the Court concurred with him on some of the crucial points of the decision, while the remaining four agreed with him on the other crucial points. The result was a five to four decision on all major issues, but Justice Powell was the only member of the Court consistently on the majority side. Hence, Justice Powell, whose position was fully shared by no other justice, wrote the majority opinion.

There were three major positions taken by members of the Court: that of Justice Powell; that of Justices Brennan, White, Marshall, and Blackmun, voiced in an opinion by Justice Brennan; and that of Justices Stevens, Burger, Stewart, and Rehnquist, voiced in an opinion by Justice Stevens. The three remaining opinions were supplementary. Justice Marshall gave an impassioned account of past discrimina-

---

134. I am not supposing that every sentence of the *Bakke* decision contains a deontic operator, but the Court's opinion as a whole aims at telling Bakke and the regents what they should, should not, may, or may not do. The dissenting opinions have a similarly deontic aim, although they purvey not actual duties but the duties that would have held if the majority of the Court had agreed.

135. This clause, with its neighbor the Due Process Clause, reads: ". . . nor shall any State deprive any person of life, liberty, or property without due process of law, nor deny to any person within its jurisdiction the equal protection of the laws."

tion against black Americans; Justice Blackmun added some general reflections; and Justice White argued against the propriety of a private individual's bringing suit under Title Six. In what follows, I shall ignore these supplementary opinions and concentrate on the opinions of Justices Powell, Brennan, and Stevens.

The questions at issue in this case were definitely deontic in nature. Should Bakke have been allowed to compete for the sixteen reserved seats? If so, should Davis be compelled to admit him or only to reconsider his admission? Is a program that makes crucial distinctions solely on racial grounds permissible? Is a program that considers other factors as well as race permissible? These questions quickly leave behind the particular question of Bakke's admission to the Davis program and rise to more general concerns. The Court, despite the disagreement of the Stevens bloc, ended up setting a policy, even though no one could be sure just what that policy was. The decision was then, in my sense of the words, legislative as well as judicial. We should therefore expect to see both legislative and judicial principles of deontic pragmatics at work.

The three-way division of the Court evinced considerable argument among the justices, since each of the three main groups tried to justify its understanding of crucial matters of obligation and permissibility. Much of the argument consists, as one would expect, of citing favorable precedents and dismissing adverse ones. But there is also an unusual amount of forthright deontic reasoning, making that decision well worth our study. For deontic reasoning employs the principles of deontic pragmatics.

JUDICIAL REASONING AND DEONTIC PRAGMATICS

In previous chapters, I examined in some detail the functioning of each of the eighteen maxims of deontic pragmatics. By examining the maxims one by one, however, I presented a somewhat misleading picture of my subject, for usually more than one maxim applies to any given example of deontic speech. Even with the examples I used when arguing for the individual maxims, more than one maxim often applies. We need to see how the eighteen function *as a group.*

The situation is even more complex when a person is deciding which deontic speech to make. Here different maxims—and even the same maxim applied to different particulars—can justify distinct and incompatible courses of action. And one should not suppose that the maxims of deontic pragmatics are the only factors in the person's decision. Considerations of politeness, propriety, interest, and many other factors might well be relevant.

In looking at the *Bakke* decision, I will be closely examining three quite incompatible opinions, each of them buttressed by arguments making extensive use of the maxims of deontic pragmatics. That sounds as if I'm getting ahead of myself. We are to see how the justices used principles of deontic pragmatics in resolving an important conflict, but we have not yet looked at how conflicts of maxims should be resolved. But what to do when maxims conflict is not easy to determine. As I shall argue in chapter 12, the only method we have for resolving conflicts is to employ an incomplete set of rules of thumb, limited in scope. There is no escape from the exercise of practical wisdom, steeped in the details of the case under consideration.[136]

However, I think the *Bakke* decision is unusual in one major respect: the justices all appear to have reached their respective conclusions on primarily moral grounds.[137] They do use the principles of deontic pragmatics, but not so much to *reach* their decisions as to *justify* those decisions.[138] If so, our look at how the justices argued pragmatically in the *Bakke* case will not serve as a paradigm for a general look at how to resolve conflicts in decision making.

I am claiming two things here. First, the justices in this case reach their decisions for a number of reasons, and the pragmatic principles play a relatively minor role among these reasons;[139] and second, the justices in their opinions tend to set out their positive cases without

136. This general way of regarding conflict resolution in judicial cases was suggested by a reader for Brown University Press.

137. I do not mean to suggest that pragmatic principles *generally* play only a minor role in determining Court decisions. It is a peculiarity of the *Bakke* decision that all the major opinions present their authors as taking the moral high ground. I take this moral earnestness seriously.

138. This may sound as if I am adopting the position of those legal realists who believed, in Ronald Dworkin's words, that ". . . judges actually decide cases according to their own political or moral tastes, and then choose an appropriate legal rule as a rationalization" (*Taking Rights Seriously* [Cambridge, Mass., 1977], 3). But I believe the justices in the *Bakke* case tried hard to decide on the basis of what they took to be morally compelling grounds; that they disagreed on what those grounds were impugns neither their positions nor the objectivity of moral values.

139. That is, their reasons tend not to be the principles of pragmatics as such. Universalizability and Proportionality, however, are also principles of justice, and as principles of justice they are often important in forming the positions of members of the Court.

really answering the arguments of the justices opposed to them.[140] In the *Bakke* decision, then, although the maxims might conflict, the justices really don't.

I am suggesting that the principles of deontic pragmatics function in the *Bakke* decision rather like Aristotelian practical syllogisms. If you hold the relevant major premiss and the needed minors, Aristotle claims that you will act. Aristotle's analysis is plausible, as long as the practical reasoner holds no other competing premisses. But Aristotle provides little help with the troublesome situation where a person has reason to take any of several different and incompatible actions. This difficulty has led a number of people to suggest that Aristotle's doctrine of the practical syllogism can explain why a person has acted but not how a person chooses what to do. The practical syllogism then enshrines after-the-fact analysis, not the factors in making actual decisions.

Much the same situation apparently holds in the *Bakke* decision: The justices' pragmatic arguments are primarily reasons for the conclusions they reached on mainly moral grounds. When one of the justices in the *Bakke* decision appeals to consistency with precedents, or with the legislative history, or with important facts about our society, he is using one of the rules of deontic pragmatics. A fellow justice then disagrees with him and makes his case by arguing for consistency with different precedents, different aspects of the legislative history, or different facts about society. The two are, in a sense, arguing past one another, not with one another. For there is no contradiction between giving a reason for doing one thing and giving a reason for doing a quite incompatible thing. In the *Bakke* case, there is reason to favor Bakke's side, and there is reason to favor that of the regents. There is

140. When the justices do try to come to grips with each others' points, the argument is usually fairly feeble. As I shall note, Justice Stevens, in the *Bakke* decision, rests much of his argument on the legislative history of Title Six of the Civil Rights Act. He believes that the legislators who passed Title Six clearly meant to rule out all discrimination by race, as the language of Title Six itself suggests. Justice Powell has no better response than that "isolated statements of various legislators, taken out of context, can be marshaled in support of the proposition that [Title Six] enacted a purely color-blind scheme. . . ." Justice Powell does not show that the statements in question are in fact isolated from the main current of legislative statements on the subject, nor does he show that a fuller context would give a different meaning to those statements. He obviously prefers to put forward his own case. Certainly, justices of the Supreme Court do argue with one another. But the arguments all too often seem to be of the form: "My brother has forgotten [or: has paid insufficient attention to] this." Then comes the positive case once again.

also reason to favor a compromise, such as that Justice Powell worked out. Since there is reason to favor each of these three incompatible positions, one cannot, by stressing the reasons behind one's favorite position, do much damage to the opposition.

Consequently, I suggest that the Supreme Court justices in the *Bakke* case should have been more destructive—in their reasoning, I hasten to add! It is not enough for them to make a case for the side they favor. They must show what is wrong with the other side or sides. As I look at the *Bakke* case, I will try to make up for the justices' shortcomings by calling attention to where they misuse the principles of deontic pragmatics. To bring commonly used rules to public awareness and to expose their status might help people use those rules with a higher degree of sophistication.

However, destructive criticism is not sufficient to determine the proper outcome of a complicated case such as that of Allan Bakke.[141] Nor should anyone expect it to be sufficient. Since we can give reasons for more than one competing position, it would be surprising if destructive criticism left only one position standing. In the *Bakke* case, all three main positions, I believe, survive my criticism. Enough of Justice Powell's reasoning survives that one can say that he has built a case; but so have Justices Stevens and Brennan, and they come out with quite different positions from that of Justice Powell.

The Supreme Court's decision in the *Bakke* case has been roundly blasted from all sides as a compromise, a political opinion that seeks to make a distinction where none is to be found. I think, on the other hand, that the position taken by the Court's shifting majority, as expressed in Justice Powell's opinion, is thoroughly defensible and even right. But the considerations I have raised so far make it clear that to defend the Court's position is to go beyond the employment of deontic pragmatics, even when we add destructive argument to the arsenal.

But if deontic pragmatics does not determine which of the three positions deserves to win out, how should the justices have made that determination? Strictly speaking, the answer to this question, since it is not given by deontic pragmatics, is irrelevant to the theme of this book. But a few words will not hurt.

What the justices turn to are substantive principles of justice, along with visions of the social good. Justice Powell, for example,

141. And, of course, destructive reasoning was not responsible for forming the positions of the three groups of justices. As F. H. Bradley pointed out, the fact that one stranger does not know the way across an unknown bog hardly implies that a second stranger must.

begins one section of his opinion with the words: "Moreover, there are serious problems of justice connected with the idea of preference itself" (298). It is an important occasion when a Justice speaks of justice and not merely of the state of the law. The justices are all political animals, and as such they sound slightly embarrassed invoking such high-flown notions as justice and the social good. But they do it, and for good reason. Ultimately, they have no other way of reaching justified conclusions. For this reason, the impassioned opinion of Justice Marshall, who traces the long and shameful history of racial discrimination, is thoroughly appropriate. If the ultimate basis for deciding the *Bakke* case is the justices' sense of justice and their vision of a better society, Justice Marshall is right to remind them of the dead weight of the past.

Unfortunately, justice and the social good are not always working on the same side. In many of the most bitterly divided cases in the past, the Supreme Court has struggled over the relative weight to put on these two major considerations. Nowhere is this more clear than in the Court's decisions about strict liability. Justice Frankfurter's opinion in *United States* v *Dotterweich* rests entirely on the social good: "Such legislation [*viz.*, the Pure Food and Drug Act] dispenses with the conventional requirement for criminal conduct—awareness of some wrongdoing. In the interest of the larger good it puts the burden of acting at hazard upon a person otherwise innocent but standing in responsible relations to a public danger."[142]

On the other side, compare Justice Murphy's dissent: "It is a fundamental principle of Anglo-Saxon jurisprudence that guilt is personal and that it ought not lightly to be imputed to a citizen who, like the respondent, has no evil intention or consciousness of wrongdoing. . . . Before we place the stigma of a criminal conviction upon any such citizen the legislative mandate must be clear and unambiguous."[143] Frankfurter and four other justices voted on grounds of social good to confirm the conviction of Dotterweich. Murphy and three others dissented strongly, on grounds that

142. *United States* v *Dotterweich* 320 U.S. 277 (1943), pp. 280–81. A recent case that explicitly bases itself on *Dotterweich*, without even restating Justice Frankfurter's argument (or Justice Murphy's heated objections), is *U.S.* v *Cassaro, Inc.*, 443 F.2d 153 (1st Cir. 1971), especially p. 157.

143. *United States* v *Dotterweich*, p. 286. I believe that Justice Murphy is right, and that the Court made a dreadful error in the *Dotterweich* decision. Justice Frankfurter totally fails to explain why punishing Dotterweich is likely to have any beneficial effect on society. Indeed, as with the *Lindberg* case discussed earlier, it seems more likely that the net effect will be to discourage people from engaging in an important profession— in this case, the pharmaceutical industry.

it is unjust to convict a person who lacks *mens rea*. The same battle between justice and the social good has been fought out many times in the Court.

And it was fought out in the *Bakke* case. It is not an oversimplification, I think, to say that four justices (the Stevens group) were most strongly aware of the injustice done to Allan Bakke by the Davis affirmative action program. Four more justices (the Brennan group) thought primarily of the evil effects of racial discrimination, and the social need to find some way to mitigate those effects. Both considerations are vitally important; for this reason, neither group can quite understand how the other can fail to see the transcendent obviousness of its position.[144]

Justice Powell's opinion tries to balance both concerns. He sees an injustice done to Bakke, and he therefore sides with those who would rectify that injustice; but he sees the social value of affirmative action programs, and he therefore finds a way to let such programs continue. As my analysis will indicate, I am not sure that the particular way Justice Powell finds is ultimately defensible. But what makes his opinion importantly right, I believe, is his attempt to find a balance between two warring but vital principles.

And where does deontic pragmatics fit in? We will see the eighteen principles at work in what follows. But they are used to build cases, to justify decisions ultimately based on justice and the social good.

ANALYSIS OF THE ARGUMENTATION IN THE *BAKKE* DECISION

Let us now look at how the three groups of justices tried to justify their answers to the six questions that form the outline of the *Bakke* decision.

---

144. This may sound to some as if the Stevens group upheld principles, while the Brennan group plumped for policies, to use Ronald Dworkin's distinction (*op. cit.*, pp. 82–84). If it were so, then I would agree with Professor Dworkin's prescription for such cases: principle should win (p. 84). But the policy advocated by the Brennan group provides perhaps the only way to achieve in our society what Professor Dworkin calls a matter of principle: "that a minority has a right to equal respect and concern" (p. 82). The battle is therefore really one between principle and principle, between competing rights of individuals. I think this analysis correct even though Dworkin, commenting on an earlier reverse discrimination case, argues that the plaintiff suffered no infringement on his rights (pp. 225–29).

1. Does the language of Title Six add anything to the guarantees already present under the Equal Protection Clause?

The first question raises the issue of the scope of the guarantees provided by Title Six. Both Justice Powell and the Brennan group hold that Title Six guarantees nothing beyond what was already provided by the Equal Protection Clause.

Justice Powell backs up this conclusion by a brief look at the legislative history of Title Six (284–87). He concedes that "isolated statements of various legislators, taken out of context, can be marshaled in support of the proposition that [Title Six] enacted a purely color-blind scheme, without regard to the reach of the Equal Protection Clause." But he argues that the entire debate, if read in the light of the problems Congress was attempting to solve by enacting Title Six, supports a narrower interpretation of that legislation. He notes, for example, that supporters of Title Six consistently held that the bill enacted constitutional principles, and that the possibility of affirmative action programs working an inequity on a majority was, at that time, purely hypothetical.

Justice Powell is imputing to Congress a minimalist effort as well as a regard for the virtue of consistency. Congress, according to this reading, was legislating no further than necessary to meet the current needs. It should not be regarded as providing for situations barely thought of at the time. Justice Powell thus invokes the rule of Minimalism.

Justice Brennan reaches the same conclusion as Justice Powell, but by a considerably more complex process (328–55). After a somewhat lengthier look at the legislative debate on Title Six, Justice Brennan considers three more factors that support his reading: the administrative rules used to interpret Title Six after it was enacted; subsequent congressional and administrative actions, presumably intended to be in conformity with and furtherance of Title Six; and various decisions of the Supreme Court itself that "strongly suggest" Justice Brennan's reading (350). Justice Brennan therefore appeals strongly to the notion of consistency among deontic pronouncements, and hence to the maxim of Theoretical Virtue.

Justice Stevens, on the other hand, points out (as had Justice Powell) that Title Six certainly appears to rule out any discrimination by race such as occurred in the *Bakke* case. The burden of proof, he argues, therefore lies on those who argue for a narrower interpretation of Title Six. They must show either that the language of Title Six misstates the congressional intent or that Bakke, as a private person, has no right to bring suit (412–13). Justice Stevens concludes that neither of these has been shown. He cites the same legislative history as the other justices, but what appeared isolated and out of context to Justice Powell is clearly central to Justice Stevens. Until this point, Justice Stevens's argument is an invocation of the principle of Straightforwardness. The intent of Congress should normally be taken as embodied in the actual language of the legislation, and it takes a strong argument to establish the contrary in any given circumstance.

The Stevens opinion makes an additional useful point: ". . . [I]t seems clear that the proponents of Title VI assumed that the Constitution itself required a colorblind standard on the part of government, but that does not mean that the legislation only codifies an existing constitutional prohibition" (416). That is, even if the court decides that the Fourteenth Amendment does not require colorblindness, it does not follow that Congress took the same view of that amendment. Hence, Congress might well have considered itself to be spelling out the guarantees of the Equal Protection Clause in enacting Title Six, while in fact it was adding to those guarantees. Justice Stevens is making a point about consistency, but by implication the point applies to the other deontic virtues. One can assume that a legislative body will, in most cases, try to be consistent in its enactments, just as one can assume that it will try to be straightforward, minimalist, factual, and the like. One cannot always assume, however, that the legislative body will succeed in these attempts. Congress might try to be consistent, but that is no ground for asserting that it will be consistent.

All three of the opinions show in their answers to the first question a high regard for the principle of Judicial Economy. For all are clearly trying to decide a case in a way that will carry out the legislative aim. Determining what that aim is, is clearly another question, and one on which the justices divide.

In addition, the numerous citations of the congressional debate seem to presuppose that Congress had no hidden agenda. To that extent, all three groups invoke the principle of Straightforwardness. But as I indicated above, it is Justice Stevens who most strongly invokes Straightforwardness by his insistence that the Court, barring strong evidence to the contrary, must assume that Congress said exactly what it wanted to say.

Similarly, all three opinions can be said to have invoked the rule of Theoretical Virtue in their regard for consistency. Justice Brennan puts the heaviest emphasis on this rule, by seeking a reading of Title

Six that is consistent with past Court decisions as well as with administrative and congressional actions. I regard Justice Brennan, like Justice Stevens, as making a point about the burden of proof: namely, that if all sorts of people understand a law in a single, consistent way, their understanding must be presumed correct unless there is contrary evidence.

Notice how the three opinions, by concentrating on different rules of deontic pragmatics, come to quite opposed conclusions. Each opinion displays deontic rationality, even though no one could rationally adhere to all three opinions at once.

One might regard the argument between the Stevens bloc and the other justices as a dispute over the principles that make up the rule of Judicial Review. Where the Stevens group stresses the need to take the language of Title Six as clearly expressing the intent of Congress, the other justices stress consistency with precedent.

2. If the answer to question 1 is "yes," does Title Six mandate an admissions process that takes no account of race?

Justice Stevens's opinion is the only one that must face this question, since it was the only opinion to give an affirmative answer to the first question. Once can easily anticipate that Justice Stevens's answer to this question will be in the affirmative as well. Since, in his view, the plain language of Title Six prohibits a government-funded body from making discriminations based on race, and since there are no compelling arguments that this plain language does not represent congressional intent, the Davis program is clearly impermissible. Moreover, any admissions program to a federally funded facility must be color-blind.

It is clearly crucial to Justice Stevens's reasoning to determine whether there are compelling arguments showing that congressional intent is not accurately embodied in the language of Title Six. Justice Stevens is surely correct in his contention that the burden of proof is on those who wish to show a more restricted congressional intent, but Justices Powell and, especially, Brennan do try to shoulder that burden.

The reasoning of the Stevens opinion is ultimately a little disappointing, since it gives no detailed consideration of the four considerations Brennan so carefully discusses. All Justice Stevens provides is a quick glance at the congressional debate, without studying the subsequent administrative, legislative, and judicial history of Title Six and related matters. The Stevens opinion suffers from inadequacy in his use of the rule of Judicial Factuality, for he gives insufficient notice or no notice at all to some relevant facts.

3. If the answer to question 1 is "no," does the Equal Protection Clause mandate an admissions process that takes no account of race?

Only Justice Powell and Justice Brennan answered this question. Since Justice Stevens reached a decision on Title Six alone, his group did not participate in the written debate on the Equal Protection Clause. Once again, Justices Powell and Brennan agree on the answer—in this case, a qualified "no"—but they differ somewhat in their attempts to justify that answer.

Justice Powell and Justice Brennan agree that the Fourteenth Amendment creates a strong presumption, but not an absolute barrier, against an admissions process that considers racial differences. A sufficiently strong justification for such a process can overcome the presumption, but because the presumption against taking racial differences into account is so strong, judicial scrutiny of any procedure that does consider race must be careful and exacting.

Justice Powell's way of justifying this conclusion is quick (287–91). The Fourteenth Amendment, he says, explicitly guarantees to all within a state the equal protection of the state's laws. "The guarantee of equal protection cannot mean one thing when applied to one individual and something else when applied to a person of another color. If both are not accorded the same protection, then it is not equal." Up to this point, Justice Powell sounds as if he is about to find in the Fourteenth Amendment the absolute prohibition on a race-conscious admissions program that Justice Stevens quarried out of Title Six. Instead, Justice Powell falls back on the precedent of *Korematsu*, the famous (or infamous) case that grew out of the forced resettlement of United States citizens of Japanese ancestry during World War II. That decision held that "all legal restrictions which curtail the civil rights of a single racial group are immediately suspect. That is not to say that all such restrictions are unconstitutional. It is to say that courts must subject them to the most rigid scrutiny."[145] In line with this precedent, then, Justice Powell concludes that what is called for in the present case is not a total prohibition of race-conscious admissions programs on constitutional grounds but rather strict judicial scrutiny of each such program.

145. 323 U.S., p. 216, quoted on p. 291 of the *Bakke* decision.

Justice Powell is giving what seems like a straightforward reading of the Equal Protection Clause. But one wonders whether he then substitutes consistency with the *Korematsu* precedent for consistency with his own reading of what the Fourteenth Amendment requires. To say that the guarantee of equal protection cannot mean different things when applied to persons of different color is not merely to say that we should be very suspicious of such applications. Justice Powell's opinion could use a bit more theoretical virtue here.

Justice Brennan again takes a more tortuous route than Justice Powell but reaches the same conclusion (356–62). Justice Brennan begins by noting that the *Bakke* case lacks three usual characteristics of those practices that call for strict judicial scrutiny: (1) no fundamental rights are involved; (2) lumping whites together does not create a class with any of the "traditional indicia of suspectness"; and (3) according to the university's representation, racial classifications are not irrelevant to the school's purposes (357).[146] But Justice Brennan adds, rightly, that even when these marks are missing, strict scrutiny might still be necessary.

Justice Brennan provides a two-part rationale for invoking strict scrutiny in equal protection cases. First, he observes that the Court has recognized that decisions based on gender have worked against a disadvantaged group in society, and he suggests that decisions based on race might have the same effect.[147] Second, Justice Brennan points out that a person cannot change his race, and that it is a "deeply rooted" principle in our society that the state should not approve, sanction, or sponsor any improvement in a person's position based on such immutable factors. Consequently, the *Bakke* case calls for strict judicial scrutiny.

Justice Powell, then, thinks that the Fourteenth Amendment obviously requires strict scrutiny, and he relies on the *Korematsu* precedent to show that no more is needed. Justice Brennan, on the other hand, finds it necessary to argue that the provisions of the Fourteenth Amendment are strong enough to require strict scrutiny. There is no question of a blanket prohibition in his view, and his argument (355–60) never hints at finding one.

Justice Brennan, although yielding to none in his regard for con-

146. The "traditional indicia" phrase is quoted from *San Antonio School District* v *Rodriguez*, 411 U.S. 1, 16–17 (1973), p. 28.
147. An odd thing about this argument is that, although it is based on past Court opinions, the chief citation (360) is from a *dissent* in *Kahn* v *Shevin*, 416 U.S. 351, 357 (1974).

sistency, as shown by the quantity of his citations, is clearly using an extended version of the consistency principle when he cites the analogy of gender. His use of the analogy is an implicit invocation of the maxim of Universalizability.[148] For Justice Brennan fails to find a relevant difference between gender discrimination and race discrimination. His argument is therefore that the Court should treat like cases alike.[149]

The second prong of Justice Brennan's argument for strict scrutiny also blends consistency with universalizability. He seems to argue something like this: We have certain methods of dealing with cases in which immutable characteristics are involved; this is such a case; therefore, we should use those methods. The interesting thing about this argument is that Justice Brennan is calling for consistency with principles of our society, not with past Court decisions. Perhaps Justice Brennan thinks of his "deeply rooted" principle as a social fact. If so, he is invoking the rule of Judicial Factuality.[150]

148. Clearly, Justice Brennan is here invoking universalizability as a *moral* principle, not as a pragmatic one. He is arguing that discriminatory legislation is vicious, not that it fails to fulfill the legislative purpose. Likewise, throughout this chapter, when I speak of justices invoking principles of pragmatics, I do not mean to suggest that they invoke them *as* principles of pragmatics. But recognizing that Brennan's moral judgments are not, as it were, free floating but do have a pragmatic justification (even if Brennan himself is unaware of the fact) adds to our understanding of his position.

149. Justice Powell (on pp. 302–3) rejects the analogy of gender. The regents had claimed that, according to past Court decisions, gender discrimination does not call for strict scrutiny.

150. Ronald Dworkin suggests a somewhat different model for construing Justice Brennan's thought: ". . . [I]nstitutional history acts not as a constraint on the political judgment of judges but as an ingredient of that judgment, because institutional history is part of the background that any plausible judgment about the rights of an individual must accommodate. Political rights are creatures of both history and morality: what an individual is entitled to have, in civil society, depends upon both the practice and the justice of its political institutions" (*op. cit.* p. 87). But unless one ascribes to Professor Dworkin the implausible belief (which, as far as I can see, he never states) that judges should cite all relevant political history that does not offend against justice, I find no major difference between his position and mine. He asks us to take the background as, so to speak, built into the structure of political rights; to cite the background is then to cite the law. I am suggesting instead that citing the background is following a practical principle, aimed at carrying out one's deontic objectives; but that hardly prevents some political facts from being principles of law or morals as well. If anything, my emphasis on carrying out normal deontic objectives might provide a necessary test for determining *which* facts from the political background are indeed built into the law. (I am indebted to a reader for Brown University Press for calling Professor Dworkin's position to my attention.)

Justice Brennan appears uneasy with his argument from immutable characteristics. If our society really demands that the state not advance people for factors outside their control, Justice Brennan notes, one would expect legislators to heed that demand. But, he adds, "this is not necessarily so" (361). Justice Brennan's point seems to be that a legislature might properly fail to heed the supposed public demand not to legislate on the basis of immutable characteristics, as long as the legislature is practicing "benign discrimination" in favor of blacks, and as long as the burden of that discrimination falls upon the most "discrete and insular" groups of whites. Justice Brennan adds that no legislature can practice such benign discrimination if doing so infringes anyone's rights under the Fourteenth Amendment. But if legislatures do not, in fact, hesitate to legislate on the basis of immutable characteristics, these considerations are useless in establishing a public demand that they not pass such legislation. At most they show that such a demand is not impossible.[151]

Justice Brennan's conclusion is more convincing than his arguments. He observes, and experience surely bears him out, that there is a "significant risk" that racial classifications, even when intended to be benign, will bring evil effects. Therefore, he concludes, ". . . to justify such a classification an important and articulated purpose for its use must be shown." Justice Brennan, if I understand him rightly, is saying that to suppose that a law's benign purpose will keep it from achieving evil results is to neglect some relevant facts. Bad results have occurred in such situations; therefore someone— namely, the Court—must monitor every such law. This argument has some difficulties, but it is an interesting use of the principle of Factuality.

Justice Powell agrees that a benign purpose is not enough to prevent injustices from occurring. He gives two reasons for reaching this conclusion. In the first place, to construe the Equal Protection Clause as placing no restraints on discrimination as long as that discrimination is benign would be both novel and (according to a footnote on page 295) self-contradictory. On the point of self-contradiction, Justice Powell cites Alexander Bickel's *The Morality of Consent*: "Those for whom

---

151. The "benign discrimination" and "discrete and insular" phrases come from a partially concurring opinion by Justice White in *United Jewish Organizations* v *Carey*, 430 U.S. 144, p. 174. Ronald Dworkin finds no merit in Justice Brennan's argument from immutable characteristics: "This proposition has been decisively rejected throughout American law and politics" (*Law's Empire* [Cambridge, Mass., 1986], 394).

racial equality was demanded are to be more equal than others."[152] Besides the usual call for consistency with precedent, then, Justice Powell is using the Orwellian quotation from Bickel to call for a principle that is self-consistent and that treats all persons alike—a principle, that is, that uses two (by now) familiar pragmatic maxims.

Second, Justice Powell contends: "Moreover, there are serious problems of justice connected with the idea of preference itself." He lists three such problems: that a seemingly benign purpose might not in fact be so; that preferential programs, by reinforcing common myths, can actually retard the progress of a disadvantaged group; and that it is inequitable to make those who did not create injustices to a group bear the burden of remedying those injustices (298). The first two do not particularly seem to be problems of justice, but are problems of understanding and of practicality, respectively. They require at most that one not embark on a program of benign discrimination without first giving the matter due thought.

But the third point is a true problem of justice. Although it receives only a sentence from Justice Powell, he is surely right to call it "serious." In fact, I believe this question of equity is the underlying problem of the *Bakke* case. Is it fair for an innocent party to bear the costs of remedying injustice?

It is Justice Brennan's awareness of this problem of fairness, I believe, that impels him to argue, rather unconvincingly, that Davis's rejection did not stamp Bakke as inferior in any way and will not affect him throughout his life in a way similar to the effect of segregation on black schoolchildren (375). Justice Brennan, that is, believes he must show that Bakke wasn't really damaged by the rejection from the medical school. For Bakke to have been damaged in the quest for advancement of minorities would be unjust. And that injustice is Justice Powell's point.

In raising this issue of justice, Justice Powell is invoking the rule of Proportionality—although as a moral, not a pragmatic, principle. It looks as if Bakke is the victim of a sanction, and there is no justification at all for his being treated in this way. No wonder Justice Brennan thought it necessary to downplay the severity of that sanction. For the less severe the sanction, the smaller the violation of Proportionality.

---

152. Alexander Bickel, *The Morality of Consent* (New Haven and London, 1975), 133. One wonders how seriously Justice Powell really takes the claim of self-contradiction. Would he say that a true self-contradiction in legislation calls only for strict scrutiny? "This legislation is logically absurd, so we should be careful in applying it . . . "?

4. What would suffice, under the Equal Protection Clause, to justify an admissions process that takes account of race?

If there is indeed a presumption against classifying according to race, under what circumstances can that assumption be overcome? Justice Powell finds his answer in previous Court decisions. He quotes from *in re Griffiths*, 413 U.S. 717, 721–722: ". . . to justify the use of a suspect classification, a State must show that its purpose or interest is both constitutionally permissible and substantial, and that its use of the classification is 'necessary. . . to the accomplishment' of its purpose or the safeguarding of its interest" (305). Justice Powell makes no attempt to justify the claim that the presence of these conditions is sufficient to justify a racially based admissions process. Consistency with precedent is enough for him.

Once again, Justice Brennan does more, in providing detail if not justification. He uses a number of precedents to come up with the vague test of an "overriding statutory purpose"—a phrase that itself derives from a previous case, *McLaughlin* v *Florida*. Then he tries to sharpen the test so that one can actually determine in a particular case whether a statutory purpose is overriding or not. Justice Brennan's sharpened test has two prongs: ". . . a state government may adopt race-conscious programs if the purpose of such programs is to remove the disparate racial impact its actions might otherwise have and if there is reason to believe that the disparate impact is itself the product of past discrimination, whether its own or that of society at large" (369).

The first prong of this test is clear enough; but Justice Brennan's own acknowledgment that benign intentions might lead and have led to unjust results proves this part of the test inadequate to justify adoption of a race-conscious program. The second prong of Justice Brennan's test is a tougher matter, both to establish and to justify. Justice Powell, in a footnote on page 269, is appalled: "The breadth of this hypothesis is unprecedented in our constitutional system . . . . Not one word in the record supports this conclusion [i.e., that were there no discrimination in society, minority members would have scored well enough to beat out Bakke for available places in the Davis facility] and the authors of the opinion offer no standard for courts to use in applying such a presumption of causation to other racial or ethnic classifications."[153]

153. Here Justice Powell is clearly engaging in some destructive criticism, but he is not so much destroying the argument Justice Brennan gives as pointing out the absence of any backing for that argument.

Justice Powell is saying the second prong of the Brennan test contains a bad counterfactual. As a piece of judicial legislation, the test is simply inapplicable, or at best one can apply it only in a capricious and inconsistent manner. Justice Brennan should have invoked the rules of Consequences and Minimalism; he would then scrap legislation that leads not to fulfillment of the legislative end but to frustration.

Where does Justice Brennan get his counterfactual test? It appears almost by magic on page 365 in the course of a contention that the Court has held race-conscious remedies for past discrimination to be permissible, whether or not the courts had previously made an official finding of discrimination and whether or not the past discriminatory acts violated the Equal Protection Clause. Justice Brennan claims that the presence or absence of past discrimination by Davis is irrelevant. He adds that "although it might be argued that, where an employer has violated an antidiscrimination law, the expectations of non-minority workers are themselves products of discrimination and hence 'tainted,'" this fact, too, is irrelevant: race-conscious remedies are permissible.

At this point, Justice Brennan introduces the second prong of his test: "If it was reasonable to conclude—as we hold that it was—that the failure of minorities to qualify for admission at Davis under regular procedures was due principally to the effects of past discrimination, than [sic] there is a reasonable likelihood that, but for pervasive racial discrimination, respondent would have failed to qualify for admission even in the absence of Davis' special admissions program" (365–66).

I find it hard to discover any principles of pragmatics that Justice Brennan has used in arguing for the second prong of his test, for I find it hard to discover any argument at all for that counterfactual! Appearing as it does at the end of a paragraph devoted to a quite different matter, the test appears an utter *non sequitur,* and its application to Bakke's situation cries in vain for substantiation. And this is quite apart from the fact that, as Justice Powell complains, the test is probably unworkable, anyway.

Hence, Justice Brennan's answer to this fourth question, although initially much more detailed and promising than that of Justice Powell, ends in severe disappointment.[154]

154. For much the same reason I find Ronald Dworkin's method of settling the *Bakke* case disappointing. In *Law's Empire (op. cit.)* Dworkin argues: "Racial discrimination that disadvantages blacks is unjust, not because people cannot choose their race, but because that discrimination expresses prejudice" (p. 395). Dworkin assumes only that discrimination sprang, perhaps many years ago, from prejudice, not that those who profit from discrimination today must themselves be prejudiced. His argument is dubious for several reasons. First, not every fruit of an evil tree is poisoned. Prejudice

5. Is there a purpose that fulfills the tests given in question 4 and that could help justify an admissions program that takes account of race?

What purpose might an admissions program have to allow it to take account of race? According to Justice Brennan, it is enough for a school to discriminate in admissions if its goal is to help remedy the effects of past societal discrimination (362). There need not be past discrimination by the school itself.

Justice Brennan's reading of various school desegregation decisions by the Court leads him to conclude that the mere elimination of discrimination, provided that such discrimination is substantial, harmful, and chronic, is "a compelling social goal justifying the overt use of race." The word 'compelling' suggests that Justice Brennan regards such a goal as overriding all sorts of other interests and considerations. (An interesting question, which he does not discuss, is whether there are any individual rights that this goal would not override.)

Justice Brennan's argument is primarily one of consistency with precedents. He must show that many of these precedents really do apply to the *Bakke* case, for some of them are dubious. For example, in many of the cases Justice Brennan cites, there had been a previous judicial finding of discrimination against the group seeking to apply a race-conscious remedy; there had been no such finding against the University of California regents. Justice Brennan contends that to require a judicial finding of discrimination as a prerequisite for allowing a race-conscious remedy would be self-defeating, for it "would severely undermine efforts to achieve voluntary compliance with the requirements of law" (364). He seems here to be calling upon the rules of Consequences and perhaps of Legislative Economy and Minimalism.

If we turn next to Justice Powell's answer to this fifth question, we find him employing a far subtler and more complex analysis than he has given up to this point. Justice Powell finds five candidates

---

that occurred many years ago has had many effects, and we cannot assume that they are all bad. Second, Dworkin needs to make a counterfactual claim little better than that of Justice Brennan: that had earlier Americans not been prejudiced, specific cases of discrimination would not exist today. At least, Dworkin would have difficulty showing that benign discrimination disadvantaging blacks, if there is such a thing, could only have resulted from prejudice. Third, Dworkin's theory applies to the *Bakke* case only if the discrimination that disadvantaged Allan Bakke was itself not the result of prejudice. I don't know how to show that. Deeds often reveal motives, but they don't so easily reveal the absence of certain motives.

for the role of a constitutionally permissible and substantial purpose achievable only through procedures taking overt account of race (306 and footnotes). The first of these five, Justice Powell himself brings forward as a possible consideration in some cases, while the other four were argued by counsel for the regents.

Justice Powell suggests that one purpose for a color-conscious admissions program might be to make up the defects of culturally biased testing or grading procedures (306, footnotes). This purpose is a sort of appeal to general considerations of fairness and equity, and in providing it, Justice Powell is effectively invoking the rule of Judicial Equity. He is providing a method by which a group hitherto without redress for a certain evil, can find that redress. Justice Powell adds that such a means for redress is not present in the case of Allan Bakke. For nothing supports the notion that the purpose of the Davis program was to account for culturally biased procedures. As Justice Powell remarks, if this had been Davis's purpose, there would be no point in setting aside precisely sixteen seats for minority members. The school would then have violated Minimalism and Legislative Economy (306, footnote).

Counsel for the regents had suggested that Davis's purposes were: to help eliminate the traditional underrepresentation of some minority groups in medical schools and the medical profession; to counter the effects of societal discrimination; to provide more physicians for communities that in the past have lacked adequate medical care; and to give Davis the benefits of an ethnically diverse student body (306). Justice Powell takes these up in turn.

First, Justice Powell insists that the goal of gaining a certain percentage of minority students simply because they are minority members is "discrimination for its own sake" and impermissible under the Constitution (307). Here I think he badly overstates his case. For adding minority members is a different goal from subtracting majority members, even though the one entails the other in a nongrowing student body. It was not, in the language of the Principle of Double Effect, the goal of the Davis facility to discriminate against whites. That discrimination was only a foreseen but unintended consequence of Davis's action. Therefore, there was no discrimination for its own sake, if that phrase has anything like its normal meaning.

When he turns to the purpose of eliminating the baneful effects of past societal discrimination, Justice Powell is again severe. He stigmatizes "societal discrimination" as an "amorphous concept of injury that may be ageless in its reach into the past" (307). He contends that the Court in the past has stepped in only when there have been findings of specific violations of the Constitution or of the positive law. But Justice Powell does not merely cite precedent to make his case against using race-conscious admissions procedures to help remedy past societal discrimination. The crucial sentence (308–09) in his disagreement with Justice Brennan on this critical point is: "Without such findings of constitutional or statutory violations, it cannot be said that the government has any greater interest in helping one individual than in refraining from harming another." Justice Powell appeals here not to precedents but to justice. More particularly, he invokes the principle of Proportionality, for he argues in effect that there is no justification for the sanctions that are to fall on certain majority members. Justice Powell is also implicitly appealing to the principle of Universalizability, for he holds that like cases, or at least cases that have not been shown to be unlike, will be treated differently if the government helps one person at another's expense.[155]

I will ignore the sharp battle of footnotes over whether any or all of Justice Brennan's precedents are relevant. Instead, I turn to Justice Powell's disposal of the next goal: increasing the number of physicians in areas that have lacked adequate medical care. Justice Powell allows that this might be a compelling reason for allowing race-conscious procedures, but his admission is tentative and of little effect. For he argues, following the lead of the California court, that there is no reason to think that the Davis admissions program will meet this goal, much less that it is the best or only available means for doing so (310–11). The Davis rule might adhere to Legislative Factuality and Legislative Economy, but the regents need to prove that it does.

Finally, Justice Powell considers the one stated goal of the University that, he thinks, might provide the sort of purpose needed to justify a racially conscious program. This goal implies that the presence of an ethnically diverse student body in a university yields certain genuine benefits. If this goal is indeed a permissible interest for a university, Justice Powell believes, then it is a matter of academic freedom and hence of First Amendment rights for such an interest to be constitutionally protected (311–315).

Justice Powell cites a 1967 case, *Keyishian* v *Board of Regents* to emphasize that "academic freedom . . . is of transcendent value to all

---

155. It is no contradiction to say that, in appealing to Universalizability and to Proportionality, Justice Powell is appealing to principles of justice; for although these are maxims of deontic pragmatics, as I have shown, they are also important principles of justice. For the relation between deontic pragmatics and ethics, see chapter 14.

of us . . . [and] is therefore a special concern of the First Amendment"
(312). The quotation from *Keyishian* explains this "transcendent value"
as stemming from the nation's need for leaders "trained through wide
exposure to that robust exchange of ideas which discovers truth 'out of
a multitude of tongues, [rather] than through any kind of authoritative
selection.' "[156]

But even if safeguarding academic freedom is an overriding
national purpose, Justice Powell insists, the regents must show two
more things: that an ethnically diverse student body is a factor in producing a "robust exchange of ideas"; and that such a robust exchange
promotes academic freedom. Otherwise, the Davis program violates
Minimalism, Legislative Economy, and perhaps even Straightforwardness.

Justice Powell undertakes to make the regents' case for them, but
he provides little evidence to back up that case. He says (312–13)
that "a diverse student body" is widely believed to promote an excit-
ing academic atmosphere, and he quotes the president of Princeton
University as claiming that such diversity might be a powerful source
of "improved understanding and personal growth." He provides no
further evidence, and what he provides is not enough.[157] I am afraid
that, at a crucial point, Justice Powell's opinion runs a strong risk of
offending against the maxim of Factuality.

6. Does a program such as the Davis one, in which race is the sole
factor, meet the tests of question 4?

Justices Powell and Brennan have now set up the general machinery by which each will reach a conclusion about the legality of Davis's
admissions procedure. If some goal overrides the presumption against
race-conscious policies, may the University of California set aside six-

---

156. *Keyishian* v *Board of Regents*, 385 U.S. 589 (1967), p. 603. I do not find it obvious
how the national purpose of training leaders is connected to the guarantees of the First
Amendment; nor does Justice Powell pursue the point.

157. President Bowen of Princeton claimed that it is good to have a student body diverse
in many ways. Even if he is right, it might not be good to promote a particular sort of
diversity—such as ethnic diversity. Further, many of the past leaders of this country
were trained among others of their race, sex, and cultural background. There is no strong
evidence that they lost out on something educationally important by their training.
Finally, as one who tried to teach philosophy at Columbia during the upheavals of
the late 1960s and early 1970s, I doubt that every robust exchange of ideas promotes
academic freedom.

teen seats in the Davis medical school for ethnic minority members in order to reach that goal?

For Justice Brennan, the answer is clearly yes. We have seen him propose a two-pronged test: ". . . a state government may adopt race-conscious programs if the purpose of such programs is to remove the disparate racial impact its actions might otherwise have and if there is reason to believe that the disparate impact is itself the product of past discrimination, whether its own or that of society at large" (369). Justice Brennan claims that Davis's program unquestionably meets this test. That past discrimination has indeed been a factor in the underrepresentation of minority groups in the practice of medicine is unquestionable, and Justice Brennan cites some significant data to bolster the point.

The second prong of the test, as Justice Brennan applies it to the specific case in question, is "whether the Davis program stigmatizes any discrete group or individual and whether race is reasonably used in light of the program's objectives" (373). The second clause here, with its standard of "reasonable use," is far more permissive than Justice Powell's requirement that the means toward an acceptable goal be shown essential for achieving that goal. Justice Brennan finds that the Davis admissions program satisfies the "reasonable use" test (373–74). The Davis procedure does not stigmatize either whites as a group or Bakke as a person, it does not clearly hurt the minority groups it is intended to help, it seems well adapted to fulfilling its goals—more so than at least one alternative (376–78)—and it follows an acceptable procedure in setting aside a specific number of seats for minority members.

As far as I can determine, Justice Brennan does not apply his counterfactual test: whether, if there had been no discrimination, past or present, and no affirmative action, Bakke would not have been admitted to Davis. Had Justice Brennan done so, as Justice Powell comments, he would have had a hard task establishing just what would have happened in a situation so different from that of the real world. As a result, Justice Brennan has no trouble finding that the Davis program meets his test; of course, he implicitly drops a crucial part of the test from its first appearance (on 365–66). While following the maxim of Use of General Rules, then, Justice Brennan leaves one rule out.

Justice Powell also seeks to decide this case by subsuming it under a general rule. But Justice Powell, as we have seen, does not allow race-conscious admissions procedures with the broad goal of helping erase the effects of past societal discrimination. The only acceptable goal he finds is the much narrower aim of achieving a diverse student body, and he believes the means toward that goal must be not merely reasonable but necessary. It is no surprise that the Davis program, which overcame the Brennan low hurdles with ease, trips on these high hurdles.

Justice Powell suggests that the minority quota used by Davis, by keeping groups of students from competing with one another for seats, actually works against genuine diversity (315). That is dubious sociology. Regardless, one can hardly suppose a program such as Davis's to be a necessary means toward the kind of overall diversity Justice Powell is seeking. So Davis's program flunks the "necessary means" test.

Justice Powell goes on to suggest that other programs, which try to achieve genuine diversity by considering race as one factor in admissions, might be acceptable (although they hardly seem to be *necessary* means to his end). He cites Harvard as an illustration. But Justice Powell does not even attempt to show that the Harvard way is necessary to achieve the Harvard purpose.

Justice Powell is clearly apprehensive that someone might accuse him of failing to treat like cases alike, as the rule of Universalizability requires, for Justice Powell wonders aloud whether an admissions program such as Harvard's is simply a more subtle and sophisticated version of the one at Davis. Both programs make some admissions decisions on the basis of the applicant's race. A person who is turned down from Harvard College might not even know that his race is responsible for someone else's being accepted instead of him.[158] At least Bakke knew why he was turned down! The moral and legal status of the Harvard program are not above question.

Justice Powell's answer to the charge of failing to treat like cases alike (318) is that the Davis program shows a "facial intent to discriminate." "No such facial infirmity exists in an admissions program where race or ethnic background is simply one element—to be weighed fairly against other elements—in the selection process." And so the cases are not alike, after all.

But that answer by no means disposes of the problem. A facial infirmity is presumably one that is obvious, present on the very face of the program. Now if an intent to discriminate is present in the

---

158. Justice Brennan makes this point on page 379. This is one instance in which one justice succeeds in putting forward a useful criticism of another justice's position.

Harvard program, why should it matter that the intent is not obvious? An intent is no less right or wrong for its being concealed. More important, Justice Powell simply assumes there is a method of fairly weighing a candidate's race against other factors. But how can one possibly assign a weight to race and call it the fair weight? As Justice Brennan noted, a person cannot change his race, but he can change the breadth of his experience prior to application for a college program. Is it fair to count mutable factors more heavily than immutable ones, or vice versa? If we sound egalitarian and count them all the same, we are at best succumbing to a vague republicanism and treating factors as if they were persons, to be given equal justice under the law.

Justice Powell, then, is far from showing that the Harvard program has virtues that make it acceptable where the Davis one is unacceptable. But the important aspect of his conclusion is not his embracing of the Harvard program in particular, but his willingness to allow that some program might, by providing a necessary means to a genuinely diverse student body, be acceptable, even if it considers the candidate's race a factor. The test is a severe one, but it can be met.

This concludes my look at the *Bakke* decision. We have seen the justices use a number of the principles of deontic pragmatics, individually and together. More than once, their use of the same principles, working on the same laws and precedents, has led them to radically diverse conclusions. This should come as no surprise. To use a principle of reasoning is not necessarily to reason well, any more than to cite a precedent is to use it properly. But the *Bakke* decision shows that when we do attempt to talk intelligently and reasonably about deontic matters, pragmatic principles are always in play.

12 When Rules Conflict

H. P. Grice tells us that in a conversation we should provide the information required. Robin Lakoff tells us that in a conversation we should be polite. And Jane Austen tells us: "Marianne was silent; it was impossible for her to say what she did not feel, however trivial the occasion; and upon [her sister] Elinor, therefore, the whole task of telling lies when politeness required it always fell.[159]

Like so many passages in Jane Austen's novels, this one is not exactly free from ambiguity. To be sure, the author seems to be endorsing Elinor's position that politeness must at times take precedence over truth-telling, but the word 'lies'

159. *Sense and Sensibility* (London, 1811), chap. 21.

is a bald one. I am sure Elinor herself would not have used that term to describe her polite little fictions. Jane Austen could be suggesting that Marianne's side in this difference between sisters is anything but despicable.[160]

The rules of pragmatics can yield conflicting advice, and well-meaning people often disagree over which rule should take precedence in a given situation. In the conflict between telling the truth and being polite, most of us keep a foot in both camps. I suppose that, most of the time, I tell polite lies, with Elinor, but I think I feel rather more guilty doing so than she does. And at other times, when the lie is too egregious, I expect I do, with Marianne, take refuge in silence, change the subject, or blurt out the truth. How do I, and how should I, decide which course of action a given situation calls for?

In the constant conflict between the demands of politeness and those of truth-telling, cases in which one side is clearly superior do occur, but they are relatively uncommon. The considerations that enter into our determinations of what to do are matters of degree: How harmful will the truth be? How transparent will an evasion seem? How great a departure from the truth is required? How important is the matter? How harmful will the exposure of my lies be to others and to myself? These are only some of the many factors involved, and none seems to admit of a precise answer. It is no wonder that these considerations rarely lead to a clearly marked course of action.

We could apply Durkheim's remarks on a similar calculus:

> Now these utilitarian calculations, though they be exact, are too intel-ligently contrived to have had any great effect upon the will; the elements are too many, and the relations uniting them too confused. To hold them all united in awareness and in the wished-for order, all our available energy is necessary, and there would be none left for action. That is why, as long as interest is not immediate and apparent, it is too feebly felt to set activity in motion.[161]

Durkheim is surely right about the phenomenon, even though his quasi-mechanistic explanation is open to doubt. We do not usually go

160. D. W. Harding points to a number of cases in which Jane Austen quietly drops a subversive word or phrase into a seemingly innocuous context. See his "Regulated Hatred: An Aspect of the Work of Jane Austen," *Scrutiny* 8 (1940): 346–62; reprinted in Ian Watt, ed., *Jane Austen: A Collection of Critical Essays* (Englewood Cliffs, N.J., 1963), 166–79.

161. Émile Durkheim, *The Division of Labor in Society*, trans. George Simpson (with a slight emendation) (New York, 1933), 417.

through elaborate calculations of utility but tend to follow our interests only when those interests are clear. The same seems to be true in any conflict between telling the truth and being polite. Even if we could by an elaborate calculation weigh all the factors in a particular case to determine what to do, no one is likely to make such a calculation, much less act upon it. Unless some factor stands out very clearly, habit and the path of least resistance are likely to be our guides.

To say that we don't go through an elaborate process of calculation is, of course, not to say that we should not do so. But if the arithmetic is complex and the factors nebulous, there seems little point in asserting a duty to act in accordance with what calculation reveals to be the best course of action, unless that duty is mandated by the rules of the particular moral or legal code to which one subscribes.

I expect Elinor did not even think twice about most of her social lies. When she first meets her future brother-in-law, he rattles on and on. "Elinor agreed to it all, for she did not think he deserved the compliment of rational opposition." More lies from Elinor, with no evidence of compunction.[162] Marianne would have been shocked; but then, Marianne in a similar situation would have been just as much a creature of her own habit.

When the rules of pragmatics conflict in particular situations, then, we should not expect to be able to determine how people either will or should react—unless one element or another is remarkably clear-cut and important. Nevertheless, it is significant that there are clear-cut cases. There are times when only a Kant would dogmatically refuse to lie from altruistic motives, and there are occasions when only a habitual liar would think that politeness requires a falsehood.

We therefore need to consider two important questions: "What principle or principles make a case clear-cut?" and, "Can any such principle, once known, help us settle, in a satisfactory manner, cases that are not clear-cut?"

The clue to answering the first of these questions comes from the fact that the rules of pragmatics arise from speaking to some purpose. If one wishes to inform, one generally follows Grice's rules; if one wishes to be polite, one generally follows Lakoff's rules; and if one wishes to affect people's actions in a certain way, one generally follows the eighteen rules of deontic pragmatics. When conflicts between pragmatic principles occur, we should expect to settle them, if we can

162. Jane Austen, *op. cit.*, chapter 36.

do so at all, by looking to the goal or goals a given speech act is meant to achieve.[163]

The simplest conflicts are those in which two rules from the same branch of pragmatics give different advice. For in such cases, the ultimate goal is often the same, whichever rule one decides to follow. The question is therefore which of the two rules will, in a particular case, be most likely to produce that ultimate goal. If the primary goal of deontic speech is to affect people's actions in a certain way, then when the rules of deontic pragmatics conflict, one should consider which course of action is most likely to have the desired effect. Sometimes the choice of the more effective course of action is obvious. When it is, the case is clear-cut.

The rule of Judicial Review, for example, asks us to impute or accept particular obligations only when those obligations are imposed in accordance with general rules that are consistent, clear, applicable, simple, modest, universalizable, and proportional. That sounds marvelous, but rules that meet those high standards are not always to be found. When the only legislation available to decide a case contains material flaws, should we use it in making our decision? The principle of Use of General Rules insists that we should, the principle of Judicial Review that we should not. Two principles of deontic pragmatics thus conflict.

What should we do in such a situation? That depends on how flawed the legislation in question is, as well as on the precise nature of the situation itself. If the trumpet gives an uncertain sound, many factors determine whether we should troop to the colors. But if the legislation is so bad that its application would be of no use in affecting people's behavior in the desired manner, applying it would be a foolish legalism. On the other hand, should the flaws be relatively minor and the goal to be achieved important, it is equally foolish to refuse to apply the legislation.

The sort of case that immediately comes to mind when I think of such conflicts involves the Exclusionary Rule for evidence in a criminal trial. Suppose important evidence has been gathered in a way that is tainted. Should the judge throw out that evidence along with any further evidence that might have resulted from the tainted procedures? Legally, these questions are still very much up in the air. But is there a common-sense answer?

---

163. This way of resolving conflicts was pointed out to me by Mary Gore Forrester.

I believe that, on some occasions, there is. Suppose that the crime was grave and the taint minor. For example, police in good faith used a wrongly dated search warrant to discover solid evidence of responsibility for a terrorist bombing that killed many innocent people. It hardly seems sensible to ban such evidence. On the other hand, the use of Gestapo methods to produce evidence is rarely, if ever, permissible. These cases are clear-cut, I suggest, if the judge considers her goal in determining them. Suppose her goal is the public good. Surely that good is not well served by allowing vicious criminals to go loose on a technicality, any more than it is well served by allowing the police to use torture on suspects.[164]

But although there are, I believe, cases in which evidence clearly should or should not be excluded, the situation is usually not so clear-cut. Some people have argued for "good faith" exceptions to the Exclusionary Rule, but faith is rarely clearly good or clearly bad. If the police use a faulty procedure, they usually could have done better; and the fault in the procedure is often material in producing the evidence. On the other hand, the gravity of the charge may make some irregularities of procedure excusable up to a point, but what is that point, and which are the irregularities? Surely Star Chamber methods are out, but that still leaves a great deal of latitude to the judge.

We may draw the same conclusions from other clashes of the eighteen maxims. For example, in my examination of the *Bakke* decision, I found members of the Court constantly invoking the eighteen maxims to support diametrically opposed conclusions. Presumably, the justices all had the same overall goal of meting out equal justice under the law, but that goal did not point the way to a clear-cut solution.

Also, legislators can face a choice of ways of attaining their goals. One proposed bit of legislation might sacrifice something of proportionality, while another might give up a measure of economy. In such an instance, about all that is clear is that whatever principle a legislator sacrifices, she had better not give up too much, or the goal will not be worth attaining. That consideration will help with some, but not many, decisions.

For another type of example, consider a typical conflict among judicial rules—the classic problem of the ethics of research. Should researchers be held liable for false results, even when the work leading

164. Of course, if the Exclusionary Rule or some substitute is in force in the judge's jurisdiction, and a ruling that denies the force of that rule will therefore be overturned on appeal, the judge must remember that she has no duty to be ineffective. But even an overturned ruling can have propaganda value.

to those results was properly and conscientiously done? Do researchers have a duty to uncover the truth? The rule of Judicial Factuality says that they do, while the rule of Judicial Publicity says they do not. In the event that one tries to codify the ethics of research into rules, Legislative Factuality and Publicity would conflict. The goal of all, let us suppose, is that research be well and properly done, but when there is a conflict it is rarely clear which rule to follow to achieve that goal.

In this matter, much depends on the greatness of the error relative to the level of research, on the accuracy of any equipment used, and on the use to which the results are to be put. A physician who in good faith announces what turns out to be a worthless cure for a given disease could have had his research plagued by improbable coincidences. Surely the unpleasantness and danger of the disease and the difficulty of coming to grips with it will be factors in any decision about whether the physician deserves censure. The goal of insuring good research is hardly sufficient to determine that decision in more than a very few cases.

Until now, I have been supposing that, in a conflict between two principles of deontic pragmatics, a person has a single goal. That is not always the case. By choosing which conflicting principle to follow, you might also be choosing which way you will try to affect people's behavior as well as the ultimate purpose of that behavior. For example, a researcher might not be interested in whether her research is well and properly done. She might care only about the comforts her position brings her. That need not mean she is a poor researcher, of course. Likewise, a person judging the case of any researcher who innocently came up with false results might have other motives for his decision besides a concern that research be well done. He might decide from pity or perhaps jealousy.

When each conflicting deontic principle carries its own goal or goals, clear-cut cases are even less likely to occur. Now you must weigh not only means but goals to reach a decision. Even if you are able to calculate which action you will take in a particular case, that does not necessarily help you determine which action you should take. One goal might be more desired but less desirable than another.

When the principles of deontic pragmatics conflict, therefore, we may conclude that people do well to take into account the goal or goals they hope to accomplish in making their speech acts. But rarely does this consideration of goals allow them to decide what they either will or should do. To regard the problem of the ethics of research as a conflict among pragmatic principles is to take one step, but only a step, toward solving the problem. One might even argue that the likelihood of a general solution is more remote than ever, because we can now see that there is good deontic justification for both sides in the controversy.

To put the point another way: The eighteen maxims, by spelling out the meaning of deontic rationality, give the people who employ them a way of justifying their deontic speech. When those rules conflict in a particular case, each side has some justification, just as the attitudes of Elinor and Marianne are both perfectly defensible. Only in clear-cut cases in which one goal or one means is clearly preferable to any alternatives is it obvious which justification is the stronger. But when the choice of either goals or means is not obvious, the maxims of deontic pragmatics provide little help in making or justifying a particular choice. The student of deontic pragmatics might gain knowledge of the nature of the conflict between maxims but is no better able to resolve that conflict.

There are even fewer clear-cut cases when the rules of deontic pragmatics clash with rules from other branches of pragmatics, for in such conflicts, the overall goals of the possible actions are diverse. The goals must form a mixed lot, because the aims of informative speech acts, polite speech acts, deontic speech acts, and all the other types of speech acts that give rise to the branches of pragmatics are themselves distinct.

It is easy to imagine situations where a person has a choice between making a deontic speech that expresses what the speaker believes to be the truth and making a speech that, instead, follows the rule of Theoretical Virtue. The person might believe that only an unclear, immodest rule, inconsistent with the others, can point out what should be done in the situation. As an example, consider how most people would act in the type of conflict that arose between Elinor and Marianne. There are certainly times when the goal of telling the truth does and clearly should outweigh the goal of influencing people to act in a certain way. Likewise, there are times when the situation is the reverse and only a fanatic would oppose telling an effective white lie. In such cases, one's course is obvious. But they are the exceptions.

In the average case, I suspect most people do well to choose the marginally better course of action, in full knowledge that one's perception of what seems better is deeply colored by habit. Can we regard this observation as a meta-rule? If so, it surely offends against Theoretical Virtue, for it is not very clear, not very consistent with our deontic pragmatic maxims, and above all not very easy to apply. Yet, this meta-rule seems to capture the truth about the Elinor–Marianne dilemma. My duty to set out the truth here clashes with my duty to make my deontic speech (in this case, my deontic meta-speech) accord with theoretical virtue.

We can find a less fancy and more common example of conflict between the principles of conversational pragmatics and those of deontic pragmatics in people's attitudes toward beggars. Imagine a person confronted by a group of beggars asking for help. He genuinely believes he has a duty to assist these people, who are clearly ill fed and inadequately clothed. But he thinks he should not extend charity to all beggars, even to all ill-fed and inadequately clothed beggars, on the grounds that doing so will be harmful to society in the long run. My prospective philanthropist honestly believes it is his duty in the present case to act in a way he could not universalize. Is the speech, "You should feed and clothe these beggars," one to which he should assent or not? Judicial Review, making use of Universalizability, provides one answer; the rule of truth-telling gives another. It is hard to see how weighing the goal of conversation against that of deontic speech will help resolve the philanthropist's dilemma.

Likewise, the maxims of deontic pragmatics can clash with those of politeness. Universalizability presents an obvious sort of example: it is not always polite to remind a person that, from the point of view of deontic considerations, he counts the same as everybody else. Especially in this country at this time, when we are bombarded by messages from sources as diverse as Mr. Rogers and the latest pop-psychology manual, all calling on us to celebrate our own uniqueness, it seems downright rude for someone to insist on treating everyone alike.

For that matter, "laying down the law" is itself often thought to be most impolite. I could give the widest publicity possible to some excellent deontic legislation and be thoroughly out of turn in doing so. In a friendly game of Monopoly, we all know what to think of the player who has the rules at his fingertips! Which is more offensive: the young punter who did not know the rules of the river, or the skillful, arrogant, and titled detective who loudly upbraided him?

To be sure, there are occasions when the goal of affecting behavior is so important that nobody thinks politeness should get in the way. When a legislator has a choice between a law that treats all alike and a law that politely caters to the prejudices of a privileged class, the proper decision is rarely in doubt. But once again, such occasions are exceptional.

So, sometimes one should say what one thinks, at other times one should say what is universalizable or theoretically virtuous. Sometimes one should be polite, at other times one should give publicity to universalizable legislation. What one should do in a particular case is often obvious and often not. Knowing when to quote the rules is often far more important and difficult to achieve than knowing the rules themselves.

When the eighteen maxims conflict with the principles of other branches of pragmatics, therefore, one should try to compare the goals of each projected speech act. But rarely will this process give more than marginal assistance in determining the proper outcome.

Sometimes principles of deontic pragmatics conflict with rules whose adoption is not intended to serve some purpose. For example, a person might decide to tell the truth at all times, quite apart from any consideration of the consequences of that decision. She might think that truth-telling is simply and obviously right, or that God or nature commands truth-telling. She might tell the truth in a particular case out of habit, or even out of a sort of weakness of will. When the maxims of deontic pragmatics conflict with any non-goal-directed rules, it is hard to see how the cases can be clear-cut. One projected action has a goal, but another does not, so one can hardly compare goals. And a rule that is not goal-directed need not override all others; even if it does, that does not help decide which course of action is proper.

Consideration of means and goals therefore is of real help in a conflict between maxims of deontic pragmatics whenever there is a single goal involved. When there is more than one goal, however, or when the eighteen maxims conflict with other pragmatic maxims, there is less point to considering means and goals. And when the conflict is with non-goal-directed rules, searching for comparisons— perhaps by treating those rules as if they are aimed at some goal—is futile.

Perhaps we can find some other meta-rules, along with that of weighing goals and means, to help resolve conflict situations. One candidate is the following: When one possible action has clear advantages over other choices with respect to one or more rule of pragmatics, and when none of the other choices has a clear advantage over that action with respect to any rule of pragmatics, one should choose that action. This meta-rule seems acceptable, but trivial. If I can tell the truth without any breach of politeness, I should no doubt do so. But the meta-rule in no way helps me in a conflict between truth-telling and politeness.

A more likely candidate for a meta-rule emerges from a closer look at the clear-cut cases. For example, we might discover that all such cases are settled in accordance with a certain kind of principle—in particular, with a moral principle.[165] But the rules I can distill from clear cases are neither very useful in solving conflicts nor particularly moral. Let me list three such meta-rules:

1. A minor violation of one principle, generally speaking, is better than a major violation of another.
2. It is better to violate one principle than more than one, other things being equal.
3. If one can gain a clear advantage by adhering to Rule A without incurring any disadvantage that one could avoid by adhering to Rule B instead, one should adhere to A.

Such rules could wear a moral aspect when the conflict is exclusively a moral one. When the conflict is prudential or political, however, I see no grounds for saying that a settlement in accordance with such principles is morally praiseworthy.

This point can be clarified by looking once more at the type of case where one has the choice of applying either a rule whose manner of adoption is flawed or a rule whose matter violates our maxims. Suppose one has the option either of subsuming a particular event under a rule whose manner is slightly flawed or of subsuming it under a rule whose matter is greatly flawed. The choice in favor of the rule with the imperfect manner is obvious, and the principle by which I made the choice equally obvious.

But what kind of principle allowed me to make the choice? That, I contend, depends entirely on the kind of conflict; and, until now, I have not said anything to specify just what sorts of rules are conflicting in my example. Well, I was presenting a problem in etiquette. I have a choice of ways to set the lunch table: one that applies a rule issued in the slightly irregular way; the other that uses a rule that is massively complex and unclear. No doubt, I will choose to apply the former rule. But is it morally proper to do so? Morality seems beside the point.

When one option has the advantage of being more moral and another of being more practical, it is still harder to characterize the principles on which we decide clear-cut cases. One rule, let us say, works a minor violation of the maxim of Proportionality and thus

165. This possibility was suggested to me by Mary Gore Forrester.

proves slightly unjust to some people. The alternative works no injustice, but its adoption requires a massive violation of Straightforwardness, to the obvious practical detriment of all legislation. I expect most of us would opt for the rule working the slight injustice, on the principle that a minor violation is preferable to a major one. But is this principle a moral one, a prudential one, or what? Neither, it would seem—only a mere matter of ordinary common sense, very hard to justify.

Even if we cannot characterize the principles by which we decide clear-cut cases, that hardly means they must be useless. Perhaps we can derive meta-rules, whatever their nature, that will help with difficult problems. Unfortunately, any meta-rules I have found simply don't help in the hard cases. It does no good, for example, to know when one is faced with a choice between two major violations that one should prefer a minor violation to a major violation. In such a situation, if one applies rules at all, they can only be the substantive rules of a given deontic system.[166]

That reference to substantive rules brings up a most important point. I do not mean to suggest that when my eighteen maxims conflict with each other or with other principles, we have no way to resolve the conflict or to resolve it properly. Indeed, we do usually have some method of resolution available. But that method of resolution is rarely a matter of simply understanding and applying meta-rules that have no connection with any particular system of ethics, law, or the like. Unless the case is very clear-cut indeed, our resolution of it usually makes some use of substantive principles.

The ancient Persians might, for example, have chosen to value truth-telling over politeness. But if they did not make the value of truth-telling absolute or that of politeness nonexistent, conflicts would have occurred. The Persians would have resolved those conflicts in accordance with their substantive principles of evaluation. And I can find nothing in the neutral ground of pragmatics to approve or disapprove their resolutions.

There are, of course, various theories of rational conflict-resolution that claim not to depend upon substantive principles. Such theories must do no violence to the data they try to explain, however. In particular, the rules that apply in clear-cut cases are surely among those that, on any reasonable scheme, should apply. No acceptable theory

---

166. Bernard Rollin made this point in a question period following a speech that he made in 1985.

throws out the principle of preferring minor to major violations, for example. Now if we cannot specify that the principle of preferring minor violations is moral, can we discover even the meaning of the word 'should' in the claim that we should employ that principle? Even more important, if we cannot apply this obvious rule to conflict situations, do we have any reason to suppose that less obvious rules will be any more applicable? I think not.

Consider the egalitarian theory that each principle should count equally in a decision. From this principle, we could derive our preference for a minor over a major violation, as well as our preference for a single violation over a multiple one. But the egalitarian theory runs foul of the fact that the importance of pragmatic rules is not a constant but varies with the type of situation. In etiquette, for example, the rule of Distribution plays very little role, whereas in law its role is major. Further, we find that the importance of Judicial Factuality varies with the severity of the sanction involved. In a capital case, it is surely the most important constraint, whereas in a lesser case, other considerations often take precedence. Vary the circumstances and different maxims come to the fore.

That, again, is only how things are, not necessarily how they should be. I have not demonstrated that we should not be egalitarian with respect to our maxims, only that we are not. But if I am right, the burden of proof falls on the egalitarian, who must show that our practice is wrong. And, as I have suggested, it is hard to think of any sense of 'wrong' that will cover the case, for the principles of decision making do not seem to be exclusively moral, prudential, or anything else.

I conclude that the prospects for rational resolution of a conflict between a principle of deontic pragmatics and some other rule, a resolution that makes no use of substantive principles, are fairly dim. I have tried to show when there are clear-cut cases, and how these arise, but such cases offer little help in dealing with the vast majority of conflicts.

This conclusion is neither original nor surprising.[167] The belief that, when genuine problems arise in an object study, meta-theory can step in and settle the dispute is at best moribund. Meta-theory can help us see when a dispute is not genuine, and it can help clarify the positions of the disputants, but its practical use ends there.

---

167. However, it is often worth putting out a considerable amount of effort, only to determine that one will not be surprised!

My conclusions might strike some as altogether too gloomy. Indeed, I could be trying so hard to avoid making excessive claims for deontic pragmatics that I end up seriously understating my own case. But I do not think so. To call the maxims that come into conflict pragmatic is, I think, valuable and revealing, and I will have more to say on that subject in the next chapter. But the study of deontic pragmatics teaches us little more than what we already know about solving genuine conflicts.

13 Pragmatics versus Logic

The eighteen maxims I have discussed in this book are, I believe, basic principles of the pragmatics of deontic language. They therefore form no part of the meaning or the logic of deontic statements. In this chapter, I shall explain why I think such a classification of the eighteen rules is useful and justified. The chapter takes up two related questions. First, does it really make any difference whether we classify the eighteen maxims as part of deontic pragmatics or part of deontic logic? And second, can we apply tests to discover which classification is correct, and if so, what are the test results? We will look at these questions in turn.

WHAT'S THE DIFFERENCE?

I doubt whether any reader will suffer from the suspense evoked by my first question. If I didn't believe it made a difference for us to classify the eighteen maxims under pragmatics rather than logic, I would have had no reason to write this book. And if you hadn't suspected I might be right, you wouldn't have read this far. But belief and suspicion are not enough. We need to see just what difference it does make if we classify the maxims one way rather than another.

At the outset, I need to make clear that the reader can expect no logically airtight arguments from this chapter. If you choose to regard the eighteen maxims or any subgroup of them as part of the logic or the semantics of deontic sentences, your position is logically consistent—but so is the belief that the sun revolves around the earth. To defend my position, all I can do is show that, based on present evidence, the best theory of deontic speech acts places the eighteen maxims in with the pragmatics of those acts. For the dividing line between pragmatics and semantics is not a clear one, nor is it always easy to find. Particular items shift across the fuzzy border, so that what appeared a pragmatic matter at one time might just as clearly seem logical at another.

The ways in which such shifts are accomplished are complex. People have tried to derive the meanings of terms from what speakers mean to do with their words, but such efforts have not met with much success. Although we cannot chart with precision how yesterday's pragmatics have become today's semantics, however, we still know that it has happened.

Bernard Rollin has imagined a mob of screaming Chinese, intending to insult Gerald Ford but under a misapprehension about English insults, yelling, "Next year in Jerusalem!"[168] Even half a million Chinese shouting together will not convert the meaning of this phrase to an insult. But by the same token, a metaphor used as an insult for long enough ("You ass!") will sooner or later lead to a new entry in the dictionaries under 'ass'.

When a phrase is undergoing such a shift, it is hard to see which side of the border it should be placed on, and some terms and phrases have lingered in no man's land for centuries. H. P. Grice, in his classic article, "The Causal Theory of Perception," raises the question of

---

168. Bernard Rollin, *Natural and Conventional Meaning: An Examination of the Distinction* (The Hague, 1976), 41.

whether "S can do A" implies "S has not done A." Grice suggests that we do best to regard the relation between these phrases as a pragmatic implicature rather than a logical implication.[169] That suggestion is far from a logically compelling refutation of the claim that nonperformance is built into the very meaning of 'can'.

No tests can therefore determine once and for all whether the eighteen maxims are pragmatic or semantic in nature, for we construct by our theories the border between pragmatics and logic. Nature does not force a classification upon us. Although one theory might test out better than another, we know enough by now to avoid claiming that a given theory has been conclusively and irrefutably established.

If you wish to build my eighteen rules into the very meaning of a deontic system, then, feel free to do so. That concession is, as we shall now see, very minor. For if the eighteen maxims are made part of deontic logic, then any violations of the maxims are logical absurdities. They should not be condemned as impractical, much less vicious, but are like errors in arithmetic. One needs a better deontic calculator to avoid them. But with each of the eighteen maxims, we discovered occasions when a person had good reason to violate the rule. Far from exhibiting mistakes in deontic arithmetic, such occasions suggest that it is the person who sticks rigidly to the eighteen maxims in all circumstances who is absurd.

Now an obvious response is that I need to state my eighteen maxims more carefully. When rules are properly stated, perhaps we will find no exceptions. I am not sure, however, that by adding another few epicycles to the theory of deontic logic we will take care of all the exceptions. And even if we manage the task, a theory that regards the eighteen maxims as part of deontic pragmatics will remain simpler and more obvious than its counterpart.

Nor will packing the justified exceptions into the eighteen maxims explain all the salient facts we have uncovered. For example, we noted that perhaps the most common basis for what seems a justified violation of the eighteen rules is the presence of an overriding external goal. If the eighteen rules are pragmatic, they exist to serve the purposes of deontic speech, and we are aware that an external goal can and occasionally should override those purposes.

My theory thus explains a fact the logical theory does not, for how

---

169. H. P. Grice, "The Causal Theory of Perception," *Proceedings of the Aristotelian Society* 35, suppl. (1961); reprinted in R. Swartz, ed., *Perceiving, Sensing, and Knowing* (Garden City, N.Y., 1965). The reference is to p. 460 of the Swartz volume.

can an external goal even appear to justify deontic behavior that is illogical? Consider a Kantian, who bases his substantive moral theory on universalizability. What can the Kantian say to the person who treats herself more severely than she does others? He should and will say that she ought not to behave in this manner. But for him to explain that her behavior is self-contradictory, absurd, and therefore not the result of a truly moral belief is to go too far. When the eighteen rules have a moral significance, breaking them leads to morally blameworthy behavior, not to behavior that cannot be classified under the rules of morality.

Further, if the eighteen maxims are reformulated to disallow any justified exceptions, the result is either rules too broad to be of use or a narrow and cramped account of deontic speech. Consider the ethical position of St. Augustine, which provides duties that subjects are unable to perform. Either this position is logically acceptable, in which case the rule seems to be that 'ought' implies 'can' except for when it doesn't, or it does not count as ethics at all. In neither case do we have any explanation of the *viciousness* of St. Augustine's ethics. Clearly, although some violations of the eighteen maxims are justifiable, most are instances of bad legislation and blameworthy decisions. If all violations of the maxims are illogical, we have no explanation of the fact that some are reasonable and others not.

Someone might claim that it is always one's duty to be reasonable and avoid illogicality. The apparently justifiable exceptions are either not exceptions or not justifiable. Some philosophers have had the bad habit of defining away what they don't like. If morality is defined as a species of rationality, then an irrationalist ethic becomes a contradiction in terms. Yet people live by irrationalist ethics even though they cannot live by irrationalist mathematics. When they build bridges by irrationalist methods, the bridges collapse, but when they build their lives by similar methods, the lives might prosper. The duty of rationality in morals is therefore not obvious—it takes much proving.

Proof is especially called for if the content of rationality includes our eighteen maxims, with the added complications of disallowing any justifiable exceptions and of being part of the logic of deontic speech. A duty to adhere to such a system of complex rules is unlikely on its face.

Finally, to regard the maxims as part of deontic logic or semantics puts them on a "take it or leave it" basis. The general usefulness of each of these rules becomes irrelevant to their justification. They are justified only if one can prove they are part of the structure of deontic utterances. But we have found for each of the eighteen maxims a clear justification tied to the purpose of deontic speech. To invoke this discovery and use that justification is to make the maxims a part of deontic pragmatics. On the theory that the eighteen are part of deontic logic, the discovery is a curiosity and the attempted justification otiose.

With my theory, I have a good answer to anyone who asks, "Why should we follow these rules?" But someone who makes the rules part of the logic or semantics of deontic speech can only answer, "Because those are the rules of the deontic game."

I have one more reason to count the eighteen maxims as part of deontic pragmatics rather than deontic logic. A number of tests attempt to capture the often unclear difference between implicatures, based on pragmatic rules, and implications, based on logic. According to these tests, the eighteen maxims give rise to implicatures and, therefore, are pragmatic in nature. But these tests deserve a section of this chapter to themselves. We have already seen, I believe, that it does make a difference whether we call the maxims pragmatic or logical. Now we need to consider how we tell which is which.

HOW CAN WE TELL?

H. P. Grice was the first to give a set of tests for nonconventional implicatures—that is, for those characteristics of speech acts that allow us to draw inferences based not on logic but on rules of pragmatics. Jerrold Sadock has transformed Grice's tests into a group of four.[170] As we should expect, Sadock's four tests cannot define precisely the fuzzy border between pragmatics and semantics. But if we apply the tests to my eighteen maxims, we find good reason to place the maxims safely on the pragmatics side of the border. These are the four tests:

1. Calculability: We can use a nonconventional principle to work out implicatures, and linguistic experience will confirm our results. Since the same is true for conventional principles and meaning-implications, calculability does not distinguish the two.
2. Cancellability: We do not contradict ourselves if we state a sentence while explicitly denying its nonconventional implicatures. The same is not true for meaning-implications.

170. Jerrold Sadock, "On Testing for Conversational Implicature," in P. Cole, ed., *Syntax and Semantics*, vol. 9 (New York, 1978), 281–97.

3. Nondetachability: There is rarely any way of restating a sentence while removing its nonconventional implicatures, except through explicit cancellation. There is never any way of doing so with meaning-implications.
4. Reinforceability: A nonconventional implicature can be stated explicitly without the speaker's being redundant. The same cannot be said of a meaning-implication.

Of these tests, the second and fourth provide good ways of separating pragmatics from logic, while the first and third are of little use. Let us look more closely at how these tests work.

The test of calculability reflects the ordinary belief that general rules, which can be syntactic, semantic, pragmatic, or any combination of the three, underlie and help explain a particular utterance or set of utterances. These rules, whatever they might be in the particular case, give rise to a set of expectations on the part of the listener. In accordance with the rules, the listener is able to anticipate to some degree the nature of the utterance.

There is an obvious analogy here with reading music at first sight. If a pianist is familiar with the conventions of the classical period, he should have little trouble sight-reading a Haydn sonata. He might be wrong in his expectations of what the next phrase will be, but his errors will be reasonable and his playing will not differ too widely from the score. The situation with speech is similar, although the number of speech rules and, hence, both the complexity and the fallibility of our anticipations is much greater than with sight-reading music.

If the eighteen maxims are rules at all, then, we should be able to use them to calculate implications or implicatures, and the results should accord with our experience. Also, we should be able to determine the effect of speech that violates those maxims. I have done just that in the chapters on the individual maxims. We looked at situations, real and fictional, and by using the maxims, I said quite a bit about those situations. I need not repeat it here. My experience confirms my account both of situations in which people employ the maxims and of situations in which they ignore or break them. I expect that, on the whole, the reader's experience does the same.

I have therefore been applying the test of calculability throughout this book, and the subrules of Deontic Rationality pass the test. That they are rules governing speech acts is therefore certain. But the test of calculability cannot tell us what sort of rules they are.

To find out, we must try the test of cancellability. I shall try it on the inference people often draw from "I ought" to "I will try."

In his introduction to a translation of Plato's *Protagoras*, Gregory Vlastos contends that the assertion, "It would be (morally) better for me to stop smoking, but I shall not," is neither self-contradictory nor "logically odd": "It is just morally pitiful."[171] My assertion that I ought to stop smoking will surely lead others to expect that I will at least try to quit the habit. But if Professor Vlastos is right, as I think he is, this expectation can be explicitly cancelled without incurring any self-contradiction. One might wonder why anyone would bother to say that he ought to stop smoking if he has no intention of trying. But one can easily think of circumstances that would render the remark reasonable: perhaps he is trying to impress a rich, tobacco-hating relative.

Logical implications cannot be cancelled, then, but pragmatic implicatures can. By this test, reasoning from "I ought" to "I will try" is licensed by an implicature, not an implication. And the rules that give rise to the implicature, primarily the rule of Straightforwardness, are therefore pragmatic rather than logical.

But the test of cancellability does not give guaranteed results, for a logical contradiction need not announce its presence to the speaker. The sentence, "I am going to construct, in accordance with the rules of Euclidean geometry, six different types of regular solid," hardly looks self-contradictory, yet it is. By the rules of logic, it therefore implies anything you please. Furthermore, people are perfectly capable of believing and acting upon self-contradictory thoughts. A logical implication might then give rise to no expectations, and even if it does, a person might believe that those expectations can be explicitly cancelled.

Further, when neither logic nor common sense proves an implication or implicature cancellable, we might decide to rank the rule that gives rise to the implication or implicature as a deeply rooted pragmatic one. Then again, we might not. Think of all the philosophers who have found logical oddity where Vlastos finds only moral pitifulness. One group finds a logical implication, another, a pragmatic implicature. It is hardly a matter of certainty which group is right. A nose for logical oddity is no more trustworthy than a nose for witches. The answer probably depends on which overall theory is better.

---

171. Plato, *Protagoras*, trans. B. Jowett (rev. M. Ostwald) (Indianapolis, 1956), xliii, footnote 54.

These considerations clearly apply to our eighteen rules. The eighteen, if they are rules of pragmatics, should give rise to cancellable implicatures rather than logical implications; but we might not be able to decide with assurance in any particular case whether we have the one or the other.

For each of the eighteen maxims, I have found situations where the rule can reasonably be set aside. In such situations, it seems reasonable to expect that an explicit cancellation could be added to the particular deontic utterance in question. For instance, recall the legislator who voted for the Noble Experiment in the hope and expectation that Prohibition would fail dismally. His action was therefore a violation of the rule of Straightforwardness. Now this legislator could, without contradicting himself, issue the following statement: "I do not anticipate that anyone will conform his conduct to this legislation, nor in voting for it was I trying in any way to get anyone to do so." Such a rider is politically foolish, but it does not contradict anything in his vote. By the rule of cancellability, then, Straightforwardness ranks as a pragmatic maxim.

Or again, recall the many exceptions to the rule of Judicial Publicity under martial law in time of national emergency. A military court, in finding a person guilty of sedition, might explicitly say: "We do not, in this finding, suppose that you either knew or reasonably could have known that what you did was against the law and liable to punishment. Nevertheless, imperative reasons of state demand that you be punished." Such a remark is unpleasant and very much open to abuse, but no self-contradiction is apparent; *raison d' état* has been given as a justification for punishments. Judicial Publicity is then a rule that gives rise to cancellable implicatures.

By making due reference to part 2 of this book, we can find similar cases for each of the eighteen maxims. For we found that each of them can be reasonably set aside in particular circumstances. When those circumstances occur, explicit cancellation is intelligible if not always sensible.

The test of nondetachability is of little relevance in distinguishing logical implications from pragmatic implicatures, for there is no way to restate a sentence so that it no longer carries its logical implications. Detachability, not nondetachability, would have to be a feature of implicatures, if we are to distinguish them from implications. Further, as Sadock points out, the test of nondetachability has some special problems. To apply it, we have to be able to tell when two sentences mean the same thing. But it is all too easy for someone to find (or presume) some shade of difference between seemingly synonymous expressions. As Quine has emphasized, a precise test for synonymy is something of a chimaera.[172]

Can we restate sentences so that implicatures based on our eighteen maxims are absent? If we count sentences containing explicit disclaimers as such restatements, then it is obviously possible with each of the maxims.[173] For each of the eighteen, we have said, yields cancellable implicatures. And since for each maxim there is some case to which it fails to apply, a sentence that contains an explicit disclaimer makes sense in such an instance.

But if we do not count those cases for which we cancel implicatures, I cannot come up with any good instances of detachability. There seems no way of saying that Jim ought to be kinder to Sarah without affording the presumption that I, who issue this edict, believe it to be in accordance with the facts about the world. The same seems true with implicatures based on maxims other than Factuality.

The test of detachability, or nondetachability, therefore gives us no further help than the test of cancellability offered. Indeed, I suspect that the test of detachability is never of any worth. For where there seems to be genuine detachment, it is reasonable to claim that the original statement and its supposed paraphrase are not synonymous.

The last of the four tests, reinforceability, is Sadock's own. It depends on the notion of redundancy, which seems hard to define without drawing on the ill-defined concept of synonymy. As a result, cases tested by the rule of reinforceability might give divergent results, if the testers have different intuitions about what is redundant. Without a test for synonymy, our intuitions of redundancy must remain unrefined and open to some question.

Still, Sadock's test could help account for some clear cases. The point of the test is that an explicit statement of a logical inference, when one has already stated the grounds for that inference, is redundant, but the same is not true for implicatures based on pragmatic rules.

We need to weaken that claim, however. For an explicit statement of a logical inference to be redundant in any normal sense of that term, the inference can only be an obvious one. The conclusion of one of Lewis Carroll's long and jumbled-up sorites comes as a surprise for

---

172. Sadock, *op. cit.*, p. 289. W. V. Quine, "Two Dogmas of Empiricism," in his *From a Logical Point of View* (New York, 1963), 24–27.
173. This point is made by Jerrold Sadock, *op. cit.*, p. 290.

most of us, not as a superfluous addition. And if one makes 'redundancy' a technical term, meaning "containing only information that could be deduced from information one is already in possession of," then one can never be sure that any piece of information is not redundant. In that event, the test is unusable.

But if we suppose that Sadock's test distinguishes implicatures only from obvious logical inferences, the test has some usefulness. "It's raining, and you had better bring an umbrella—and by the way, it's raining," is a redundancy if anything is. With an implicature, this sense of redundancy is missing. "Maybe I will," carries the implicature, "Maybe I won't," but there seems no obvious redundancy in saying, "Maybe I will and maybe I won't." After all, a person who hears John say, "Maybe I will," has every right to suppose that John is unsure of what he is going to do. But even if John is in fact certain of his course of action, he has not spoken falsely, even though his speech greatly misled us. For the information John has conveyed by "Maybe I will" does not imply "Maybe I won't." Hence, as with other implicatures, there is no redundancy.

Sadock notes that, while inferences based on implicatures yield no redundancies, those based on presuppositions do. [174] It is surely redundant, for example, to say: "It's incredible to think that Jones ran the mile in less than 3 minutes 50 seconds, and, by the way, Jones did run the mile in less than 3 minutes 50 seconds." We therefore have some means of distinguishing presuppositions from implicatures.

What happens if we apply this test of reinforceability to inferences based on our eighteen maxims? We can begin with an instance displaying the principle that 'ought' implicates 'can'. Suppose I say to a friend of mine, "You really ought to visit your sick old grandmother." By Kant's Principle, I should say this only if he is able to visit her. But there seems nothing at all redundant in adding the statement, "You are perfectly able to do so, you know." Rather, the additional remark serves to reinforce the implicature.

The same is true in other, now-familiar instances. A judge who says, "You should have driven at no more than 55 m.p.h.: that's the law," is not being redundant. Yet, by Judicial Use of General Rules, she would not have rendered this deontic judgment unless it is in accordance with the law. Her saying, "That's the law," reinforces the implicature. Or if I say to a child, "You shouldn't take a bigger piece of cake than Sally got," it would hardly be redundant to add a few

---

174. Sadock, *op. cit.*, p. 294.

remarks about the virtue of not treating one's self as an exception. According to the test of reinforceability, then, it does seem proper to list our eighteen deontic maxims as part of pragmatics rather than of logic.

In sum, then, of Sadock's four tests only cancellability and reinforceability help determine the nature of our eighteen maxims. Those two tests both point toward regarding the eighteen as part of pragmatics, although neither separately nor together are they close to deciding the point once and for all. Sadock's tests are therefore indicators, but only indicators, that I was right to regard the maxims as pragmatic. In that respect, they are like the arguments I gave in the first section of this chapter. As I warned at the outset, I do not and cannot have a logically tight proof of my position.

Pragmatics or logic—does it matter, then? In a sense, it doesn't really matter, for one can consistently hold either position.

But in that same sense, it doesn't really matter whether one regards the earth as going around the sun or the sun as going around the earth. Both astronomical theories are possible, and both can be made to yield the desired results. However, one theory is simpler, requires fewer curlicues, and demands that we accept fewer unexplained facts than the other.

The same is true with the classification of our eighteen maxims. My purpose in this chapter has been to show that the theory listing the eighteen as part of deontic pragmatics is, in a number of ways, better than any alternative that makes them part of deontic logic or semantics.

14 Deontic Pragmatics and Ethics

In chapter 1, I explained that this book had its origin in an attempt to answer the perennial student question about ethics, "Who cares?" In this final chapter, now that I have laid out and argued for the eighteen maxims of deontic pragmatics, it is time to use the results of this book to construct a satisfactory answer to that perennial question.

Of course, as I noted in chapter 1, the worth of this book is not dependent on the success of this final chapter. The structure of deontic pragmatics is a topic worth exploring for its own sake. If I have laid bare that structure, then this book has succeeded in its major aim. Still, it would be a valuable extra if the study of deontic pragmatics provided a good reason for people to be moral. In this final chapter, I shall try to provide that good reason. But the subject is huge, and a single chapter can be no more than suggestive. Single examples here must take the place of extended discussion. I do not flatter myself that this book says anything like the final word on its subject.

WHY WE SHOULD BE MORAL

In this section, I try to justify the proposition that persons, taken collectively, should be moral. In the next section, I shall take up the proposition that *each* person should be moral.

My justification in this section is strictly limited in its scope by two considerations. First, there is much more to moral language than statements of what a person morally ought to or may do. Sentences about goals and purposes or sentences about particular virtues, for example, neither openly contain deontic terms nor can obviously be equated with sentences that do contain deontic terms. Yet they do have a major role to play in moral language.

Second, even among the overtly deontic statements of any moral code we find substantive principles that are more than just an application of the eighteen maxims. If two competing moral codes conform approximately equally to the eighteen maxims of deontic rationality but differ in those substantive principles, the maxims cannot justify our adhering to one code rather than the other. By the same token, the maxims provide no method for making a rational choice among several codes that conform equally to the eighteen maxims.[175]

Despite these qualifications, I believe I can show that people ought to be moral, provided that the morality in question satisfies my eighteen maxims. If this is not enough to please an all-out ethical absolutist, at least it answers the ethical relativist, the skeptic, and the moral nihilist.

In fact, I am not merely trying in this section to sketch an argument against one mistaken position. There are at least five kinds of ethical relativism that I have heard people (and not just students)

---

175. This concession is not as damaging as it might appear to some readers. Although more than one moral code might get through the net of my eighteen maxims, those maxims are strong enough to screen out racist codes, capricious codes, and the like. As I noted in chapter 10, pp. 153–154, the maxims screen out all the truly vicious codes of which I am aware.

espouse, along with moral skepticism and moral nihilism. Following the precept that one should know one's enemy, I shall set out those mistaken positions.

1. Ethical Relativism: the belief that acts are good and right only for the person or persons who commit them, and that this goodness or rightness is the product of the tendency of an individual or group to approve of those acts.[176]

   Ego relativism: the belief that an act is good or right for a person if, only if, to the extent that, and because the person tends to approve of the act.

   Alter relativism: the belief that an act is good or right for a person if, only if, to the extent that, and because some other person or persons tend to approve of that act.

   Divine relativism: the belief that an act is good or right for a person if, only if, to the extent that, and because God or some god or gods tend to approve of that act.

   Group relativism: the belief that an act is good or right for a person if, only if, to the extent that, and because there is a group to which the person is taken to belong and that tends to approve of that act.

   Privileged-group relativism: the belief that an act is good or right for a person if, only if, to the extent that, and because a specific group tends to approve of that act.

2. Moral skepticism: the belief that we have no reason to think that a person is bound by the constraints of morality, however these might be understood.
3. Moral nihilism: the belief that we have good reason to deny that a person is bound by the constraints of morality, however these might be understood.

People who ask, "Who cares?" might be espousing any of these positions. In fact, they often hold more than one: some people are ego relativists at one time, group relativists at another, moral skeptics at

---

176. As Plato was fond of pointing out, a formulation such as this is ambiguous. Is what is good for X what is in X's best interests, or is it what X thinks is in X's best interests, or is it what X would under certain conditions think is in X's best interests? The ambiguity in formulation, however, does not seem to affect my argument.

still another, and absolutists on Sunday morning. Other people are sure it's all relative, but they seem able to accept fuzzy versions of incompatible theories simultaneously. In any event, any argument for being moral must speak to the various forms of relativism, skepticism, and nihilism if it is to have a chance of being effective.

Anthropologists should note that I have classified at least one form of ethnocentrism as a kind of ethical relativism. Some people believe that the standards of their group are the proper norms for everyone to follow, solely because those are the standards of their group. Such persons are both ethnocentrists and privileged-group relativists. This ethnocentrism is very different from the ethical absolutism that holds that certain standards are correct for everyone, whether or not any group actually lives by those standards. Some people have argued for group relativism by holding up ethnocentrism as the only, and horrible, alternative. But it should be clear not only that there are plenty of alternatives to group relativism, but that ethnocentrism itself can be a type of relativism.

Now let us suppose a bright student asks, "Why *should* I be moral? Who cares about morality anyway?" I would answer with the following argument:

1. Morality is, at least in part, a deontic undertaking.
2. Deontic undertakings are intended to serve some purposes and fulfill some functions.
3. These purposes and functions give a person good reason to engage in the deontic undertakings in question.[177]
4. There are therefore good reasons to engage in morality; and this answers the nihilist and skeptic.
5. But if a deontic undertaking is to be effective in fulfilling its purposes and functions, it must adhere closely to the constraints of deontic rationality. Too great a deviation from the eighteen maxims renders a deontic undertaking ineffective in obtaining the ends for which anyone engages in it.
6. It is pointless and silly to engage in an undertaking because it

---

177. As a reader noted, this statement suggests that we have reason to follow the dictates of any deontic undertaking, not just of morality. I think we do. But it hardly follows that we have equally good reason in a certain context to be polite as to be moral, for example. How good the reason is depends upon the kinds of purposes to be served and functions to be fulfilled.

aims at some end, if one has reason to think that the undertaking will be ineffective in obtaining that end.

7. Therefore, there is reason to engage in morality only if one has reason to think that the morality in which one engages is deontically rational. Hence, by step 3, one has reason to think that the morality in which one engages is deontically rational; and that answers the relativists.

This argument supports a position that is to some extent absolutist, for it supposes that there are standards by which all moral codes can and should be judged. These standards are the eighteen maxims of deontic pragmatics. According to the argument, a person has good reason to follow a moral code that accords with the maxims.

Further, the argument supports a position that at least sounds absolutist because it supposes that the maxims allow people to justify at least some of their statements under a deontically rational moral code. A code embodying the eighteen maxims will normally also contain substantive principles that are not merely applications of the maxims. The argument suggests that even these substantive principles can be taken as morally binding, as long as they do not engender conflicts in particular cases with the eighteen maxims. One can pragmatically justify entire codes containing many substantive principles, even though one cannot give pragmatic justifications for each such principle singly.

But the position the argument supports is also, to some extent, relativist. For it nowhere supposes that only one moral code can pass the test of deontic rationality. And if two or more moral codes pass the test, the argument gives us no way of choosing between the two.

It might seem as if my argument makes too much of linguistic facts, for the fact that moral language might be used to preserve society hardly implies that a moral society has certain institutions.[178] But pragmatics has to do with the *effects* of utterances; and those effects are events in the world. My argument is not that moral language creates the institutions of society. Rather, I claim that *if* our deontic utterances are to have their intended effects, there must be social institutions that conform to certain rules. And if those institutions do conform to the eighteen maxims, the society then has a defensible morality.

178. This objection was urged by a reader for Brown University Press.

Enough of what I take my argument to show. Does the argument succeed? The last three steps of the argument, and in particular step 5, have formed the major theme of this book. I see no need for a rehash here. If what I have said in the preceding chapters is correct, then an ethical relativist who is neither a moral nihilist nor a skeptic should accept some absolute principles—the eighteen maxims.[179] But that still leaves steps 1–4 to be examined, if I am to answer the moral nihilist and the skeptic. Strictly speaking, to do so is to step outside the specific task of this book, which was to outline deontic pragmatics. But I began the book in hopes of answering the question, "Who cares?" Unless I can indicate how I would answer both skeptic and nihilist, I will not have completed my task.

There are, I admit, real difficulties with those first four steps. For instance, step 3 is ambiguous in an important and troublesome way. Even if a person, as a member of a society whose moral code is deontically rational, has reason to obey that code, that same person will sometimes also have reason to disobey the code. An individual might even consider that, as long as only he and perhaps a few others get away with disobeying the code, he can enjoy all the benefits of society without fulfilling any of its precepts. If so, then I might have explained why *people in general* should be moral; but the question remains, "Why should *I* be moral?"[180]

Yet another problem claims our attention. If a person has a moral obligation to his society's code as long as it embodies the eighteen maxims, what if any obligation does he have to a code that does not do so? Is he totally free to wage war on his society? I shall return to St. Augustine, Lt. Broderick, and the American Bar Association when looking at this problem.

In what remains of this chapter, therefore, I shall give my answers

179. I have refuted, to be sure, only what Bernard Williams calls a "vulgar and unregenerate form" of ethical relativism. Yet, as Williams adds, this same extreme position is "both the most distinctive and the most influential form" of ethical relativism (Bernard Williams, *Morality: An Introduction to Ethics* [New York, 1972], 20). Philosophers who call themselves ethical relativists are usually more sophisticated than their brethren in the social sciences; but if the undoubted popular appeal of ethical relativism depended on general acceptance of philosophic formulations, that appeal would be minimal. Certainly, the student relativists of my first chapter have no qualms about the extreme position, even though to Williams it is "possibly the most absurd view to have been advanced even in moral philosophy" (Williams, p. 20).

180. I am indebted to a reader for Brown University Press for insisting on this point.

to these two questions. I shall also answer two other important problems that arise from the first four steps of my argument. The four questions are:

1. What is the purpose of moral language and of moral institutions in general? (Step 2 in the argument claims that deontic undertakings serve some purposes. What are those purposes in the case of moral deontic undertakings?)
2. Even if people in general have reason to obey the precepts of a justified moral code, why should an individual be moral? (Step 3 says that the purposes and functions give *a person* good reasons to engage in morality. Why is this true for individuals? Why is it not just a claim that holds for most, but not all, members of a given group?)
3. What is the relation between the moral and the deontic, and more particularly, between moral language and deontic language? (Step 1 says that morality is, at least in part, a deontic undertaking. What part? How does a moral 'ought' differ from a generic 'ought'?)
4. What if any moral obligation does a member of a society have if the society's code is not deontically rational? (The argument tells us what we should do if our code is deontically rational, but we might not always be so lucky.)

Answers to the first three questions will constitute my justification of steps 1–4 in the argument, while an answer to the fourth will clean up a particularly untidy loose end. When this chapter is done, we should have at least the outline of a good answer to that never-ending question, "Who cares?"

THE PURPOSE OF MORAL INSTITUTIONS AND LANGUAGE

Social scientists, at least since Émile Durkheim, are in general agreement that the presence of a shared morality is of crucial importance for a society. Feelings and expressions of obligation serve a social purpose, and this purpose is often said to be no less than the maintenance of society.

Bernard Williams quite properly warns that such a claim runs two opposed risks. A social scientist might simply identify a society as a group having certain shared values; if so, his claim that those values maintain the society is trivially true and vacuous. On the other hand, the social scientist might claim that maintaining a society is necessary for the continued physical existence of that society's members. Such a claim is far from trivial, but it seems prone to exaggeration and hard to establish.[181] Williams does believe, however, that "there is room for such claims as that a given practice or belief is integrally connected with much more of a society's fabric than may appear on the surface, that it is not an excrescence, so that discouragement or modification of this may lead to much larger social change than might have been expected."[182] The thesis of social scientists is then not as straightforward as they might believe, but it is not necessarily a hopeless muddle, either.

In this section, I shall look at an example of a social practice in a relatively primitive society. I believe that this example, although problematic in important respects, bears out Williams's point: that despite the twin dangers of vacuity and exaggeration, a social scientist has reason to think that the practice I discuss is "integrally connected" with the society's fabric.

My example is taken from A. R. Radcliffe-Brown's classic study of the Andaman Islanders.[183] Radcliffe-Brown examined a number of Andamanese customs while arguing for the value of a shared morality. Perhaps the most interesting customs concern the supposed protective power of inanimate objects.

The Andamanese used fiber from the *Hibiscus tiliaceus* for rope in hunting turtles, leaves of *Myristica longifolia* for canoe paddles needed in hunting turtles, and leaves from *Tetranthera lancoefolia* for arrow shafts in hunting wild pig. *Hibiscus* and *Myristica* were of no use for hunting wild pig, nor apparently was *Tetranthera* of any value for hunting turtles.[184] The Andamanese believed it was dangerous to eat certain foods, including turtle and pig.[185] But *Hibiscus* and

---

181. Williams, *op. cit.*, pp. 21–22. I am indebted to a reader for Brown University Press for pointing me to Williams's remarks.

182. Williams, *op. cit.*, p. 22.

183. A. R. Radcliffe-Brown, *The Andaman Islanders* (New York, 1964).

184. Radcliffe-Brown does not make this last point explicitly. Ibid., pp. 259–61.

185. As one reader of this book pointed out, the Andamanese belief in the danger of eating turtle meat might be a false one. In any case, if there is real danger, the Andamanese way of averting that danger was probably ineffective. That is a flaw in the example. But one can say that the Andamanese *belief* in the danger of eating turtle meat is real enough. Perhaps it would have been best for the society if that belief were expunged, but the customs of the Andamanese did at least provide a way, if not necessarily the best way, for the natives to incorporate turtle into their diet.

Myristica had the power to lessen or remove the danger from eating turtle, *Tetranthera* from eating pig. Turtle flesh must therefore be cooked over *Hibiscus* wood, and an initiate who eats turtle must be seated on leaves of either *Hibiscus* or *Myristica* and must hold a bunch of these leaves. On the other hand, *Tetranthera* wood and leaves must be used for similar purposes when one eats pig.[186]

The connection between the supposed powers of these trees and the social uses to which they are put is obvious. Radcliffe-Brown comments: "Not only is the protective power of these substances explicable by the fact that they are things on which the society depends in its daily life, but the special uses of each of them as amulets are only explicable when we consider the different uses to which they are put as materials."[187] The practice of eating one's turtle while seated on *Hibiscus* leaves is therefore not simply a quaint custom, indulged in for unfathomable reasons. Rather the eating customs of the Andamanese were a way, if not necessarily the best way, of coping with a situation brought about by their beliefs about dangerous foods. There is an explanation of their custom and it is a fairly straightforward one.[188] The explanation, however, requires us to consider the value of the turtle in the physical life of the community and the communal nature of turtle hunting.[189]

The claim that cooking turtle over *Hibiscus* wood helped preserve Andamanese society does not appear to be a vacuous one.[190] If the phy-

186. Radcliffe-Brown, *op. cit.*, pp. 259–61.

187. Ibid., p. 261.

188. Not that the explanation would recommend itself to most Western scientists! It generalizes from a causal connection: Without *Hibiscus*, there would be less (and perhaps no) turtle to eat. (This connection, in turn, depends upon the Andamanese having discovered that *Hibiscus* makes the best rope fibers for catching turtles, and that use of rope fibers is the best way open to the Andamanese to catch turtles.) The generalization seems to be that whatever has to do with turtles should therefore make use of the power of *Hibiscus*.

189. One reader points out that, since there is no danger in eating turtle, the Andamanese custom is a violation of my maxim of Factuality. As such, it would seem of dubious help in an argument to get people to obey moralities that conform to the eighteen maxims. But no moral code will be perfectly deontically rational. And this violation of Factuality seems unlikely to have widespread effects, unlike (say) laws predicated on a belief in important differences among races.

190. A reader for Brown University Press is surely right, however, in noting that the claim looks like a grossly inflated one. One can allow a social value to institutions, such as the dietary customs of the Adamanese, without making the preservation of each such institution a matter of life or death to the society. "Helping to preserve the society" is then an acceptable phrase only if one concedes that the degree of help might be rather small and that the same degree of help might be obtained by other means.

sical life of the Great Andamanese was largely dependent on a diet of turtle and pig, then whatever lessened the availability of those foods would have caused major changes in the Andamanese society.[191] This is surely a causal claim, not a matter of definition. And if the use of the right wood was indeed believed to take away the danger of eating those foods, the effect of changes in eating and cooking customs might well have been to lessen the availability of pig and turtle.[192] This, too, is a causal claim. The thesis that these customs played a role in preserving Andamanese society is therefore causal, testable, and far from vacuous.

We are likely to define the Great Andamanese society by its relatively isolated location, by various kinds of transactions among the islanders, and by their diet. But I see no need to include in the definition their folk beliefs about the right branches on which to sit while eating different foods. One could imagine these beliefs being replaced by an entirely different set of beliefs without our being forced to the conclusion that a new society had taken the place of the old. For instance, one could imagine islanders deciding to eat turtle while seated on *Tetranthera* leaves, in an effort to frighten off jealous pig spirits intent on ruining the turtle harvest.

However, given the strong association in the islanders' minds between *Hibiscus* and turtle, anything that tended to reduce belief in that association and in the resulting magical power of *Hibiscus* was likely to impinge upon the turtle harvest. In this way, maintenance of a set of beliefs about what one should do is definitely of use in the (nontrivial) preservation of a society.

The major features of this illustration do not depend upon the particular nature of Andamanese beliefs. That the Great Andamanese happened to cook turtle over *Hibiscus* rather than *Tetranthera*, that they invoked the power of the wood directly instead of misleading evil spirits, is no more than an interesting fact about these people. The fact

191. Again, I am not arguing that the Andamanese practices were the best way of dealing with their beliefs about the dangers of eating turtle. Large-scale changes, by the same token, are not necessarily harmful to a society. But it is no argument against the claim that a practice is useful to the good of a society to say that another practice would be even more useful.

192. Of course, the Andamanese might have lost their cooking customs while, at the same time, losing their belief in the danger of eating turtle and pig. In that case, there might have been no real change in the food supply. Or the Andamanese might have found new ways of removing the danger from these foods. One cannot, then, say that the loss of present cooking and eating customs *must* harm the society; but it is very likely to do so, for folk beliefs are not lost nor are folk customs adequately replaced as easily as a rationalist might hope.

that whichever custom they held played a useful role in preserving their society has much wider implications.

An example such as this one supports the thesis that the precepts of a shared morality, at least in a simple society, individually serve a social purpose that is intimately bound up with the survival of the community. In this instance, what is at stake might be the sheer physical survival of the community's members, at least to the extent that their survival depended on the provision of turtle and pig meat. Other examples suggest that what is at stake often is not physical survival but rather the maintenance of a society in anything like its current form.[193]

No doubt, it would be hard, perhaps impossible, to come up with similar explanations for the precepts of more developed societies and make any show of scientific accuracy. But the illustrations from the Andamanese at least suggest that in more developed societies, precepts as a whole probably help maintain and integrate society, even if not all the precepts do so individually.

There is then a purpose in having a shared morality in a society. And that purpose does seem to be the continuation of the society in at least something like the form it has had.

Obviously, most of the time it is to any individual's interests that his or her society be maintained. The benefits of the society's continuance are obvious, the dangers in its breakup are many.

A persistent tone in Radcliffe-Brown's book is his sadness at the passing of Andamanese society under the onslaught of British rule and the establishment of a penal colony. He emphasizes the effect of the breakup on the Andamanese themselves. At the time Radcliffe-Brown wrote, the aboriginal population had been cut to less than one-fifth its former size, and births were rare events. The failure of Andamanese society to continue was indeed a disaster for individual members of that society. And the disaster continued after Radcliffe-Brown's study. According to an *Encyclopaedia Britannica* article on the Andamans, the tribal culture of the Great Andamanese has been wiped out.[194] I recently heard, although I do not know this to be a fact, that the Great Andamanese themselves have now disappeared.

Now it would be absurd to suppose that the disappearance of folk beliefs about the power of different trees was responsible for this catastrophe. Such a belief would commit the sin of exaggeration

---

193. It is harder to avoid the problem of vacuity in this kind of case.

194. *Encyclopaedia Britannica*, 1970, vol. 1, p. 888.

Williams warns social scientists against—rather like his example of Welsh nationalists who claim that preservation of the Welsh language is essential to the physical continuance of the Welsh people.[195] The establishment of a penal colony and the resulting continuous contact with the outside world were probably far more important factors in the decline of the Andamanese.

But the precepts and folk beliefs of Andamanese society clearly had value to the individual in that society, a relatively self-sufficient organization dependent on the availability of turtle and pig meat. And when the precepts were gone, so was the society and, soon, so were the people. *Post hoc, ergo propter hoc*? No; but it seems reasonable to suppose that the disappearance of the shared precepts helped bring on the catastrophe.

My purpose in this section has been to argue that a person has some reason, some justification, for following the morality of his group, because a shared morality plays an important and perhaps crucial role in the maintenance of any society. Whether a person in a given instance has a sufficient justification for following his society's shared morality depends on the nature and importance of the precepts and the particular circumstances present.

WHY I SHOULD BE MORAL

I have argued that individuals gain important benefits from obeying the moral precepts of their society, as long as those precepts conform to the eighteen maxims. But perhaps an individual can gain even greater benefits by paying only lip service to the code. I might let others live up to the rules; I will break them whenever it is safe to do so. As long as most people are moral, why should I be moral?

This so-called "free-rider" problem has been around for a long time. Glaucon, in Plato's *Republic*, thinks it the common opinion that a person who could make himself invisible would have every reason to ignore the claims of justice. Socrates' answer is not overly convincing, and it takes up several books of the *Republic*.[196] I must try to do better in less space. To do so, though, I need to distinguish two types

195. Williams, *op. cit.*, p. 22.

196. Socrates in effect makes morality a matter of proper mental hygiene. Aside from the dubiousness of the medical metaphor, with its confusion of different sorts of norms, Socrates' position simply assumes that everyone will prefer this sort of moral mental health to moral mental sickness. As Sportin' Life would say, it ain't necessarily so.

of free rider. The *reasonable rider*, as I shall call her, has a good reason, other than her own convenience, for not following her society's morality in a particular case. The *true free rider* merely wishes to enjoy the benefits of her society's moral code while herself obeying that code only when safety and prudence require her to do so.

Now free riders of both stripes need to pick their spots carefully. Universalizability is, after all, one of the eighteen maxims. In the great majority of cases, I do well not to treat myself as an exception to the rules of my society. The person who makes a practice of not obeying society's rules is not likely to enjoy that society's advantages for long. But that consideration argues only that I should *usually*, other things being equal, be moral; this suggests the answer to the problem of the reasonable rider.

For let us consider the reasonable rider from a different angle. Imagine a society able and willing to insure that each of its members has enough to live on without economic discomfort, but with a distribution system that allows for sizable economic disparities among individuals. People in this society can have other interests besides obeying morality, whatever the nature of their moral code. For example, Jane finds herself in a situation where she needs to steal to avoid starvation for herself and her family. Her poverty struck suddenly and unexpectedly, and the distribution system is painfully slow in dealing with new cases. Jane knows and accepts the rules. But she weighs severe economic need against the worth of obeying her society's (and her own) moral code, and the former determines her conduct.

It would be incorrect to say that, because Jane's need was so great, she did not break the rules. To use Ronald Dworkin's useful distinction, she might have been right (on balance) to steal, but that does not mean that she had a right to steal.[197] The latter would imply that society has no justification for interfering with her theft or later punishing (or even forgiving) it. And surely it does have a justification: she stole.

Did Jane weigh matters rightly? I do not know. How severe was her need? How much longer would the creaky welfare system have taken to get to her case? Were there less drastic ways of getting food for herself and her family? These are relevant questions. One cannot say that, when weighing the shared morality against other considerations, the former should always win. Thus an individual's interests do not always coincide with society's precepts. At times it

197. Dworkin, *Taking Rights Seriously*, (Cambridge, 1977), pp. 188–90.

is impractical to follow the precepts of one's society, and I shall argue in the next section that doing so can even be immoral.

If I am right, a person does not always have an overriding reason to follow her society's precepts. On occasion, the situation is quite the reverse, and she has at least a *prima facie* obligation, whether prudential or moral or both, to act contrary to those precepts. Failure to ride would in such circumstances be unreasonable.

Hence, we can settle the problem of the reasonable rider by pointing out that she has a reason, in a typical case, to be moral, and that most of the time anyone's reason to be moral holds only if other things are equal. And the occasions on which a person does *not* have sufficient reason to be moral are exactly the same as those in which the reasonable rider dissents from her society's morality.

Unfortunately, the true free rider has nothing like Jane's need to sustain her immoral acts. She wishes only to go along for the ride, acting immorally while benefitting from the morality of others. Why should she be moral?

What held for the reasonable rider will not hold for the true free rider. The latter, like the former, prudently agrees to be moral in all but a few cases, and we have seen that morality is not the overriding concern in a few cases. But for the true free rider, these "few cases" are not the same. The true free rider eschews morality even though her society's morality is not overridden. Hence, I have not yet given the true free rider reason to give up her practices.

Jane had a good reason for her actions. But does the true free rider? The answer obviously depends upon whether a mere wish to enjoy society's benefits without bearing the normally attendant pains constitutes a good reason for immoral behavior. Does it?

I think we must concede some ground to the true free rider. Consider again the Andamanese society, in which one should cook turtle only over certain kinds of wood. I argued that this custom played a causal role in preserving Andamanese society. But another custom might have played the same role, and had the Andamanese lost their belief in the danger of eating turtle, no custom at all would have been necessary.

Now imagine an Andamanese true free rider, at least when it comes to eating turtle. If nobody is around, he cooks his turtle over whatever wood happens to be handy. He sees no point in holding or sitting on *Hibiscus* leaves as he eats. But he is careful to cover his tracks afterward. Should this free-spirited Andamanese, while by himself, follow the morality of his society? I do not see why he should.

Perhaps his solitary vices cause him great psychological damage, but perhaps they do not—he might doubt or deny his society's beliefs about the danger of eating turtle. If he is not harming himself, and if he is sufficiently careful, and if he is not in some indirect way harming his society, he has no reason to be, by the standards of his group, moral.

The morality of a group, I have argued, normally contains much more than the eighteen maxims of deontic pragmatics, even if it is consistent with those maxims. I am now suggesting that a true free rider (by definition, a person who does not yet subscribe to a given moral code and who is therefore unreachable by moral arguments) has no reason other than her own safety to obey any moral standard other than implementations of the eighteen maxims.

But what about those principles that do embody the eighteen maxims? I think the true free rider does have some reason to obey them.

In the first place, the eighteen maxims are all primarily social rules. They have to do with deontic speech, which is chiefly aimed at directing people. And, although I might use deontic speech to direct myself, I normally use it to direct others. The true free rider who violates a moral rule embodying a maxim of deontic pragmatics must then do so in public. Suppose she sets out to violate Universalizability. She then treats herself, without special justification, as an exception to the rules both she and her society expect others to obey. Is it really likely that no one will notice? Safety is not easily come by in this case.

Nor is safety the only concern. People do generally want to be part of their community and, in a general way, to uphold the interests of those around them.[198] The would-be violator of Universalizability has reason not to break the rule, as well as not to be seen breaking the rule.

Can a nonuniversalizer ever have a good reason for breaking the law? Only if the nonuniversalizer's convenience provides her not merely with *some* reason to act as she does, but with a reason that outweighs all the reasons against such action. I have argued that there are circumstances in which universalizability does not achieve its usual goal; in those circumstances one has reason not to be moral. But those circumstances define the reasonable rider. A true free rider fails to universalize, despite considerations of safety and community. One must set a high value on one's convenience to find true free riding a worthwhile venture most of the time.

198. See Mary Gore Forrester, *Moral Language* (Madison, 1982), 170–72.

Now imagine a true free rider who decides to let her caprice determine a particular case of obligation. She has no special reason to employ caprice, as had the lover whose beloved cherished spontaneity. Rather, she just feels like letting caprice take over. If she yields to the temptation, she has much to lose and, an outsider would suggest, relatively little to gain.

But in spite of these considerations, all I have done is to raise the stakes for the true free rider. What if the true free rider thinks that her prospective gains from free riding outweigh any of the losses she is likely to incur? She could, for all I know, be right.

I have no way of proving irrational the actions of any true free rider who, having considered the difficulties and dangers of her actions, decides to engage in them anyway. True free riding seems unreasonable to me, but the true free rider weighs matters differently, and I cannot prove that her method of weighing is wrong. I do think that if most would-be free riders thought a little harder, they would decide to be moral after all. But not all.

People should, other things being equal, be moral. And so should I, an individual person. Of course, other things aren't always equal, and there can be good reason for any one of us to disobey the morality of the group. Perhaps, for a few of us, convenience is sufficient reason to disobey. But on most occasions, most persons have good reason to follow the group's morality to the extent that it embodies the eighteen maxims.

THE MORAL AND THE DEONTIC

I can sum up my results so far by saying that if one's society has a morality that generally conforms to the eighteen maxims, then one has *ceteris paribus* good reason to practice that morality. The "good reason" is entirely practical, however, not moral; and that might strike many people as intensely unsatisfactory. Am I claiming that there is really no morality but only a slicked-up version of self-interest?

The relation between the moral and the deontic raises a connected problem. As I noted in chapter 1, in certain contexts the maxims of deontic pragmatics carry moral force. To violate a pragmatic maxim is to be ineffective in seeking one's goals, but to violate a moral maxim is, at the least, to deserve censure. Mention of ineffectiveness seems a bad joke when wickedness is afoot.

Nazi policy on the treatment of one's fellow man was a massive violation of the principle of Universalizability. As such, it was not an effective means of achieving the Nazis' legislative end. But does anyone who knows anything of Nazi behavior toward Jews and Eastern Europeans have the patience to allow such talk? The violation of Universalizability was morally vicious, and that is what counts.

Just what, then, is the relation between the moral and the deontic? Is it just a coincidence that at least some of the pragmatic maxims we have isolated have moral force? Or is their moral status clearly connected to their pragmatic basis, so that we are justified in ascribing moral force to those maxims and to any code that conforms to them? Unless I can show that we are justified in such ascriptions of moral force, I might have answered the question, "Who cares?" But I will not yet have touched the deeper question, "Why *should* I care?"

One obvious place to begin looking at the relations between the moral and the deontic is with the truism that many moral statements are deontic. Although much of importance in morality is not conveyed by deontic language, quite a bit is. And since all deontic statements are issued for some purpose, the issuance of moral deontic statements must be effective or ineffective. The eighteen maxims therefore apply to at least some moral statements.

But that is only to state the problem, not to answer it. For all I have said, the eighteen maxims might apply to moral deontic statements with practical force only. What converts a merely pragmatic rule into a moral one? If it is simply whim, the unreasoned choice of an individual or a group, then my triumph over relativism is utterly hollow.

Some people have argued that moral contexts and rules differ from other deontic contexts and rules by the presence or absence of rewards and sanctions. Durkheim, for example, makes the presence of sanctions part of his definition of a moral fact as "a rule of sanctioned conduct."[199] If we accept Durkheim's account, then we have an answer to the problem this section is wrestling with. When I fail to apply Proportionality, for instance, the morality of the context does not make me liable to punishment. Rather, my liability to punishment is what makes the context moral. Rewards and sanctions transmute the merely deontic and practical into the moral.

But I cannot recommend Durkheim's answer to our problem.

---

199. Durkheim, *op. cit.*, pp. 424–26. Although I am not including rewards under the heading "sanctions," it is not clear whether Durkheim means to do so.

Durkheim himself realizes that he has identified the moral with the legal and, for that matter, with the societal. Even if one thinks these should all coincide, quite clearly they do not always do so. For some people dissent from the morality of their group. Whether their dissent is justified or unjustified, rational or irrational, the fact remains that they do dissent. If the moral is merely the socially approved, the phenomenon of moral dissent from society needs an explanation.

Again, some breaches of the shared morality of a society are not breaches of law. John Stuart Mill, in *On Liberty*, makes much of this fact: "Disinterested benevolence can find other instruments to persuade people to their good than whips and scourges, either of the literal or the metaphorical sort."[200] Mill knew that society has more weapons at its disposal than those of the law. What society forbids and provides sanctions against is not always the same as what the law forbids and provides sanctions against. If there were no differences between the religious beliefs of the bulk of American society and the law of the land, then atheists would have a great deal more than social disapproval to contend with.

Not all that is rewarded or punished is then of a moral nature, nor is all that is of a moral nature rewarded or punished. If I believe that a certain type of behavior is morally vicious, I probably wish for sanctions against such behavior. But must I even do that? I might be tolerant, or smug and superior, or forgiving. And even if I do wish for sanctions, not all such wishes are effective. Moral beliefs can exist without sanctions, then, and sanctions can be imposed where there are no operative moral beliefs.

Still, one might contend that the morally deontic is that portion of the deontic which *should be* attended by rewards and sanctions, whether it is or not. These rewards and sanctions need not be state sponsored. One could allow society such metaphorical whips and scourges as Mill mentions. But this suggestion also has its difficulties. A soldier who disobeys orders receives what we might consider a well-deserved punishment. After all, the army needs to maintain discipline. But does everyone conclude that the soldier's disobedience was a breach of morality? He might have disobeyed on acceptable moral grounds and still deserve punishment.

To say that the morally deontic should be attended by rewards and sanctions is either useless or implausible. Implausibility is present when the 'should' is taken as pragmatic, for it is not always practical

200. John Stuart Mill, *On Liberty*, (London, 1859), chap. 4.

to enforce morals. But if the 'should' is moral, it is at best circular to assume without argument a substantive moral claim, presumably binding on all, as a basis for arguing that some substantive moral claims are binding on everyone.

The lack of a necessary connection between deontic statements in general and rewards or punishments is apparent from many of my examples in this book. With breaches of etiquette, for example, everything seems to depend on time and place. Yet even the prospect of a beheading is hardly enough to convert showing one's back to His Majesty into immoral behavior, however strongly one might argue that such gross conduct deserves severe punishment.

But if sanctions and rewards, or even the deserving of these, will not do the job, is there any rational explanation of the moral force I have ascribed to the pragmatic maxims? We begin to see an answer to this problem, I think, if we look at pointless breaches of nondeontic pragmatic maxims. For there, too, a surprising amount of moral force comes into play.

"Sir, will this road take me to Vilsack Road?" "Well, I think so, but I haven't lived here very long." From this little dialogue, the questioner is justified in reaching several conclusions about the respondent's speech. What justifies him in doing so is, of course, Grice's Cooperative Principle.

For one thing, the questioner assumes that the respondent is making the strongest statement he can. He therefore supposes the respondent doesn't know for sure whether the road in question will lead him to Vilsack Road. Further, the questioner assumes that the respondent's statement that he has not lived long in the area is both true and relevant. He takes it to be an explanation of why the respondent is not sure.

But what if the respondent is, in fact, quite sure that the road soon will intersect with Vilsack Road?[201] The respondent has not been lying, but he has given the false impression that he is unsure. Perhaps he has some reason for responding in so misleading a manner. But if he has no good reason, or if his misdirection is quite pointless, we condemn the respondent for more than the misuse of pragmatic conventions. He has acted immorally.

Where is the immorality in a pointless disregard of a couple of conversational maxims? Not, I suggest, in the pointlessness, nor even

---

201. It might gladden the reader to know that there is indeed a Vilsack Road, north of Pittsburgh and sometimes very hard to find.

in the particular maxims. Rather, the respondent in my little dialogue was guilty of a breach of trust, a sort of bad faith.[202]

I think some degree of immorality also attends pointless violations of the maxims of politeness. Seemingly unmotivated rudeness comes as a shock. I try to think of some reason why a salesperson should be so rude to me. If I can find no good explanation, I condemn her behavior as wrong, not just as a violation of a pragmatic maxim. She shouldn't treat people like that. And the 'shouldn't' is at least flavored with a sense of morality, because the rude salesperson has somehow broken faith with me. Her waiting on me created, or at least presupposed, a condition of trust that she has breached. I have a right, we might say, to expect common politeness.

In most conversational situations, we trust speakers not to violate the maxims of pragmatics without good reason. Where there is no good reason, or where a speaker deliberately attempts to exploit the listener's expectations for a hidden and reprehensible motive, breach of trust and immorality have entered.

Now when little hangs on the matter, the breach of trust seems minor and perhaps even nonexistent. That is why my description of gratuitously rude behavior as immoral might seem a bit harsh. After all, rudeness rarely does lasting harm. But when it does, calling such behavior immoral seems almost too mild. With the case of the person seeking directions to Vilsack Road, the matter could be very important indeed. Suppose the driver seeking directions is rushing a desperately ill person to a hospital on that road. A misleading answer in such a circumstance would be almost criminal.

If we apply these considerations to deontic pragmatics, we can, I think, explain both the presence of moral force and the importance of rewards and sanctions. By uttering a deontic statement, a person either creates or presupposes a condition of trust with those to whom he made the utterance. The content of the trust is that the speaker is obeying the eighteen maxims. If rewards or sanctions depend on the keeping of that trust, for the speaker to breach it unnecessarily is morally vicious. Judges who decide cases on caprice and not by applying rules, for example, betray their trust.

It is because they have violated their trust that I find St. Augustine's God and Lieutenant Broderick's superior officers worthy of moral

---

202. Is "bad faith" too strong an expression? I don't think so. The speaker not only deceives the listener, but the deceit occurs in a situation where the listener has a right to expect the best advice the speaker can give.

condemnation.[203] Both had their reasons for intentionally issuing obligations that could not be fulfilled, but their aim was not the straightforward one of causing people to behave in accordance with the law.

An authority might order the impossible for various reasons—to induce guilt and shame, perhaps, or to provide an excuse for vindictiveness. The army might have issued Broderick his peculiar orders as a response to political pressures from all sides. After all, both jingoists and Nervous Nellies vote. As for the Augustinian God, who knows what His motive might be? To amend a well-known phrase, none dare call it sadism!

But in the trial lawyer's dilemma, our third example from chapter 2, no question of bad faith arises. Nobody has suggested that the contradiction in the rules is either pointless or motivated by ulterior and unstated considerations. Quite the opposite: There seems to be good reason for lawyers to make the best case for their clients, and there seems to be good reason for lawyers not to countenance what they know to be perjury. No one is guilty of breach of trust here. That is why the A.B.A. rules are impractical but not immoral.

I should therefore distinguish between failing to use deontic institutions properly and using them improperly. The two usually go together, for improper ulterior motives generally underlie a failure to make proper use. In such cases, we rarely take the pragmatic standpoint and convict the person of mere deontic irrationality. But when there is no improper use but only a failure to use the institutions properly, as in the instance of the trial lawyer's dilemma, there is impracticality but not immorality.

The impracticality of being deontically irrational is, therefore, most often masked by a moral viciousness that ensues when one employs deontic institutions for improper purposes. The graver fault tends to hide the lesser one. The Nazis violated maxims of pragmatics, but their actions were vicious rather than just impractical. In condemning the Nazis, then, we do not merely complain of their inefficiency. Rather, we hold that their widespread violations of Universalizability, Proportionality, Economy, and other maxims were morally vicious. One reason for our condemnation is that their violations were a massive breach of the trust given them as legislators for the German people, and widespread death and destruction followed

---

203. See chapter 2, *passim.*

from this breach of trust.[204] The Nazis do deserve moral condemnation by all. If this statement entails that at least some moral standards are absolute, then it adequately illustrates what I believe to be the truth.

We can apply the same considerations to less grave cases, even those in which the 'ought' imposed is nonmoral. I start, however, with a relatively trivial moral duty. My son has promised to mow a certain woman's lawn, and I tell him he ought to keep his promise. I am imputing a particular duty in accordance with the general moral rule that one should keep one's promises. Unless I accept both the general rule and its application to the present situation, it is wrong of me to tell my son he should mow the lawn. By saying what he should do, I have given him reason to believe that I think his duty is what I say it is. And since I am his parent and he is not of age, I am in a position of deontic trust. My advice cannot be taken as idle and gratuitous. He has every reason to expect that I am following the applicable maxims of deontic pragmatics.

Now what if I really don't believe he should go ahead and mow the woman's grass? I am surely guilty of dealing in bad faith with my son. If it is hard work to mow that lawn, and if my only real aim is to get him out of the house so that I can sleep longer, my act deserves moral censure. And if he faces some danger by cutting her lawn at a time when an electrical storm is about to strike, my act deserves worse than censure.

We can say much the same when a breach of trust involves a nonmoral 'ought'. Suppose a widely read etiquette columnist informs her readers that every civilized person ought to use napkin rings at the table. If the columnist makes this claim only to gain notoriety and not to mold people's habits, she breaks faith with her readers. Under ordinary circumstances, so little hangs on this kind of recommendation that the columnist's sin is no worse than venial. But if it turns out that a number of poor people have gone without adequate nourishment in order to lay in a supply of napkin rings, clearly the columnist's fault is greater. If she had good reason to expect that her advice would bring about this consequence, her fault is greater still. Large-scale bad results convert a breach of trust into a moral outrage.

---

204. I do not suppose that this is the only reason, or even the principal reason, for which the Nazis deserve moral censure, nor do I mean to suggest in talking about breach of faith that only the Nazis were blameworthy.

Suppose we look at the columnist's motives rather than at the consequences of her advice. She might have given the advice about napkin rings just as a lark, or to test how powerful her hold over her readers is, or because she has secretly bought stock in napkin ring companies. Each of these motives is worse than its predecessor in departing from Straightforwardness. As the motives grow less straightforward, the act becomes more vicious.

Violation of pragmatic rules for deontic contexts can therefore render an act morally vicious, even when those contexts are not themselves moral.[205] The deeper the breach of trust and the more important the consequences, the more immoral the violation is.

If breach of trust is sufficient to convert at least some violations of pragmatic maxims into immorality, then it seems there must be some general, cross-cultural moral obligation to keep faith. For the cases I am concerned with, that amounts to a moral duty to be deontically rational. In fact, though, I do not need to assume any such cross-cultural moral obligation. For I have not argued that in every moral code some of my eighteen maxims are morally binding. I am committed only to the supposition that wherever the maxims of pragmatics are moral obligations, people have a moral duty to keep faith.

Nevertheless, many have argued for the stronger position— that a moral duty to keep faith must be present in all moral codes. Consequentialist theories have an obvious argument: in G. J. Warnock's words, "To the extent that trust is undermined, all cooperative undertakings, in which what one person can do or has reason to do is dependent on what others have done, are doing, or are going to do, must tend to break down."[206] A strong anti-consequentialist such as Kant can reach the same conclusion from quite different premises. According to Kant, "The man who communicates his thoughts to someone in words which yet (intentionally) contain the contrary of what he thinks on the subject has a purpose directly opposed to the natural purposiveness of the power of communicating one's thoughts and therefore renounces his personality and makes himself a mere deceptive appearance of man, not man himself."[207]

205. Although I cannot give a method of identifying moral contexts, I surely do know in clear cases when a context is moral.

206. G. J. Warnock, *The Object of Morality* (London, 1971), 84; cited by Charles Fried, *Right and Wrong* (Cambridge, Mass., 1978), and reprinted in part in Christina Hoff Summers, ed., *Vice and Virtue in Everyday Life* (San Diego, 1985), 294.

207. Immanuel Kant, *Tugendlehre*, trans. Mary J. McGregor as *The Doctrine of Virtue* (Philadelphia, 1964) 428–30, cited in Fried, *op. cit.*, reprinted in Summers, *op. cit.*, p. 293, footnote 1.

Even if every moral code does impose a duty to keep faith, however it might justify that duty, not every code requires that one always keep faith with every human being. Many codes and many moral theorists have sanctioned the claim that one need not keep faith with outsiders or with heretics. On this ground, the Council of Constance allowed itself to disregard the Emperor Sigismund's safe conduct and brought about the burning of John Huss. And as the Bible-quoting mountaineer explained when asked how he could justify selling a broken-down horse to an unsuspecting city man: "He was a stranger, and I took him in."

But a code that allows for breaking faith with outsiders is still likely to require that its subscribers keep faith among themselves. A moral code without this obligation is in grave practical difficulties. Perhaps it is even conceptually impossible. I do not know. At the very least, then, the principle that one should keep faith is a moral maxim found in many different codes and theories. Perhaps it can be found in all; perhaps it must be present in all.

We also find the moral necessity of keeping faith in cases where a deontic speaker obeys the eighteen maxims. For deontic speech that follows those maxims can be morally praiseworthy, even when the context is not a moral one, because it is morally praiseworthy to keep one's trust. If I give you straightforward advice that presents what I think will be best for you at the least cost to you, my action is *prima facie* morally good, even if I don't specifically consider what is morally best for you.[208] My action is better if much hangs upon the advice I give you, and it is better yet if I have some motive not to be straightforward. If I tell you honestly that you should do something, even though your doing it will harm my interests, then I deserve praise. For example, I could tell you that you should testify truthfully in a court of law, even though your doing so will lead to my being punished.

We have seen moral features arise in deontic, but not necessarily moral, contexts whenever it is important not to breach one's trust. We might even conclude that a moral context is one in which important questions of keeping faith are usually prominent, while a nonmoral context is one in which such questions usually are not of major concern.[209] If so, then a political question or a question of etiquette

---

208. Only *prima facie*, of course, because I could be giving you honest advice to further a bad cause. That was what landed Guido da Montefeltro deep in Dante's Hell.

209. But this would be an overstatement. See ahead, p. 232.

can have moral features, and it is even possible that either of these can be considered a moral context. Conversely, a moral context can, in an exceptional circumstance, present no moral feature.

Take again the instance of keeping a promise. We usually think we should keep all of our promises. But in real life, situations occur in which keeping a promise is of little or no help to any of the parties concerned. A five-year-old boy promises that, on arriving at the age of 21, he will give his best friend his favorite toy dump truck. Sixteen years later, the best friend has no interest in collecting the truck. An outsider advises, "You made a promise, and you should keep your promises." Normally, this advice would be morally correct. But because so little hangs on the matter—nothing, I think, except that keeping one's promises is a good habit—most people would not ascribe immorality to the breaker of such a promise. To give the dump truck is hardly more praiseworthy than to withhold it, so that to advise the one rather than the other strikes most people as having little to do with morality.

We have found that deontic statements that are normally not moral become so when much depends upon maintaining the good faith presupposed in making the deontic utterances. Conversely, those deontic utterances that normally are moral in nature can lack that quality in cases where little hangs on the matter.

I must not overstate my case, however. The law says that a person ought not to commit murder. This is a practically justifiable rule that, in most people's view, carries great moral force. But it is most improbable that what gives the rule its moral force is the condition of trust created between legislators and people. The condition of trust and the presence of rewards or sanctions are therefore not the only conditions under which a pragmatically justified rule can have moral force. I have by no means given a complete explanation of the factors that make deontic statements moral. Therefore, any suggestion that the moral deontic can be defined by a condition of trust and the presence of significant rewards or sanctions is an exaggeration. In the case of the law against murder, an adequate account surely has to take notice of both history and religion.

But I think I have established that, when a condition of trust exists and there is a strong possiblity of meaningful rewards or sanctions, pragmatically justified statements gain moral force. When good faith is of importance, then, keeping the eighteen maxims is vital not just to being practical but to being moral.

WHAT IF ONE'S DEONTIC CODE FAILS THE TEST?

Our final question in this final chapter addresses the other side of the coin from the previous three sections. I have claimed that you have a good reason, and often a good moral reason, to obey your moral, legal, or societal code, as long as that code is deontically rational. We now need to consider what your obligations are if your code is not deontically rational. Do you have a diminished duty to the code, no duty at all, or even a duty to try to overthrow the code?

This matter is crucially important, and I am afraid my response will prove disappointing. I cannot either justify or anathematize the supposed right of revolution. But let us see what the considerations I have raised so far indicate.

A code's compliance with the eighteen maxims is, of course, a matter of degree. Probably no existing code is in perfect compliance, nor is it likely that any code could exist in total disregard for deontic rationality. Similarly, making comparisons among codes is a risky business. All could be for the best in the best of all possible deontic codes, and yet, in principle, every precept might be a necessary evil— for any set of improvements in one area might have overall deleterious effects. To say that code A is better than code B, or that code A can be improved, is to make an overall judgment on those codes and should not result from looking at one or two precepts alone.

I suggest that the grading of deontic codes in accordance with the maxims of deontic pragmatics can never be a precise affair. If two codes are very different, but seem, as far as we can tell, to comply about equally with deontic rationality, I doubt that any Benthamite calculus will ever tell us which of the two is preferable.

People who find flaws in their deontic code, therefore, do not automatically lose any reason to uphold that code. There are all sorts of factors they must consider. How major is each flaw? Does it keep the code from fulfilling its purpose? How important is it that that purpose be fulfilled? Would attempts to remedy the flaw have even worse side effects? Is there any reason to think an adequate remedy is possible? Probable? Only if you have given careful thought to these and other critical questions are you clearly justified in reconsidering your allegiance to the code.

Of course, with open-ended codes, one rarely has to face a need to reconsider one's allegiance. There is always some hope of amendment, although the hope might at times be vanishingly thin. Even when you are able to push for amendment of faulty sections in your code, however, you should still ask the questions I just raised. The rules of Minimalism and Economy demand as much.

Nevertheless, despite all the factors that call for caution, sometimes a flaw in one's code is clearly major and crippling, while amendment is unlikely or impossible. What allegiance did a conscientious German owe to the precepts of the Third Reich? At this point I think the question of breach of trust enters once more. Have the authorities, in instituting the flawed part of the code, been guilty of bad faith?

I argued that St. Augustine's God and Lieutenant Broderick's superior officers were guilty of an egregious breach of trust. As a result, I find no pragmatic or moral reason why either a sinner in the hands of that angry God or the lieutenant should try to carry out the commands from on high. To be sure, where there is no reason, force might take its place, but force is hardly a reason. The same holds for Germans in the Third Reich. Because of the massive breach of trust committed by the Nazi leaders, the German people owed their government no duty of obedience. Only force, habit, and deception keep such a regime together.

On the other hand, suppose that one is suffering under a code imposed in a condition of excusable ignorance. The authorities who imposed and enforced laws against the practice of witchcraft during the European witch craze were in no way guilty of bad faith. Their violation of Factuality was entirely unknowing, and it is unreasonable to say that they should have known better. What should sincere disbelievers in witchcraft do? If they are brave, they try to stop or at least moderate the persecution, with possible grave danger to themselves. But I suggest they still might have reason to uphold the law as a whole, to seek its amendment but not its total overthrow.[210] Only if the authorities come to realize their breach of Factuality but continue the persecution of witches are disbelievers clearly stripped of any reason to continue their allegiance.

That I have found no reason why you should obey a superior guilty of flagrant bad faith does not mean that somebody else might not come up with such a reason. But, as I said when considering whether there

---

210. As I will insist shortly, to say that a person has a reason to do something is not necessarily to affirm that she has sufficient reason to do so. One might argue that anti-witchcraft laws in most places were applied to comparatively few people. But, as a reader noted, often such laws required citizens to aid in the discovery and punishment of witches. Under such a law, a citizen might well seek total overthrow.

might be more than eighteen maxims, all a person can do is examine any candidates when they offer themselves. More important, even if you have no reason to obey a superior guilty of breach of trust, that does not determine whether you should or should not disobey that superior. And if you do have a duty to disobey, are there limits on that disobedience? Could disobedience be active, or must it be only passive?

The fact is, I don't think my considerations in this book allow me to give firm answers to those harder questions. After all, the most I have been trying to establish in this chapter is that one sometimes has a good and morally justifiable reason to obey one's deontic code. But even a good and morally justifiable reason is not always a sufficient reason. My methods cannot determine in any particular situation that a person should obey his code, even when that code conforms to deontic rationality. Still less can I determine by my methods what you should do when you find that your code contains grave flaws.

The sum of my achievements in this chapter might seem pretty meager. In the first place, I do not claim that every precept of a given moral code, including the one to which I myself subscribe, is an absolute standard that all should follow in every circumstance. The maxims of deontic pragmatics, when they have moral force, provide only threshold conditions for moral codes and theories to meet. A code that meets those conditions is rationally and morally acceptable, but that does not entail that the specific actions it prescribes must or should be chosen by any rational and moral agent.

Again, contrasting codes can meet the threshold conditions equally well. If they do, I see no absolutist or rational way of choosing between them. Where two such codes differ over the moral worth of a given act, there are no rational criteria for choosing one claim over the other.

Further, to find that one's moral code does not meet the threshold conditions does not by itself determine what action one should take. Much, as always, depends on circumstances. For example, as I mentioned much earlier, one rarely has a duty to be ineffective.

All this sounds quite negative. Yet, my purpose in this book has been to set out and explain the working of the maxims of deontic pragmatics. One should be pragmatic about pragmatics: This study should be of use!

In fact, the results of this chapter are useful. It has been worth the effort if I have sketched a plausible argument against moral relativism, skepticism, and nihilism. The considerations raised in this chapter are necessary steps toward completing that sketch. They leave huge questions unresolved, but they make a good start in sorting out some very important matters.

What I have argued for is a highly tempered ethical absolutism. There are some absolute standards all codes should conform to — so far runs my absolutism, but no farther. I suppose this is a middle-of-the-road position. But then, that's the American way.

Appendix:
The Maxims of
Deontic Pragmatics

This appendix reprints from chapter 4 the rule of Deontic Rationality, together with the eighteen maxims of deontic pragmatics that constitute the substance of this rule. The number in front of each heading indicates the chapter in which I have discussed those submaxims.

Supermaxim of Deontic Rationality: Impose, accept, and impute obligations only in accordance with a rationally defensible structure.

5. Three Principal Submaxims:

☐ Straightforwardness: Have as the goal of deontic speech that people behave in accordance with what your utterances say they ought, ought not, may, or may not do.

☐ Consequences: In determining whether to make a deontic utterance, take into account the consequences of making that or any other deontic utterance.

□ Minimalism: Reserve deontic utterances for occasions when the goal is pressing, the likelihood of achievement high, and the availability of suitable alternatives for reaching the goal limited.

6. Legislative Rules of Manner:

□ Regularity: Have a standard method of legislative procedure, and follow that method in this legislation.

□ Publicity: Provide methods by which those who are to be bound by the legislation can know of its contents and, where practicable, of its justification.

□ Openness: Provide a method by which new legislation can be developed when cases are insufficiently or improperly determined by present legislation.

7. Legislative Rules of Matter:

□ Theoretical Virtue: Adopt only rules that are consistent with one another, clear, applicable, simple, and modest.

□ Universalizability: Adopt only rules that treat like cases alike.

□ Factuality: Do not adopt rules that depend crucially upon false statements about the way the world is.

□ Proportionality: Let the strength of obligations and the severity of sanctions be roughly proportional to the strength of the justification provided.

□ Economy: Adopt only rules the performance of which will meet your legislative ends at the least cost to those for whom you legislate.

□ Distribution: Provide a method for the distribution of goods and services, benefits and sanctions.

8. Judicial Rules of Manner:

□ Use of General Rules: Decide the case under consideration, if possible, by subsuming it under properly determined general rules.

□ Equity: Provide a method for solving conflicts, in case general rules appear to give conflicting advice or prove insufficient in particular situations.

9. Judicial Rules of Matter:

□ Judicial Factuality: Decide cases in ways consistent with the facts about the world.

□ Judicial Economy: Decide cases in a way that will carry out the legislative aim at least cost to the actors.

□ Judicial Publicity: Impute obligations only to people who knew or should have known that the obligations in question applied to them when they performed the acts in question.

□ Judicial Review of General Rules: Impute or accept particular obligations only when those obligations are imposed in accordance with general rules that are consistent, clear, applicable, simple, modest, universalizable, and proportional.

Index

Note: The location for the primary discussion of each maxim of deontic pragmatics is printed in *italics*.

241

Constitution, U.S., 82–84, 86, 102, 160,
168, 178, 179; Eighth Amendment,
102; Fifth Amendment, 22; First
Amendment, 179, 180; Fourteenth
Amendment, 160, 167, 168, 170, 171,
173, 175, 176
Constitutional rights, 27
Cooperative Principle (Grice), 33, 34, 226
Copperheads, 145
Council of Constance, 231
counterfactual conditionals, 37–41, 176,
181
cruel and unusual punishment, 109
Cum Occasione (papal bull), 20

Dante Alighieri, 138, 231
Davis, *see* University of California at
Davis
De Libero Arbitrio (St. Augustine), 19, 20
de Minimis non curat lex, 52, 71, 72
death penalty, 152–55
Declaration of Independence, U.S., 87
Defense Function Standards (A.B.A.),
27–29
deontic: code, 233, 235; judgment, 124,
126, 129–32, 206; logic, 2, 14–16, 24,
31, 36, 58, 66, 197, 199–201, 207;
operator, 160; pragmatics, 1–4, 11,
13, 33, 34, 46, 49–51, 54–56, 58, 60,
67, 70, 75, 82, 84, 85, 91, 94, 99, 110,
112, 113, 122–24, 129, 132, 134, 136,
138, 140, 141, 144–47, 149–52, 154,
155, 159, 161–64, 166, 169, 179, 183,
186, 187, 189–92, 195–97, 199, 201,
207, 208, 209, 212, 213, 222, 223,
227, 229, 233, 235, 237; speech, 1–4,
11, 13, 31, 32, 34–36, 42, 44–46, 50,
51, 55–58, 60, 61, 66–70, 73, 74, 80,
91, 94, 121, 123, 124, 127, 129, 131,
135–38, 141, 151, 152–55, 160, 161,
187, 190, 191, 198–201, 222, 231;
undertakings, 211, 214
Deontic Rationality (supermaxim), 56,
150, 202, 209, 212, 233, 235, 237
descriptive meaning, 44
descriptivism, 42
detachability (Sadock), 202, 204, 205
detachment principles, 24
deterrence theory of punishment, 106, 139
diets, 64, 111, 215, 217
diminishing deontic returns, law of, 73
Distribution (maxim), 54, 55, *113–17*, 152,
195, 238

Divorce (Henry VIII), 37
Dobu, 9, 98
Don Quixote, 92, 93
due process, 27, 160
Durkheim, Emile, 185, 214, 224,
225
Dworkin, Ronald, 162, 166, 172, 220

Economy (maxim), 54–56, 85, *110–13*,
138, 146, 151, 152, 154, 155, 177,
178–80, 228, 234, 238
egalitarian principles, 114, 183, 195
Electoral College (U.S.), 83
Elizabeth, New Jersey, 97, 99
Elizabeth II, Queen, 99, 105
Encyclopaedia Britannica, 218
epistemic logic, 24
Equal Protection Clause, *see* Constitution,
U.S.: Fourteenth Amendment
Equal Rights Amendment, 86, 87
Equity (maxim), 53, 54, 124, *129–32*, 178,
238
equity (general principle), 51, 174
Escholier, Marc, 20
ethics, 11, 17, 21, 26, 54, 92, 143, 179, 188,
189, 194, 200, 208, 213, 215
ethnocentrism, 211
etiquette, 1, 50, 53, 83, 91, 92, 104, 105,
143, 145, 193, 195, 226, 229, 231
Euclidean geometry, 203
Eve, 19, 32
ex parte Milligan, 148
Exclusionary Rule, 187, 188
excommunication, 50, 80

facial intent, 182
Factuality (maxim), 54–56, 85, *96–101*,
146, 173, 179, 180, 189, 205, 216, 234,
238
false beliefs, 9
ferrets, black-footed, 65
first-person statements, 40–45
focal meaning, 37
focal use, 37
Ford, Gerald, 198
formal mode, 42
Forrester, Mary Gore, xii, 40, 42, 187,
193, 222
Forrester, William, xii
Frankfurter, Felix, 165
Free French, 15
Free riders, 219–23; reasonable, 220–22;
true, 220–22